Writing for Radio and Television in India

Writing for Radio and Television in India

Krishan K.Kedia

CYBER TECH PUBLICATIONS
4264/3, Ansari Road, Daryaganj New Delhi - 110002
Phone : 011-43559448, Fax : 011-23280028
Email : cybertechpublications@gmail.com

Writing for Radio and Television in India

CYBER TECH PUBLICATIONS
4264/3, Ansari Road, Daryaganj
New Delhi - 110002 (India)
Phone : 011-23244078, 011-43559448,
Fax : 011-23280028
E-mail : cybertechpublications@gmail.com
Website : www.cybertechpublications.com

First Published : 2008

Reprint 2024

ISBN 978-81-7884-352-0

Price,1200.00

Printed at :

New Green Print Solutions, New Delhi 110078

Preface

This book examines the features of writing in two journalistic media: television and radio. The monograph is relevant not only to students and teachers of journalism but also to those interested generally in the field of composition studies. It offers a highly specific analysis of the differences among the writing styles for these two media--differences that are often felt by student and teacher alike but rarely described in detail. Comparative in orientation, the book examines each of the two media in all major sections: Leads; Story Structure; Sentence Structure; Word Choice; Names, Quotes and Attribution. Each of these sections discusses a number of distinct points; three columns, one for each of the media, highlight the comparisons. The section on "leads," for instance, looks at summary leads, datelines, beginning with names, the umbrella lead, an item lead, an anecdotal lead, a delayed lead, a buried lead, question leads and quote leads.

The author has put his effort in this book to make every section more clearer and understandable. Wherever necessary examples are also given, undersigned is hopeful enough that this work of him would be beneficial to the readers.

Suggestions of the readers to improve the book further are always welcome.

—Author

Contents

1

Primary Tasks and Cautions

MAKING A MEDIA LIST

Make up a media list and organise it into the following categories:

- wire services
- local print media
- local radio
- local TV
- national media

Record the name and title of each contact person (you may have more than one contact person for each organisation), the name of the publication or station, and the address and telephone number. For print media, get the name of the news editor (also called city editor, news director, or assignment editor), the features editor, and the person responsible for the community calendar or bulletin board.

RELATING TO MEDIA PEOPLE

For radio or TV, you will need the name of the assignment editor, the public service director, and the people responsible for booking talkshow guests. If you don't have the names of contact people, don't be afraid to call and ask. Be sure to get their titles, since personnel turnover can be rapid. Update the list every three or four months.

Organise media information according to whether the publication is daily, weekly, or monthly. Find out the deadlines for these publications. Also, make a list of what times your local TV news is broadcast and find out which stations do live (on the scene) reports. It will help in planning times for demonstrations or actions to know what times fit into the TV station's schedule.

Try to keep profiles of your media contacts, with comments on whether they are sympathetic or hostile to certain issues and on what issues they are interested in or have covered in the past.

MEETING DEADLINES

Reporters work against a deadline. If you call editors or reporters when they are rushing to meet a deadline, you won't get your story in the news, and you may alienate them as well.

The best time to call contacts at a morning paper is in the morning between 9:30 and 10 a.m. As it gets later, the staff will be more pressed for time. Call contacts at an evening paper in the late afternoon, when the paper has just gone out.

It is best to call radio or TV reporters as early in the day as possible if you're trying to get on an evening broadcast. Don't call after 1 or 2 p.m. for a 5 p.m. story; the staff is rushing to edit the news they already have. Talk to media people as far before deadlines as possible. Your goal is to become a resource person for the media on animal rights issues. You can do this by letting the media know you exist and by cultivating contacts.

Send a brief letter to each contact person on your media list, explaining the purpose of your group and offering information on animal rights issues. Include your group's identifying fact sheet or brochure. This alone is probably not enough to get the media to contact you-usually you have to become known in the community-but it is a start.

Try to develop and maintain professional relationships with media people in your community by being courteous and responsible. Return calls promptly-remember those deadlines! Be enthusiastic, cooperative, friendly, and always tell the truth. If you make a mistake, admit it promptly. Don't be afraid to say, "I don't know, but I can find out." Then do so.

When you send a news release to more than one person in an organisation, let each person know who else is receiving it. Nothing infuriates an editor more than to work on a story and then find that someone else at the paper is doing the same story in another section.

Reporters sometimes claim that they can't cover animal rights stories because there's no new "angle," so you've got to provide it. Use interesting visuals, such as costumes and props, in your demonstrations. Focus on the local aspects by talking, for example, about what the company that employs half the people in town does to animals, or talk about local people arrested in a national demonstration.

Never speak "off the record"; there is no such thing. Also, watch out for jokes-you could be misunderstood. Don't get bullied into a simple yes-or-no answer to a complex question. Give the facts necessary to understand the issue.

Study the professionals on national interview shows. Develop a few good phrases and examples to recite that will catch a reporter's ear. When you make a press call or send out a news release, be sure that it is for something newsworthy.

Your communications should be organised and state important points clearly and briefly. It's helpful if you understand what the media consider newsworthy. Some of the characteristics of news are:

timeliness (media are interested in what's happening today, not yesterday)

proximity (the closer the event is to the media, the more likely the media will consider it news)

prominence (if you've got well-known people involved, the media sometimes respond better)

conflict (the media love covering opposing factions)

oddity (if you're doing something for the first time, the media are more likely to respond; they get tired of the same old thing)

importance (how many people might be affected or interested).

All of these "news judgments" don't have to apply before you contact the media, but your information/event should meet most of them. Remember, the media don't like to feel "used" by anyone with a cause. Reporters want to think that what they're writing about is legitimate news and not propaganda. If your information/event isn't newsworthy, don't contact the media because you'll only anger them for wasting their time.

WRITING A NEWS RELEASE

A news release, a short announcement of a newsworthy event, is sent to newspapers, magazines, and TV and radio stations to interest them in doing a story. Because news directors receive hundreds of releases every day, yours must look professional and present the facts quickly, or it will never be read.

Here are some guidelines: Keep it short. One page is best.

Write a concise, catchy headline that summarizes the story. It should be written in the style of a newspaper headline, using active verbs.

Use the "inverted pyramid" style to write the release: Put the most important facts in the first paragraph and supporting information in descending order, so that the least important information is last.

The first paragraph should answer the five W's: who, what, where, when, and why.

Underline the text that gives the location, time, and date of the event.

The final paragraph should describe your group and reinforce your message, with a quotation from your spokesperson.

Never editorialise. Use quotations to express opinions. The quotation should be from a specific individual, not from your group, e.g., Nafisa Kumar, a spokesperson for Animal Action, says, "....."

Proofread the release carefully for grammar and spelling. Ask someone else to read it for an objective reaction. If you have the time, set it aside and look it over again the next morning. Eliminate redundancies, use short words and phrases, and simplify complex ideas.

If you've got an exciting, relevant photo, include it. Try to use a "screened" photograph. An article showing the timeliness or significance is even better.

You may also want to include black-and-white photographs, a factsheet, or a flier. If you do, at the bottom of the last page of the release write, "Attached: (list documents)."

Make it dramatic and attention-getting, but be sure you can substantiate what you say. Double-check the facts. It is virtually impossible to correct a release once it has gone out. But if you do make a mistake-especially in the time or location of an event-be sure to call and tell those to whom you sent the release.

The time you tell the press should be the ideal time for them to see your event. If your event starts at 11:00 a.m., tell the press it's a little later but ask them to arrive at the time you tell them "sharp" so that they don't arrive to find activists figuring out where to stand or discussing last week's potluck dinner and also so that they don't arrive too late.

The sample news release (click here) illustrates the proper format to use. The following tips correspond to the numbers shown on the sample.

1. Use 8 1/2" × 11" (or similar standard sized) regular weight white stationery.
2. Your letterhead should contain your group's name and address.
3. The words NEWS RELEASE should be at the top of the first page. Always refer to releases as "news releases," not "press releases." The same goes for "news conference," rather than "press conference."
4. List the name of the "contact person." Make sure that someone is always available at this number, or include both daytime and evening numbers where the contact person can be reached.

5. Type the date in the upper left-hand corner. If you have enclosed photos, note that there.
6. "FOR IMMEDIATE RELEASE" appears in the upper left-hand corner above the date.
7. The headline should be centered, underlined, and typed in capital letters. It should be placed about three inches down from the headings above it to provide space for editor's notes.
8. The body of the release should begin one-third of the way down the page.
9. Leave wide margins for reporters' and editors' notes.
10. Don't use zeroes for times (e.g., use "11 a.m.," not "11:00"), and don't use letters after numbered dates (e.g., August 22, not 22nd).
11. Indent five spaces to begin new paragraphs, and don't hyphenate words at the end of a line.
12. Never continue a release on the back of a page. Instead, end the first page with a complete paragraph and type the word "more" centered at the bottom. Number each additional page at the top. Include a topic headline and your organisation's name. Do not staple multiple pages.
13. Type all releases double-spaced using capital and lower-case letters (not all capitals).
14. At the end of the release, center any one of these closings: "-30-," "#," or "Ends."

Before deciding how and when to deliver your release, establish what you want to accomplish-do you want something printed/broadcast BEFORE the event, or do you want the media to attend and cover the event? Generally, such activities as film showings, meetings, and fund-raisers fall in the "BEFORE" category. In this case, mail your releases at least three weeks before the event. These releases are probably being sent to the "Community Calendar" or "Bulletin Board" sections.

If you're having a picket or demonstration, you want "news" coverage. In this case, try to fax or hand-deliver your news release, and distribute it only one day before the event. Schedule it to arrive around 10 a.m., and try to deliver a copy to a reporter as well as to the news editor. Be sure to note on the release who else is receiving a copy. You may need two people to hand-deliver releases-one to run inside with the releases while the driver stays with the car.

Call the news desk to inform them if you are planning a demonstration. Do not read your entire news release. Just say, "Hello, I'm calling to let you know that Action for Animals will be holding a demonstration tomorrow at 11 a.m. in front of the Leather Store at 15 MG Road. Our contact number is 011-23232879 if you'd like more information. We've sent a release to the news desk." If you have a good relationship with a particular reporter, call to say your release is coming out, or afterwards to see if he or she got it.

After the demo, assign volunteers to get the coverage. At least two people should videotape television coverage and be certain to check the newspapers for a story and/or photo. These clips can be used to send out with your next news release to show that what you're doing is "newsworthy."

If a newspaper covers your event and the wires don't, call the wires afterwards to let them know that they can pick up the story from the paper. If your event is of national interest (i.e., Supreme Court Santeria ruling, animal-to-human organ transplant), call the national television news desks to let them know they can pick up footage from the local affiliate.

MAKING A MEDIA KIT

A media kit is a packet of information to give to reporters who come to your demonstration, event, or news conference. It helps to get your message across and makes you look professional. A media kit can include any or all of the following, depending on the issue:

- a news release
- a factsheet
- black-and-white photographs and possibly colour photographs. Type the following information on a sticky label to put on the back of the photograph: what it is,

where it is, when it was taken, and who took it. Never write on the back of a photograph with a pen. The ink will rub off and damage other photographs.

- background information on or history of the issue
- copies of relevant documents
- if dealing with legislation, a copy of the bill and a summary of the main points.
- biographies of key individuals and a "mug shot" photograph (i.e., a head-and-shoulders shot) with an identifying label on the back.
- background on the organisation

Package the kit in a two-pocket folder (found in office supply stores) and put a label on the cover with the group's name and the words "Media Kit." If you have a photograph, you can put it on the cover, although it is not essential.

WORKING WITH THE WIRE SERVICES

Wire services are news-gathering agencies that sell stories to newspapers and radio stations around the country. They should be your first contact when you deliver a news release or make press calls. If you can interest the wire services, your story will be sent to all subscribing media in your area or even nationally. Popular wire services are the Associated Press (AP), United Press International (UPI), Reuters, United News of India (UNI), Press Trust of India (PTI), Agence France Press (AFP), and Deutsche Presse-Agentur (DPA). Many of the nation's largest papers-Times of India, Hindustan Times, The Indian Express, The Hindu-also have news services, which means if you interest them in your story it may be sent nationwide as well.

Getting a story "on the wire" is a valuable accomplishment. It is worth a great deal of effort to develop good relations with wire-service reporters. Many TV, radio, or print assignment editors will answer a call asking for coverage by saying, "We'll see what comes in over the wire."

To find out what wire-service bureaus are in your area, look in the telephone book or call the local newspaper office. Any reporter can tell you where the nearest bureau is. If the newspaper is a member of AP, it also submits stories to AP.

Send the bureau manager a letter describing your organisation and supply the names, addresses, and telephone numbers of your best contact people. Offer to supply information or the local angle on animal rights issues.

Always deliver two news releases to the wire services: one for the "daybook," and one for the assignment editor. Call both the daybook editor and the assignment editor.

The daybook is a listing of scheduled events for the day. Each evening and again each morning, wires like AP and UPI send the daybook to their members. Assignment editors use this list to decide how to assign reporters and camera crews. To get listed in the daybook, send your news release about one week before the event. You can still get listed in the daybook for the next day by calling the information in to the daybook editor.

You may also be able to get a photograph of your event on the wire. If you've just had a demonstration, take your roll of undeveloped black-and-white film to the photographic department of the wire-service bureau and give it to the staff along with your news release. You can come back in a few hours or the next day to pick up the negatives. If you do provide prints, they must be 8" x 10" black and white photographs-no other size will fit the machines they use to transmit the photos nationwide.

Some wires, AP and UPI for example, also have radio networks. Call the radio bureaus closest to your area. Be prepared to do an interview on the spot if they are interested. They'll tape it for use later.

DOING RADIO AND TV TALK-SHOW INTERVIEWS

Before you can do an interview, you must get the TV station interested. It helps to know the "gatekeeper" at the station: the news assignment editor. Call the station to learn his or her name and the best time of day to call. Send your news release one or two days before your event. If you call to remind them of your event, be brief and polite and don't call in the late afternoon. Your event will be more likely to get TV coverage if it involves conflict or visual interest. You can reach thousands of people through talk shows. Call in your comments to talk shows whenever animal-related subjects are discussed or during "open phone" segments. It's even better if someone from your group can be the guest on a talk show.

If your group is expecting a visit from someone with a particular area of expertise, try to get the person on a talk show. Or, try to get yourself on one. Contact the station several weeks in advance. Send a letter to the talk show director, describing your credentials or those of your speaker, what you'd like to discuss, and why it would interest the audience. Be sure to provide your telephone number.

Prepare a list of people your speaker would feel comfortable debating, in case the show wants to present both sides.

Once you are booked for the show, listen to it or watch it to see what style and format to expect. To prepare, do the following:

- Study the issue.
- Practice being interviewed. Tape yourself with a tape recorder or video camera.
- Anticipate difficult questions and plan your answers.
- Memorise good quotations, anecdotes, and facts.
- Have a friend ask you all the hard questions in a hostile, aggressive way so you can be prepared for a difficult interview.
- Decide on the five main points you want to make during the show. Memorise a fact or an example for each one.
- Try to make your five points even if the interviewer doesn't ask the "right" questions. Don't feel you're limited to just answering the questions. You can answer them and still take the opportunity to talk about one of your points. Practice saying, "The real question here is...." or, "That relates to a larger issue, which is...."
- If you're doing a TV show, dress carefully: no solid black, white, or bright red, and no patterns. Wear plain

solid colours. Green or blue films especially well. Smile, and don't fidget or touch your face or hair.

- Try to make your point in 20 seconds or less. TV news shows look for a "sound bite"-a statement that can be plugged into a 60-second story. If you take 45 or 60 seconds to make your point, your spot won't be aired, so use short sentences.
- Speak slowly and carefully (without being too slow!) and give yourself time to think before you answer the question.
- Don't say anything you wouldn't want edited out and aired separately. The reporter may interview you for five minutes, but air only 20 seconds of it. Don't worry about repeating yourself: It just increases the chance that what you want to be heard actually will be.
- If the reporter is hostile, don't get flustered and raise your voice or get shrill. Stay calm and concentrate on making those five points. Remember-the reporter is not your real audience!
- Talk directly to the interviewer, not to the audience or camera. If you steal side glances at the camera, you'll look nervous or shifty.

MAKING PUBLIC SERVICE ANNOUNCEMENTS

Public service announcements, or PSAs, are 10-to 60-second notices that radio and TV stations sometimes air in order to balance the effect of paid advertisements and to present balanced coverage of issues.

They are free to nonprofit community groups.

The four standard lengths for a PSA are 10 seconds (25 to 30 words), 20 seconds (45 to 50 words), 30 seconds (60 to 75 words), and 60 seconds (120 to 150 words). Following are some sample PSA's:

20 seconds: More people live off research today than benefit from it. The traditional use of animals in experimentation must be replaced. Animals are not "tools for research." Their use is costly, unethical, inefficient, and old-fashioned. Sophisticated non-animal methods are available. Help us support their use. [group name and address]. (21 seconds, 48 words)

20 seconds: The original motto of medicine was, "First, do no harm." Yet this year millions of animals will suffer and die in U.S. laboratories. We need to encourage the use of sophisticated computers, cell and tissue cultures, clinical studies, and mathematical models. To support progress without pain, write: [group name and address]. (20 seconds, 47 words)

Besides issue-oriented PSAs such as these, radio and TV stations will air announcements of meetings or events on a "community calendar." This is an excellent way to publicise your group's event.

Send several copies of your PSA with a typed, double-spaced cover letter to the public service director of the station. Explain the purpose of your organization and your activities, and state why the station should use the PSA.

On the top left side of the page, type the beginning date (the first day the PSA should be read), the kill date (the last day you want it read), and the length of the announcement in seconds and in words.

Find out the deadline for PSAs-it may be two or three weeks in advance. Make a follow-up call to be sure the station received it. Some stations may want to see proof that you're actually nonprofit, so be prepared to produce your paperwork. PETA also has television PSAs available on 3/4" videotape. If you would like to try to interest your local stations in airing them, please let us know.

WRITING LETTERS TO THE EDITOR

You can get great exposure for animal rights issues through letters to the editor in newspapers or magazines. Make it a point to read local papers and magazines for articles that provide fuel for a letter to the editor.

Your letter must be short: 300 words is the maximum most papers or magazines will publish without cutting. It's better for you to do the cutting than for the editor to do it. The best length is 100 to 150 words (10 to 15 typed lines).

Make the first sentence catchy, so it will get the reader's attention, and stick to one issue. The letter should be timely. If possible, send it in no more than three to four days after the article you're responding to has appeared.

The letter should be typed and double-spaced. Sign it and include your home and work telephone numbers. Some papers will want to verify that you wrote it.

Don't send letters just to the biggest paper in town. The smaller the paper, the better chance you have of getting your letter printed. Small weekly papers are an excellent way to reach hundreds or even thousands of people.

Sending in regular letters to the editor should be a priority. The exposure you get is so valuable that it is worth forming a letter-writing committee just to ensure that the job gets done.

Occasionally, you may have the chance to write an opinion piece for the local paper, especially if you are involved in a controversial campaign. These are longer articles of 500 to 800 words that summarize an issue, develop an argument, and propose a solution. Send the article to the editorial page editor with a cover letter explaining why you feel it should be printed. The article has a better chance of getting printed if it is signed by someone prominent, even if you wrote it for him or her.

APPOINTING A SPOKESPERSON

You should appoint a spokesperson for each event. Members of your group should be prepared to answer media questions with a brief sentence and then direct further questions to the spokesperson. This helps prevent the local TV station from interviewing the most inarticulate or ill-presented person.

Your group must decide ahead of time what the spokesperson should and should not say and have ready all the available facts. The group leader does not necessarily have to be the spokesperson.

The spokesperson should be well dressed and have media kits available. If the demonstration involves people wearing costumes, the spokesperson should not be in costume. Though you must appoint a spokesperson, everyone at the event/protest should be familiar with the topic, as reporters will often want a second comment from others involved.

SETTING UP A NEWS CONFERENCE

A news conference is a good way to fall flat on your face unless you have a really important story. It's usually better to hand-deliver or mail a professional-looking media kit with a news release. Hold a news conference only when:

- The media can benefit from it more than from photographs and news releases.
- You have important or newsworthy people available to present your story.
- Experts will be available to answer questions.
- The story involves something that has to be seen to be understood.
- The press is inundating you with telephone calls, and rumours must be dispelled.

Use this format when holding a news conference:

- Start promptly-soft news at the designated hour, hard news after five minutes.
- Begin the conference with a concise statement from your spokesperson.
- Explain material available to the press.
- Call on the expert to read a short statement.
- Answer questions.
- End the conference on time. It should not last more than 30 or 40 minutes. Reporters will ask further questions if they wish.
- Hold the conference in a location convenient to the media, such as in a downtown hotel, and provide light refreshments. The best time is at 10 or 11 a.m.

If possible, issue invitations one to two weeks ahead of time by sending a "media alert." Explain the details of the conference and what will be addressed. If you are holding the conference right away, alert the media by telephone. Call the wire services to get it on the daybook.

Be careful to allow only media, not the general public, to enter the room. Assign someone to check media IDs at the door.

Be sure to have media kits prepared. Hand them out as soon as reporters arrive. If a major statement is being made, you may want to issue the news release after the statement.

After the news conference, follow up with media inquiries as quickly as possible. Make every effort to accommodate requests for personal interviews. Deliver news releases and media kits to media who were invited but did not attend. Tell radio stations that your spokesperson is available for a telephone interview.

2

Screenwriting

INTRODUCTION

Screenwriting refers to the art and craft of writing screenplays for film or television. Writing for film is potentially one of the most high-profile and best-paying careers available to a writer, and as such, it is perhaps the most sought after. It is increasingly difficult to make a living as a Hollywood screenwriter, but that does not stop tens of thousands of people from trying every year, as the capricious nature of the film industry makes it possible for a complete unknown to launch a career simply by writing a commercially-appealing screenplay and getting it into the hands of the right people.

STATUS OF SCREENWRITERS IN THE INDUSTRY

Historically, screenwriters have had a low social position in the film industry. Despite the fact that a screenwriter is often the genesis of a project, directors-not writers-frequently get their names associated with the films they make (as in, "a film by..."). Screenwriters usually do not get this honour, unless the screenwriter is also directing. Before Alfred Hitchcock, the reverse was the case. The Writers Guild of America agreed to make an exception for Hitchcock, which other directors took advantage of (and insisted on using "a film by...") and gradually screenwriters were marginalized in this respect.

However, the situation has improved dramatically as the resurgence of the independent film in the late 20th century gave new rise to the idea of the screenwriter as the amateur, and creative generator of cinematic product. In the past few years, news of multi-million dollar screenplay deals is a sign of increased respect for the role of the screenwriter in film production.

Recently, the Writers Guild of America (WGA), the labour union representing writers in the American film and television industries, has made great efforts to limit the use of the "a film by" title in the credits of motion pictures, to preserve the respect for level of input made by the writers. (See: WGA screenwriting credit system.)

THEORIES ON WRITING A SCREENPLAY

Writing a screenplay requires the creativity of a storyteller and the skills of both the dramatist and the filmmaker. Because of the particular combination of skills and standards required by the motion picture industry, many writers find screenwriting more challenging than writing novels or other narrative fiction.

Fundamentally, the screenplay is a unique literary form. It is like a musical score, in that it is intended to be the basis of other artists' performance, rather than standing on its own merits. For this reason, a screenplay is often written using pre-determined technical jargon when describing stage directions. Nonetheless, a good screenwriter will use interesting visually-descriptive language when setting up a scene or its characters so as to conjure up images. There are several main screenwriting theories which help writers approach the screenplay by systematizing the structure, goals and techniques of writing a script. There are also numerous screenwriting programs available to help a screenwriter set up scenes and keep track of structure. Scenes are usually short and dialogue clipped, i.e., the way people actually speak in real life. The First Act is typically anywhere from fifteen to twenty pages leading to a major conflict. Second Act--the story--is about seventy pages. The Third Act or resolution is the rest. [See Act structure (Film)] Screenplays are usually one-hundred-and-twenty pages in length, or two hours, a page of screenplay roughly corresponding to a minute of movie.

The most common kinds of theories are structural. Screenwriter William Goldman is widely quoted as saying "Screenplays are structure." The first, most basic theory of screenwriting is Aristotle's Poetics, which explains the Three Act Structure. The Three Acts are Beginning, Middle and End, or more functionally, Setup, Complication and Resolution. A common way to paraphrase the Three-Act structure is "get your character up a tree, throw rocks at him, then get him down out of the tree." Many screenwriters also draw inspiration from Joseph Campbell's Monomyth which also employs a variation of the Three Act Structure.

SYD FIELD

Screenwriting guru Syd Field wrote the seminal book Screenplay, and posited a new theory, which he called the Paradigm. Others refer to it as the "Three Act Structure". Field noticed that in a 120-page screenplay, Act Two was notoriously boring, and was also twice the length of Acts One and Three. He also noticed that an important dramatic event usually occurred at the middle of the picture, which implied to him that the middle act was actually two acts in one. So the Three Act Structure is noted 1, 2a, 2b, 3, resulting in Aristotle's Three Acts divided into four pieces.

Field also introduced the idea of Plot Points into screenwriting theory. Plot Points are important structural functions that happen in approximately the same place in most successful movies, like the verses and choruses in a popular song. In subsequent books, Field has added to his original list, and students of his like Viki King and Linda Seger have added to the list of Plot Points. Here is a current list of the major Plot Points that are congruent with Field's Paradigm:

Opening Image: The first image in the screenplay should summarize the entire film, especially its tone. Often, writers go back and redo this as the last thing before submitting the script.

Inciting Incident: Also called the catalyst, this is the point in the story when the Protagonist encounters the problem that will change their life. This is when the detective is assigned the case, where Boy meets Girl, and where the Comic Hero gets fired from his cushy job, forcing him into comic circumstances.

Turning Point 1: The last scene in Act One, Turning Point One is a surprising development that radically changes the Protagonist's life, and forces him to confront the Opponent. In Star Wars, this is when Luke's family is killed by the Empire. He has no home to go back to, so he joins the Rebels in opposing Darth Vader.

Pinch 1: A reminder scene at about 3/8 the way through the script (halfway through Act 2a) that brings up the central conflict of the drama, reminding us of the overall conflict. For example, in Star Wars, Pinch 1 is the Stormtroopers attacking the Millennium Falcon in Mos Eisley, reminding us that the Empire is after the stolen plans to the Death Star that R2-D2 is carrying and that Luke and Ben Kenobi are trying to get to the Rebel Alliance (the main conflict).

Midpoint: An important scene in the middle of the script, often a reversal of fortune or revelation that changes the direction of the story. Field suggests that driving the story towards the Midpoint keeps the second act from sagging.

Pinch 2: Another reminder scene about 5/8 through the script (halfway through Act 2b) that is somehow linked to Pinch 1 in reminding the audience about the central conflict. In Star Wars, Pinch 2 is the Stormtroopers attacking them as they rescue the Princess in the Death Star. Both scenes remind us of the Empire's opposition, and using the Stormtrooper attack motif unifies both Pinches.

Turning Point 2: A dramatic reversal that ends Act 2 and begins Act 3, which is about confrontation and resolution. Sometimes Turning Point Two is the moment when the Hero has had enough and is finally going to face the Opponent. Sometimes, like in Toy Story, it's the low-point for the Hero, and he must bounce back to overcome the odds in Act 3.

Showdown: About midway through Act 3, the Protagonist will confront the Main Problem of the story and either overcome it, or come to a tragic end.

Resolution: The issues of the story are resolved.

Tag: An epilogue, tying up the loose ends of the story, giving the audience closure.

FINAL THOUGHTS

Perhaps the most daunting theory of screenwriting comes from Pulitzer Prize-winning screenwriter David Mamet, who has advised that a screenwriter should simply read Aristotle's Poetics and write a lot until they get good at it.

Professional screenwriters often recognize the importance of learning about style, craft and structure by reading the screenplays of popular/successful movies.

The time necessary to write a screenplay varies widely upon the writer and the circumstances. Professional television writers frequently are called upon to write an hour-long script in less than a week. Some major movie scripts have literally taken years of rewrites before they are ready. Most professional writers can complete two to three original screenplays in a year.

SCREENPLAY FORMAT AND ELEMENTS OF THE SCREENPLAY

A screenplay has very rigid set of standardizations in place, beginning with proper formatting. These rules are in part to serve the practical purpose of making screenplays uniformly readable "blueprints" of movies, and also to serve as a way of distinguishing a professional from an amateur---if a screenplay doesn't follow the simple rules of formatting, it is generally disregarded as a lesser product, regardless of content.

Most screenplays are expected to be written in 12 point Courier or Courier New typeface, with no bolding or italicizing. Specific elements and formatting defined below.

Screenplay Format

This section describes the components used to build-up a screenplay.

Title Page

The title page of your screenplay is the first clue to a producer that you're either a professional or an amateur. The title should be about 20 lines down the page and either underlined or in quotation marks. Two lines down, in the same font, should be the words "Written By", "Adapted From (insert title here)", or just plain "By". In the bottom corners put contact information, as well as any copyright information. In shooting scripts, the title page contains in the upper right corner a list of every set of revisions distributed thus far.

Some writers are tempted to insert eye-catching fonts or images on the title page. However, such deviation from industry standards is seen as unprofessional and is not recommended.

Scene Headings

Scene headings (or slug lines) define the beginning of a new scene in a screenplay. They either begin with "EXT."---if the scene is an exterior, or takes place outdoors---or "INT."---if the scene takes place indoors.

Following this descriptor, the name of the location of the scene should appear in all caps (example: "BOB'S PLACE"). This is followed by a space, a hyphen, another space, then the time of day (example: "-DAY," "-NIGHT," "-EVENING," etc.). The finished heading should read something like "INT. HOUSE-DAY". Scene headings have a margin of 1.5 inches (37 mm) from the left, 1 inch (25 mm) from the right.

Scene numbering: It is rare that you will find a "spec script" (speculation script, the one written by a screenwriter, before it is sold) with the scenes numbered. This is a tool added later in the production as the "spec script" becomes a "shooting script." The numbers are generally found immediately to the left of the scene heading.

Action

Two lines below the scene heading and with the same margins, the action begins. Action describes what can be seen on the screen, and is always in present tense. Here, screenwriting varies most from standard fiction writing, in that elaborate prose describing the feelings of a character is to be avoided. When introducing a character, the character's name should appear in all caps (example: "Bob turns and sees JOAN, whom he has never seen before."). Afterwards, capitalize according to standard grammar.

Page Breaks

Scene headers, dialogue cues, and transitions-in (such as FADE IN:) should never appear at the bottom of a page. When a paragraph of action or dialogue is split across pages, the break should come between sentences and not before the second line of the paragraph. When dialogue is split, (MORE) should appear at the bottom of the first page, aligned vertically with the dialogue cue. The cue should be replicated on the subsequent page, with (CONT'D) appearing alongside it.

Dialogue

In screenwriting, dialogue refers to anytime a character is speaking, even if it is a monologue. A dialogue "cue" is the name of the character speaking, with a margin of 4.2 inches (107 mm) from the left of the page. The name should be in capitals letters in cues. Unless there is a parenthetical (see below), dialogue is placed one line below the cue. The standard length of a dialogue line is 35 characters starting at 3.1 inches (79 mm). Hyphenation of words in a dialogue is frowned upon.

Parentheticals

To show minor actions or revealing body language, a parenthetical, or subtext, is placed after the cue and either above or within the dialogue, within rounded brackets. e.g:

Jack

I can get a better price.

(to Megan)

Let's bounce!

The margin for parentheticals is 3.7 inches (94 mm) left, 1 inch (25 mm) right. Many script readers prefer limited use of parentheticals. They are also looked upon unfavourably by actors and directors, especially when they become too specific about emotions or actions.

Transitions

Transitions are short descriptions describing how the film will move from one scene (or image within the scene) to the next. They are justified to the right side of a properly formatted screenplay, and followed by a colon. Some of the most common transitions seen in screenplays are:

- CUT TO:-Indicates a direct transition (cut) to a new scene, or to a new shot within a scene. If a scene header follows the cut, this transition is usually omitted.
- DISSOLVE TO:-Indicates a dissolve, where one scene gradually fades into another. Dissolves are commonly used to indicate the passage of time.
- INTERCUT WITH/INTERCUT BETWEEN:-Indicates that a sequence of cuts back and forth between two scenes is about to begin. Subsequent transitions between the two scenes are indicated with the transition BACK TO:. Intercuts are commonly used when portraying telephone conversations, or to contrast action taking place in two locations at the same time.

Intercut example:

INT. ADULT BOOKSTORE--DAY--INTERCUT

Max is on the phone by the register, ringing purchases.

MAX

(into phone)

Dino Velvet... yeah, he's like the

John Luc Godard of S+M flicks,

supposed to be a real weirdo.

WELLES (O.S.)

(from phone)

A weirdo making S+M films? Who'd

have thought it?

MAX

(into phone)

His stuff comes out of New York.

WELLES (O.S.)

Speciality product.

Dialogue and Description

The following is an example from an unproduced screenplay which may give the reader an idea of how a scene without camera angles can be descriptive, and perhaps even poetic, so as to convey the proper time frame (1910) and/or feeling:

A BUNCH OF GARDENIAS

makes a sudden burst of BRIGHT RED. A hand removes each petal--one at a time. The petals fall on the ground.

Following the petals--

A part of a woman's SHOE is seen. It is strangely ornate with a shabby heel.

Giggles erupt, and the extravagantly painted face of a very young prostitute appears.

Her hand is at the arm of a man who is older by at least a couple of decades.

Imagery

Imagery can be used in many metaphoric ways. In The Talented Mr. Ripley, the title character talked of wanting to close the door on himself sometime, and then, in the end, he did. Rain is commonly used to express a character feeling depressed, while sunny days promote a feeling of happiness and calm. Use imagery to your advantage to sway the emotions of your audience and to clue them in to what is happening.

Imagery is well defined in City of God. The opening image sequence sets the tone for the entire film. The film opens with the shimmer of a knife's blade on a sharpening stone. A drink is being prepared, The knife's blade shows again, juxtaposed is a shot of a chicken letting loose of its harness on its feet. All symbolising 'The One that got away'. The film is about life in the favelas in Rio-sprinkled with violence and games and ambition.

Character

It is very important to develop your characters, because that is who the viewers will be relating to. Characters, especially major characters, should be original and interesting. A character's true nature is revealed by his or her actions in overcoming obstacles.

Dialogue

Dialogue is very important to the film industry, because there are no written words to explain your characters or the plot; it all has to be explained through dialogue and imagery. If your script has weak dialogue, there is a good chance it will lose a reader's or viewer's interest. Make your dialogue sharp, snappy, and easy to follow.

Plot

While the story is what will be told (narrative); the plot is how the story will be told (narration). This vocabulary is not indisputable, though. Sometimes in literature story and plot are used exactly the other way round. Develop your plot before you begin work, write a treatment or a short outline for a film and follow it, but feel free to branch out in other directions if you feel that it would make your script more interesting.

ACT STRUCTURE (FILM)

Act structure explains how a plot of a film story is composed. Just like plays (Staged drama) have 'Acts', critics and screenwriters tend to divide films into acts; though films don't require to be broken down as such in reality.

Whereas plays are actual live performances that need 'breaks' in the middle for change of set, costume, or for the artists' rest; films are recorded performances shown mechanically and therefore don't need actual breaks. Still they are divided into acts for reasons that are in aesthetic and structural conformation with the original idea of Act in theatre. Act breaks in a film are usually very obscure for lay audience and only a trained person can detect the ending of one act and the beginning of the other in the progression of a movie.

The idea of Act structure is of more value while writing a Screenplay than watching a film, though the Act breaks are never actually written in the final copies of screenplays. But television scripts called Teleplays almost always include clear denotions as such.

Act is the broadest structural unit of enacted stories. The most common paradigm in theatre, and so in films, is that of the 'Three-Act structure' proposed by Aristotle. It simply means that any story has a 'beginning', a 'middle' and an 'end'. Playwrights and screenwriters divide their stories into three major parts viz. 'Set up', 'Confrontation' (alternatively called as 'conflict' or 'complication') and 'Resolution'. These form the basic three acts of any performance-staged or screened.

Though various theories have been proposed and debated, the Three-act structure stands as the most popular one. Also, this is what Hollywood has discovered and proved as the most successful. The rest of the world cinema may have its own ways of looking at the plot.

The 'Three-Act Structure'

According to Hollywood, feature films are considered as audio-visual narrative forms which can be seen in distinct parts called 'Acts'.

It follows that the enacted story opens with the introduction of characters and situations, backdrop, locale etc. It creates interest in the audience and takes them to feel concerned as to what the real problem is and what may happen with it. Plays, and screenplays, usually revolve around main characters- the 'Protagonist' and the 'Antagonist' who engage themselves into a battle. That is "Set up".

The next part-and considered to be more important-is complication of the problem of the story. It intrigues the audience all the more, giving them more and more information and putting various points of view for imaginative comparison. This eventually leads to higher points of audience interest. Because this second Act of most screenplays adds all the possible dramatic values to the plot, this is considered to be the core of the same. The Antagonist and the Protagonist try and experiment with all their strengths (and weaknesses of the other) to win the battle. That is "Confrontation".

This takes us to the third-and the most important-act, the "Resolution". This means it tends to 'solve' the problem (-s) of the story developed so far. But this is not obvious, as it is expected to bring the 'climax' (or a series of climaxes) to give the audience the pay-off. The tool usually implemented is a 'do or die' situation where doors of escape for either or both of the two characters go on closing one by one, leaving them with only a thin chance that demands the fullest exploitation of their qualities and energies. This so called jaw-dropping, breath-taking, arm-rest-grabbing moment for the audience leads to the final outcome of the entire plot. And it is usually the triumph of the good (Protagonist) over the evil (Antagonist), with rare exceptions.

Limitations

This framework can not be rigidly applied to all the film stories, and there are a good proportion of Hollywood movies that defy this theory. Many films follow this pattern only to a subtle extent, where their genre demands a more delicate handling. Screenwiters and Script doctors have tried to provide alternative ideas, which again are open for debate. As said earlier, cinema across the world and 20th century has evolved its own ways of putting a story. Also, this theory may not be fit for non-fiction films like documentary or corporate films, which may not have a 'plot' at their base with 'characters' and all their 'actions and speeches' predecided, like the feature films have. Such non-fiction films require their own forms of arrangement.

What is important here is that ideas of Act structure help us understand films better. More importantly, these are 'tools' of the screenplay writers who can break down the story at hand and play with various ways of presenting it to find the best possible one. Experts have gone long way ahead in dividing plot to even smaller structural units and they keep working to find the most effective formula of structuring a film story.

BECOMING A SCREENWRITER

Handling Writer's Block

Many writers get to the page and get stuck. Writer's block is what happens when you have the desire, but just can't think of what to write. The key to working through this kind of block is to push through it. Pick a time of day that works for you and write, write, write. Take time out. Relax. Let your screenplay ferment for a while. Watching movies, reading books of the same genre can spark that jolt of creative writing you've been looking for. Writer's block is quite common, both for new writers as well as tenured.

Some say writer's block is simply a lack of research. It is in the writer's best interest to know the world about which he or she is writing backwards and forwards. Meaning, if you don't know what to write, perhaps it's because you don't know what you're writing about.

Editing

Every writer knows that editing is an essential part of writing. Rewrite your piece several times until you are satisfied with the final product. Not only check spelling and grammar, but rewrite scenes to develop them more fully. But always check spelling and grammar. If there is improper spelling or grammar in a piece, an agent, producer, or other person that you are submitting it to will strongly judge it. Bad spelling prejudices people against work, and they are less likely to accept it.

Screenwriting Software

Various pieces of software are available to help screenwriters adhere to the strict formatting conventions (as described above):

- *Celtx-Free*-Open Source scriptwriting software. Linux version available.
- *Cinergy Script Editor*-Free Windows-based script editor program offered in conjunction with a full suite of non-free production management tools under the name Cinergy Motion Picture Production System.
- *Dream a Script*-All in one Screenwriting Software.
- *Final Draft*-Integrated professional scriptwriting software.
- *Montage*-Screenwriting Software for Mac OS X.
- *Movie Magic Screenwriter*-Integrated professional screenwriting software.

- *NTCore Screenwriter*-A little freeware software with autocompletion.
- *Practical Scriptwriter*-Requires no knowledge of script formats.
- *Rough Draft*-A simple script and creative writing word processor. Free (donationware).
- *Scenario*-Modern, intuitive interface with full 30-day trial.
- *Scriptbuddy*-Web-based screenwriting software.
- *Script Right Mobile Edition*-screenwriting software for Pocket PC and Palm OS
- *Scriptware*-The first scriptwriting word processor with real-time formatting/pagination
- *Sophocles*-Screenplay and production management software.
- *Script Smart*-Microsoft Word templates.
- *Totally Write Development Suite*-A four-module program created by professional writer Jeffrey Alan Schechter to streamline the story development and screenplay structure process.

The first screenwriting software was SmartKey, a macro program that sent strings of commands to existing word processing programs, such as WordStar, WordPerfect and Microsoft Word. SmartKey was popular with screen writers from 1982-1987, after which word processing programs had their own macro features.

COPYRIGHT PROTECTION FOR SCREENPLAYS

In the United States, completed works may be copyrighted, but ideas and plots may not be. Any document written after 1978 in the U.S. is automatically copyrighted even without legal registration or notice. However, The U.S. Library of Congress will formally register a screenplay, and some sources claim that if a work is not registered with the Library of Congress, then it is not possible to file for copyright infringement. For the purpose of establishing evidence that a screenwriter is the author of a particular screenplay (but not related to the legal copyrighting status of a work), The Writer's Guild of America registers screenplays. Since this service is one of record keeping and it is not regulated by law, other organizations can register screenplays as well, such as The Creators Vault. While there are benefits to registering a screenplay, it is considered amateurish and a faux-pas to include mention of copyright or guild-registered status anywhere on the screenplay itself.

Screenplay

A screenplay or script is a blueprint, written by a screenwriter, for a film or television program. Screenplays can be original works or adaptations from existing works such as novels. A screenplay differs from a script in that it is more specifically targeted at the visual, narrative arts, such as film and television, whereas a script can involve a blueprint of "what happens" in a comic, an advertisement, a theatrical play and other "blueprinted" creations.

The major components of a screenplay are action and dialogue, with the "action" being "what we see happening" and "dialogue" being "what the characters say". The characters, when first introduced in the screenplay, may also be described visually. Screenplays differ from traditional literature conventions in ways described below; however, screenplays may not involve emotion-related descriptions and other aspects of the story that are, in fact, visual within the end-product. For more details on the contents of screenplays, see Screenwriting.

In the United States, the Writers Guild of America (WGA) has final control on who may be awarded screenwriting credit for a screenplay in a union production. The WGA is one of several organizations in the U.S. and worldwide which recognize screenplays with awards.

A script for television is sometimes called a teleplay.

Screenplay Format

There is no unique "rule" for the writing of a screenplay, but throughout the world, within the relevant industries, several conventions are adhered to.

Film

Motion picture screenplays intended for submission to mainstream studios, whether in the US or elsewhere in the world, are expected to conform to a standard typographical format known widely as studio format which stipulates how elements of the screenplay such as scene headings, action, transitions, dialogue, character names, shots and parenthetical matter should be presented on the page, as well as the font size and line spacing.

One reason for this is that, when rendered in studio format, most screenplays will transfer onto the screen at the rate of approximately one page per minute. This rule of thumb is widely contested-a page of dialog usually occupies less screen time than a page of action, for example, and it depends enormously on the literary style of the writer-and yet it continues to hold sway in modern Hollywood.

There is no single standard for studio format. Some studios have definitions of the required format written into the rubric of their writer's contract. The Nicholl Fellowship, a screenwriting competition run under the auspices of the Academy of Motion Picture Arts and Sciences, has a useful and accurate guide to screenplay format. There is also a compact, quick-reference chart with format specifications and examples called the Screenplay Format Guide from ScriptBuddy. Most screenwriting software comes with a set of templates for various screenplay formats which are more or less standard. A detailed description of correct screenplay format can be found here.

Traditionally, a screenplay should be 90-110 pages long. Comedies and children's films tend to weigh in at the lower end.

Screenplays are almost always written using a monospaced font, often a variant of Courier although other fonts are sometimes seen, including those intended to resemble the output of an old battered typewriter such as a Remington Portable.

Television

For American TV shows, the format rules for hour dramas, like CSI, and single-camera sitcoms, like Scrubs, are essentially the same as for motion pictures. The main difference is that TV scripts have act breaks. Multi-camera sitcoms, like Two and a Half Men, use a different, specialized format that derives from radio and the stage play. In this format, dialogue is double-spaced, action lines are capitalized, and scene headings are capitalized and underlined.

The script format for documentaries and audio-visual presentations which consist largely of voice-over matched to still or moving pictures is different again and uses a two-column format which can be particularly difficult to achieve in standard word processors, at least when it comes to editing.

PHYSICAL FORMAT

American screenplays are printed single-sided on three-hole-punched letter sized (8.5 x 11 inch) paper, and held together with two brass brads in thé top and bottom hole. The middle hole is left empty. In the UK, double-hole-punched A4 paper is often used, although some UK writers use the US letter paper format, especially when their scripts are to be read by American producers, since otherwise the pages may be cropped when printed on US paper. Despite the use of double-punched paper, it is common to see scripts in the UK held together by a single brad punched in the top left hand corner. This makes it easy to flip from page to page during script meetings and may have something to do with the taller page of A4.

Screenplays are usually bound with a light card stock cover and back page, often showing the logo of the production company or agency submitting the script.

Increasingly, reading copies of screenplays (that is, those distributed by producers and agencies in the hope of attracting finance or talent) are distributed printed on both sides of the paper (often professionally bound) to cut down on paper waste out of environmental concerns. Occasionally they are reduced to half-size to make a small book which is convenient to read or put in a pocket; this is generally for use by the director or other production crew during shooting.

Although most writing contracts continue to stipulate physical delivery of three or more copies of a finished script, it is common for scripts to be delivered electronically via email. Although most production companies can handle scripts in most formats, it is better practice to supply scripts as a PDF file where possible. This is because it gives the writer final control over the layout of the script, which may otherwise vary depending on what fonts and/or paper size the recipient uses to print the script out. The formatting software programs listed at the bottom of this article produce industry formatted standard screenplays in PDF.

WRITING ON SPEC OR ASSIGNMENT

Screenplays can be written either on "spec" (speculative) or as assignment ("Commissioned"). The Variety language dictionary defines "spec script" as "a script shopped or sold on the open market, as opposed to one commissioned by a studio or production company."

Writing on Assignment

Assignments are commissioned by production companies or studios on the basis of pitches from producers or writers, or literary properties they already own. Most established writers do most of their work on assignment and will only "spec" scripts which they think no-one will pay them to write, or if they cannot find assignment work.

There are exceptions: some very famous writers only write on spec because they know that they can get a better price for their work this way. Other writers spec scripts that they care deeply about so that they do not have to bend to the whims of executives and producers.

An assignment may be for an original screenplay, or for an adapted screenplay based on another work such as a novel, film, short story, comic book, magazine article or, increasingly, video game. It may also, however, be for a rewrite of an existing script, and in fact this is how a large proportion of writers in the modern studio system make their living. Rewriting scripts is an art in itself and an extremely lucrative one at that: it is not unknown for trusted writers in the higher echelons of the industry to receive $200,000 a week (2004 numbers) for their efforts. $50,000 per week is not uncommon.

Rewriting is difficult because executives often have very clear ideas about what is wrong with a script, however, they are usually unable to provide detailed prescriptions for ways it can be fixed. This is not surprising, because screenwriting is not the expertise of the executive, but of the screenwriter. The writer is therefore usually expected to come up with a detailed prescription for how the script can be improved, and then execute this in a timely fashion. During the process of choosing a writer to rewrite a script the executives may ask several writers for their 'take' and choose the one who appears to have the greatest likelihood of moving the script forward to the point where it may be granulite for production.

Before 'going to script' a writer may be asked to write a treatment, an outline, or a step outline describing the script in various granularities of detail. Some writers resist this process and will do anything to avoid it and get down the writing the script itself; others embrace the process and even deliver fairly elaborate treatments, the so-called scriptments. It is fair to say that producers tend to be wary of the former and pleasantly surprised by the latter.

SPEC SCRIPTS

A spec script is a "speculative" screenplay, one that the Variety language dictionary defines as being "shopped or sold on the open market, as opposed to one commissioned by a studio or production company."

Spec scripts are written for various reasons:

- by writers, who hope to have a script optioned and eventually purchased by producers or studios;
- by writer/directors, who want to direct a film themselves;
- by amateur writers hoping to convince a literary agent to represent them or a producer to hire them.

Attracting Producers

The process of 'going out' with a spec script can be an extremely tense and nerve-wracking one for a writer. The writer's agent will identify a number of prospective buyers who may range from small independent producers to executives working in the major studios, and attempt to build up 'heat' under the script. The script is sent out simultaneously to all the prospective buyers, usually to be read over the weekend, in the hope of attracting a bidding war.

Within a few days it is abundantly clear whether the script is going to sell or not. If it does, the writer may receive a payment of anything from a few tens of thousands of dollars to several million. If not, the script is often dead in the water because it is now in the databases of the studios and development executives, and has been marked as having been 'passed' on.

Sample Script

A sample script is usually not intended for production, but to showcase the screenwriting skills of the author, in hopes of attracting the attention of an agent or producer. Often a spec script which fails to sell goes on to be a sample script

Many Spec scripts (short for speculative) are written independently by screenwriters in hopes of optioning and eventually outright selling them to producers or studios. Other spec scripts are written by writer-directors who plan to direct the film themselves. Many so-called "arthouse" films fall into this latter category, whereas the former category tends to be filled with "high-concept" scripts-mostly action or comedy, to which a star or A-list director can be attached.

Script Costs

Script costs can include adaptation rights, but often story rights are listed separately in the development section of a budget.

The cost of screenplays vary enormously, and there are often many different writers involved, some of which are uncredited. For example, Quentin Tarantino did uncredited rewrites for Silver Surfer and It's Pat (see Jami Berhard's Quentin Tarantino: The Man and His Movies).

Jurassic Park was adapted by the book's author, Michael Crichton, for a large undisclosed sum. His salary for Twister was 2.5 million, but there were many writers involved, not just him.

Out of a $72 million budget for the film Signs, writer-director M. Night Shyamalan was paid $5 million, most of which were however license fees for the story rights. For the film The Village (total budget: $71 million) Shyamalan received $327,500 for all writing costs including the screenplay fees for his production company Blinding Edge Pictures and costs for materials, supplies, script duplication as well as fringes. An additional $7.2 million were payed to Shyamalan for the story rights, almost three times the amount Shyamalan earned for his work as producer and director on the film.

Although the highest paid names are stars and directors and sometimes novelists who get their film adapted, a good screenwriter can command-and is worth-a large salary. Total script costs can easily be ten percent of the film's budget but, like other areas of a film, unless the writer is a star, it is unlikely for a big budget film to spend more than 5% in the script department.

For a movie with a script budget of $500,000 that is not an adaptation, written on assignment, the payments might break down as follows (referred to as "300,000 against 500,000"):

- First draft: $150,000
- First draft revisions: $50,000
- Second draft: $75,000
- Second draft revisions: $25,000
- Production bonus: $200,000

The first four payments are paid half on commencement of the writing step and half on completion. The final payment, the production bonus, is paid only if the script goes into production and becomes due on the first day of principal photography. If a script is approved for production before all the steps have been completed, the production bonus could be bigger. This means there may be an incentive for the writer not to drag out the process.

The Development Process

Once a studio has purchased or commissioned a script, it goes through the process of revisions and rewriting until all stakeholders are satisfied and ready to proceed. It is not uncommon for a script to go through many, many drafts on its journey to production. Very few scripts improve steadily with each draft, and when a certain avenue has been exhausted the writer will often be replaced and another brought in to do a rewrite. Occasionally it becomes impossible to satisfy all such parties, and the project enters development hell.

If a studio decides it does not wish to proceed to production with the script, the project enters 'turnaround'. Another studio may purchase the script from its original owner, but the script is encumbered with the development costs the studio has already incurred. At a certain point, it may simply be uneconomic for anyone to purchase the script, even if it is a very good one. This goes part of the way to explaining why some of the best scripts in Hollywood remain unproduced.

The Shooting Script

Once a script has been approved for production, camera directions and notes may be inserted by the Director, and each scene is assigned a number to provide a convenient way for the various production departments to reference individual scenes. When a scene is omitted, its number is retained labelled with "OMITTED", so that it won't be assigned to any newly added scenes.

When the shooting script is distributed, its pages are locked, meaning that any subsequent revisions will apply to the first set of revision pages. When revisions are distributed, the pages are swapped into the outstanding drafts, and the script is once again locked. The process is repeated for each new round of revisions.

Each round of revisions is distributed on different coloured paper. The progression of colours varies from one production to the next. Since rewrites often continue throughout principal photography, most shooting scripts evolve into a rainbow of gold, pink, blue, green and cherry pages.

Transcripts

A screenplay is different from a transcript. A transcript is simply a copy of what dialogue finally appeared on-screen, without regard to the original script, the stage directions or action. A full post-production transcript may also include descriptions of the action on-screen, but since it is generally not written by a professional writer but either a production assistant or a fan, it may not be particularly entertaining to read.

Many published screenplays available at booksellers or downloaded from the internet are in fact glorified post-production transcripts rather than shooting scripts. Transcripts and screenplays often differ radically because scenes are frequently re-ordered or dropped entirely during the editing process. Moreover, actors may change lines or simply improvise dialog, and many directors will make their own changes to the script on the fly during rehearsal or shooting.

It can be extremely revealing to compare a shooting script with the film as finally distributed.

Screenwriting Software

Detailed computer programs are designed specifically for screenplays, and many have templates for teleplays and stageplays. These programs have been designed to create industry standard screenplays and are used by professional screenwriters. What should be remembered is that all such software is an aid in 'formatting' of a screenplay and not the actual 'creation' of it. A number of these programs offer access to on-line screenwriter communities where you can publish your work for feedback from fellow screenwriters. Furthermore, screenwriting software is available for handheld devices (Palm OS, and Windows Mobile / Pocket PC).

SCREENWRITER'S SALARY

A typical writer's deal usually comprises:

- *Option:* Monies paid in exchange for the right (the "option") to produce--and therefore to purchase outright--a screenplay, treatment or other work within a certain period.
- *Guarantee:* Literally, the monies the writer is guaranteed to receive, whether the script is produced or not. This amount is usually divided into payments for multiple

drafts (commonly, a draft and a "set," a set being a rewrite and a polish). The guaranteed monies are sometimes referred to as the "front-end."

- *Bonus/Bonuses:* Also known as the "back-end." Typically, a production bonus is paid once the script goes into production, or, if there has been more than one writer, after the final credit has been determined. A typical contract will specify a smaller production bonus for shared credit. There may also be bonuses contingent upon budget (e.g. "if the movie's budget is greater than x...") or grosses. The cousin of the bonus is the "penalty," which might be paid by the writer if, for example, the script has not been put into production by a set date. Penalties are rarely included in writer's deals, however.

Definitions

- Five figures: under $100,000
- Low-six figures: under $300,000
- Mid-six figures: between $300,000 and $600,000
- High-six figures: over $600,000
- Seven figures: Over $1 million
- *Spec Script:* Short for "speculative." The writer writes the script without being paid, and, subsequently, tries to sell it.
- *Pitch:* The writer works up a five-to-twenty minute presentation of a prospective movie and presents it to buyers in a short meeting.
- *Assignment:* A rewrite-for-pay of someone else's script. The writer pitches his "take" much like he would an original pitch.

History of Screenwriters' Pay

- 1900: One of America's first screenwriters, New York journalist Roy McCardell, is hired to write ten scenarios (each about 90 seconds long) for $15 each (has the buying power of about $332 today).

- 1947: The original screenplay Woman of the Year is bought by MGM for $100,000 (about $950,000 today).
- 1949: Ben Hecht is paid $10,000 a week (about $77,000 today). Claims David O. Selznick paid him $3,500 a day (about $27,000 today).
- 1967: William Goldman's original screenplay Butch Cassidy and the Sundance Kid is bought for $400,000 (about $2.25 million today).
- 1972: Leonard and Paul Schrader's spec script The Yakuza is sold for $350,000 (about $1.6 million today). Paul Schrader and his agent receive 40% each; novelist Leonard Schrader, who conceived the idea for the story, is persuaded to take just 20% and a story credit.
- 1984: Shane Black sells the screenplay to Lethal Weapon for $250,000, ushering in the modern spec market.
- 1985: Ex-fireman Gregory Widen sells his university thesis screenplay Highlander for $500,000.
- 1990: Kathy McWorter-promoted by her agent as a 21 year-old wunderkind, though she was in fact 28-sells her sex comedy The Cheese Stands Alone for $1 million. This was followed by nuclear-terrorist technothriller The Ultimatum by Laurence Dworet and Robert Roy Pool and WWII action comedy Hell Bent... and Back! by Doug Richardson, both of which sold for a million dollars.
- 1990: Brian Helgeland and Manny Coto sell their nuclear-armed robot spec The Ticking Man for $1.2 million. The script was sent out with a ticking alarm clock attached.
- 1990: Shane Black is paid $1.75 million for The Last Boy Scout.
- 1990: Joe Eszterhas sells Basic Instinct to Carolco for $3 million, but is replaced by Total Recall scribe Gary Goldman when he argues with director Paul Verhoeven over explicit content. There will not be another million dollar spec script for over two years.
- 1991: Front page of Variety mourns the end of the modern spec market, announcing "the candy store is closed."

- 1992: Sherry Lansing is hired to run Paramount and spends $3.6 million in less than a week, $2.5 million for a two-page outline of Jade by Joe Eszterhas, and $1.1 million for the for the script Milk Money by John Mattson. At the time, both deals are records, respectively, for outlines and romantic comedy specs.
- 1994: After a bidding war, Shane Black is paid $4.5 million by New Line for The Long Kiss Goodnight.
- 1999: M. Night Shyamalan-who received $2.5 million for breakout script The Sixth Sense-is paid $5 million for Unbreakable, plus another $5 million to produce and direct. Later receives same sum for Signs.
- 2003: M. Night Shyamalan is paid $7.5 million for The Woods, later renamed The Village, but with a reduced fee of $3.21 million for producing and directing.
- 2004: Peter Jackson is paid the higher of $20 million aggregate or 20% of the gross to write, produce and direct King Kong. Jackson wrote the screenplay with his wife, Fran Walsh, and Phillipa Boyens.
- 2004: Bobby Florsheim and Josh Stolberg are paid $1.5 million against $2.5 million + 2% for "The Passion Of The Ark", later becoming Evan Almighty. Daily Variety reports this as the highest price paid for a spec script by unproduced writers.

Current Records

Some of the highest amounts paid to writers for spec screenplays:

$4 million:

- The Long Kiss Goodnight by Shane Black

$3 million:

- Basic Instinct by Joe Eszterhas
- Medicine Man by Tom Schulman
- The Ugly Americans (Eurotrip) by Alec Berg, David Mandel and Jeff Schaffer
- Bad Dog (unproduced) by Dale Launer

- Married in the Morning (unproduced) by Harry Elfont and Deborah Kaplan
- Panic Room by David Koepp. $2 million against $3 million.

$2.75 million:

- Mozart and the Whale (The Newports) by Ronald Bass. $2 million against $2,750,000.

$2.5 million:

- The Sixth Sense by M. Night Shyamalan
- Twister by Michael Crichton and Anne-Marie Crichton
- Jade by Joe Eszterhas
- A Knight's Tale by Brian Helgeland
- Untitled Will Davies Romantic Comedy (unproduced) by Will Davies
- Jackson (unproduced) by Brandon Camp and Mike Thompson
- The Superconducting Supercollider of Sparkle Creek, Wisconsin (unproduced) by David Koepp and John Kamps. '$2.5 million against $3.25 million with an additional deferred bonus of $1.5 million for Koepp.
- Deja Vu by Terry Rossio and Bill Marsilii. $2 million against $5 million.

$2.25 million:

- Untitled Disney Family Comedy (unproduced) by Kevin Bisch
- They Came From Upstairs (unproduced) by Mark Burton
- You, Me and Dupree by Mike LeSieur
- The Break-Up by Vince Vaughn, Jeremy Garelick and Jay Lavender

$2 million:

- The Arrangement (unproduced) by Kevin Bisch
- Stalker: A Love Story (unproduced) by Michael Carnes and Josh Gilbert

- The Worst Man (unproduced) by Michael Carnes and Josh Gilbert
- Manhattan Ghost Story (unproduced) by Ronald Bass, based on the novel by T.M. Wright.
- Radio Flyer by David M. Evans
- Forever Young by Jeffrey Abrams
- Showgirls by Joe Eszterhas
- Sacred Cows (unproduced) by Joe Eszterhas
- Reliable Sources (unproduced) by Joe Eszterhas
- Courage Under Fire by Patrick Sheane Duncan
- Tennessee (Pearl Harbor) by Randall Wallace
- River Road (unproduced) by Andrew Niccol
- The Mark (unproduced) by Rob Liefield
- Untitled Tim Herlihy Comedy (unproduced) by Tim Herlihy
- The Game by John D. Brancato and Michael Ferris
- Untitled Firestein-Pesce Action Project (unproduced) by Les Firestein and PJ Pesce
- Executive Search (unproduced) by Gerald Di Pego
- Going West (Switchback) by Jeb Stuart
- Untitled Michael McCullers Buddy Comedy (unproduced) by Michael McCullers
- Alpha (unproduced) by David Benioff
- Ghost Town by David Koepp and John Kamps
- Male Pattern Baldness (unproduced) by Joe Eszterhas. $2 million against 4.5 million.

$1.8 million:

- RPM (unproduced) by J.H. Wyman
- Stay by David Benioff

$1.5 million:

- The Passion of the Ark by Bobby Florsheim and Josh Stolberg. $1.5 million against 2.5 million.

$1.25 million:

- 99 Problems (unproduced) by Deborah Kaplan and Harry Elfont. $1.25 against $2 million.

$1.1 million:

- Milk Money by John Mattson, bought outright by Paramount in 1992.

$1 million:

- Foreplay (unproduced) by Joe Eszterhas. $1 million against $3.5 million.
- The Cheese Stands Alone (unproduced) by Kathy McWorter.

$750,000:

- Steinbeck's Point of View (unproduced) by Brandon Camp and Mike Thompson. $750,000 against $3,750,000 with an additional potential $2 million bonus cast contingent.
- Man-Witch by Bobby Florsheim and Josh Stolberg. $750,000 against $1.5 million.

ACT STRUCTURE (FILM)

Act structure explains how a plot of a film story is composed. Just like plays (Staged drama) have 'Acts', critics and screenwriters tend to divide films into acts; though films don't require to be broken down as such in reality.

Whereas plays are actual live performances that need 'breaks' in the middle for change of set, costume, or for the artists' rest; films are recorded performances shown mechanically and therefore don't need actual breaks. Still they are divided into acts for reasons that are in aesthetic and structural conformation with the original idea of Act in theatre. Act breaks in a film are usually very obscure for lay audience and only a trained person can detect the ending of one act and the beginning of the other in the progression of a movie. The idea of Act structure is of more value while writing a Screenplay than watching a film, though the Act breaks are never actually written in the final copies of screenplays. But television scripts called Teleplays almost always include clear denotions as such. Act is the broadest structural unit of enacted stories. The most common paradigm in theatre, and so in films, is that of the 'Three-Act structure' proposed by Aristotle. It simply means that any story has a 'beginning', a 'middle' and an 'end'. Playwrights and screenwriters divide their stories into three major parts viz. 'Set up', 'Confrontation' (alternatively called as 'conflict' or 'complication') and 'Resolution'. These form the basic three acts of any performance-staged or screened.

Though various theories have been proposed and debated, the Three-act structure stands as the most popular one. Also, this is what Hollywood has discovered and proved as the most successful. The rest of the world cinema may have its own ways of looking at the plot.

THE 'THREE-ACT STRUCTURE'

According to Hollywood, feature films are considered as audio-visual narrative forms which can be seen in distinct parts called 'Acts'.

It follows that the enacted story opens with the introduction of characters and situations, backdrop, locale etc. It creates interest in the audience and takes them to feel concerned as to what the real problem is and what may happen with it. Plays, and screenplays, usually revolve around main characters-the 'Protagonist' and the 'Antagonist' who engage themselevs into a battle. That is "Set up".

The next part-and considered to be more important-is complication of the problem of the story. It intrigues the audience all the more, giving them more and more information and putting various points of view for imaginative comparison. This eventually leads to higher points of audience interest. Because this second Act of most screenplays adds all the possible dramatic values to the plot, this is considered to be the core of the same. The Antagonist and the Protagonist try and experiment with all their strengths (and weaknesses of the other) to win the battle. That is "Confrontation".

This takes us to the third-and the most important-act, the "Resolution". This means it tends to 'solve' the problem (-s) of the story developed so far. But this is not obvious, as it is expected to bring the 'climax' (or a series of climaxes) to give the audience the pay-off. The tool usually implemented is a 'do or die' situation where doors of escape for either or both of the two characters go on closing one by one, leaving them with only a thin chance that demands the fullest exploitation of their qualities and energies. This so called jaw-dropping, breath-taking, arm-rest-grabbing moment for the audience leads to the final outcome of the entire plot. And it is usually the triumph of the good (Protagonist) over the evil (Antagonist), with rare exceptions.

Limitations

This framework can not be rigidly applied to all the film stories, and there are a good proportion of Hollywood movies that defy this theory. Many films follow this pattern only to a subtle extent, where their genre demands a more delicate handling. Screenwiters and Script doctors have tried tc provide alternative ideas, which again are open for debate. As said earlier, cinema across the world and 20th century has evolved its own ways of putting a story. Also, this theory may not be fit for non-fiction films like documentary or corporate films, which may not have a 'plot' at their base with 'characters' and all their 'actions and speeches' predecided, like the feature films have. Such non-fiction films require their own forms of arrangement.

What is important here is that ideas of Act structure help us understand films better. More importantly, these are 'tools' of the screenplay writers who can break down the story at hand and play with various ways of presenting it to find the best possible one. Experts have gone long way ahead in dividing plot to even smaller structural units and they keep working to find the most effective formula of structuring a film story.

PLOT POINT

In television and film, a plot point is a significant event within a plot that digs into the action and spins it around in another direction. Noted screenwriting teacher Syd Field teaches that the 'ideal' movie plot has the first plot point occurring around the 30th minute of the film, then the second one around the 90th minute. See screenwriting theories for an overview list of plot points.

Monomyth

The monomyth (often referred to as "the hero's journey") is a description of a basic pattern found in many narratives from around the world. This universal pattern was described by Joseph Campbell in his book The Hero with a Thousand Faces (1949). A noted scholar of novelist James Joyce, Campbell borrowed the term monomyth from Joyce's Finnegans Wake.

Campbell's work has been consciously applied by a wide variety of modern writers and artists, for example, in creating screenplays for movies. The best known is perhaps George Lucas, who has acknowledged a debt to Campbell regarding both the original Star Wars trilogy and its prequels.

In addition, leaders in the men's movement, notably Robert Bly and Michael J. Meade, have used Campbell's insight as a guide for personal spiritual growth.

Campbell's insight was that important myths from around the world which have survived for thousands of years, all share a fundamental structure. This fundamental structure contains a number of stages, which includes

1. A call to adventure, which the hero has to accept or decline
2. A road of trials, regarding which the hero succeeds or fails
3. Achieving the goal or "boon," which often results in important self-knowledge
4. A return to the ordinary world, again as to which the hero can succeed or fail
5. Application of the boon, in which what the hero has gained can be used to improve the world

In a well-known quote from the introduction to The Hero with a Thousand Faces, Campbell wrote:

"A hero ventures forth from the world of common day into a region of supernatural wonder: fabulous forces are there encountered and a decisive victory is won: the hero comes back from this mysterious adventure with the power to bestow boons on his fellow man."

The classic examples of the monomyth relied upon by Campbell and other scholars include the Buddha, Moses, and Christ stories, although Campbell cites many other classic myths from many cultures which rely upon this basic structure.

Summary of the Monomyth

In the monomyth, the hero starts in the ordinary world, and receives a call to enter an unusual world of strange powers and events. If the hero accepts the call to enter this strange world, the hero must face tasks and trials, and may have to face these trials alone, or may have assistance. At its most intense, the hero must survive a severe challenge, often with help earned along the journey.

If the hero survives, the hero may achieve a great gift or "boon." The hero must then decide whether to return to the ordinary world with this boon. If the hero does decide to return, the hero often faces challenges on the return journey. If the hero is successful in returning, the boon or gift may be used to improve the world. The stories of Osiris, Prometheus, Moses, Buddha, and Christ, for example, follow this structure very closely.

Campbell describes some seventeen stages or steps along this journey. Very few myths contain all seventeen stages-some myths contain many of the stages, while others contain only a few; some myths may have as a focus only one of the stages, while other myths may deal with the stages in a somewhat different order. These seventeen stages may be organized in a number of ways, including division into three sections: Departure (sometimes called Separation), Initiation and Return. "Departure" deals with the hero venturing forth on the quest; "Initiation" deals with the hero's various adventures along the way; and "Return" deals with the hero's return home with knowledge and powers acquired on the journey.

Other Formulations

Campbell's proposed structure has been expanded and modified since its conception. Many modern characterizations of it add in new steps (such as the hero having a miraculous birth) or combine or prune others. For instance, Phil Cousineau, in his book, The Hero's Journey, divides it up into the following eight steps:

1. The Call to Adventure
2. The Road of Trials
3. The Vision Quest
4. The Meeting with the Goddess
5. The Boon
6. The Magic Flight
7. The Return Threshold
8. The Master of Two Worlds

Another eight-step formulation was given by David Adams Leeming in his book, Mythology: The Voyage of the Hero:

1. Miraculous conception and birth
2. Initiation of the hero-child
3. Withdrawal from family or community for meditation and preparation
4. Trial and Quest
5. Death
6. Descent into the underworld
7. Resurrection and rebirth
8. Ascension, apotheosis, and atonement

Use of the Monomyth by Modern Artists

The monomyth has influenced a number of artists, musicians, poets, and filmmakers, including Bob Dylan and George Lucas. Mickey Hart, Bob Weir and Jerry Garcia of the Grateful Dead had long noted Campbell's influence and agreed to participate in a seminar with him in 1986 entitled From Ritual to Rapture.

George Lucas and Star Wars

George Lucas's deliberate use of Campbell's theory of the monomyth in the making of the Star Wars movies is well-documented. In addition to the extensive discussion between Campbell and Bill Moyers broadcast in 1988 on PBS as The Power of Myth (Filmed at "Skywalker Ranch"), on Campbell's influence on the Star Wars films, Lucas, himself, gave an extensive interview for the biography Joseph Campbell: A Fire in the Mind (Larsen and Larsen, 2002, pages 541-543) on this topic.

In this interview, Lucas states that in the early 1970's after completing his early film, American Graffiti, "it came to me that there really was no modern use of mythology...so that's when I started doing more strenuous research on fairy tales, folklore and mythology, and I started reading Joe's books. Before that I hadn't read any of Joe's books.... It was very eerie because in reading The Hero with A Thousand Faces I began to realize that my first draft of Star Wars was following classical motifs"(p.541).

Twelve years after the making of The Power of Myth, Moyers and Lucas met again for the 1999 interview, the Mythology of Star Wars with George Lucas & Bill Moyers, to further discuss the impact of Campbell's work on Lucas' films. In addition, the National Air and Space Museum of the Smithsonian Institution sponsored an exhibit during the late 1990s called Star Wars: The Magic of Myth which discussed the ways in which Campbell's work shaped the Star Wars films. A companion guide of the same name was published in 1997.

Chris Vogler, The Writer's Journey, and Hollywood Films

Christopher Vogler, a Hollywood film producer and writer, created a now-legendary 7-page company memo, A Practical Guide to The Hero With a Thousand Faces, based on Campbell's work which inspired films such as Disney's 1994 film, The Lion King. Vogler's memo was later developed into the late 1990s book, The Writer's Journey: Mythic Structure For Writers, This story structure is evident in a vast number of successful Hollywood films including the Matrix series.

Orson Scott Card and Ender's Game

In his book, Ender's Game, Orson Scott Card gives a very complete example of the monomyth structure, with the main character, Ender Wiggin, fulfilling all eight primary stages of it:

- *Miraculous Birth*-In a world where only two children are normally allowed, Ender is born as the third child by special government decree
- *Initiation*-Ender shows remarkable intelligence at a young age
- *Withdrawal*-Ender is removed from his family and sent to Battle School
- *Trial and Quest*-Ender learns of the threat to humanity from the Buggers
- *Death*-Ender grows despondent after his unit is broken up, and he is sent back to Earth
- *Descent into the underworld*-Ender's sister helps him feel like part of humanity once again
- *Resurrection and rebirth*-Ender refuses to play the "simulations" anymore, and ends the "game" by destroying the Buggers' homeworld
- *Ascension, apotheosis, and atonement*-Ender realizes that the simulations were in fact real and has to cope with this

The narrative structure within Ender's Game doesn't follow this structure perfectly linearly. Many elements of it are actually repeated throughout the book. For instance, the latter four steps can also describe the psychological states Ender went through after his realization of what he'd done to the Buggers.

Modern Applications of the Monomyth

Each of the seventeen stages of the monomyth (below) can be found in popular works, including movie series such as the Star Wars movies, The Matrix movies and even the anime Fortune Dogs.

DEPARTURE (OR SEPARATION)

The Call to Adventure

The adventure begins with the hero receiving a call to action, such as a threat to the peace of the community, or the hero simply falls into or blunders into it. The call is often announced to the hero by another character who acts as a "herald". The herald, often represented as dark or terrifying and judged evil by the world, may call the character to adventure simply by the crisis of his appearance.

Campbell: The Call To Adventure-"A blunder-apparently the merest chance-reveals an unsuspected world, and the individual is drawn into a relationship with forces that are not rightly understood" (Joseph Campbell, The Hero With A Thousand Faces, 51).

Modern Applications: In Star Wars, Luke Skywalker, the hero, begins the story in frustration over being unable to leave home. The heralds are the two droids who carry a message from Princess Leia. In The Matrix, the call comes in the form of Morpheus and his followers who encourage the hero, Neo, to question reality. Morpheus literally calls Neo using a cell phone.

Classic Examples: Sometimes the call to adventure happens of the character's own volition. In the story of the Minotaur, Theseus learns the tale of the beast and the terrible sacrifice to appease it, which sets him on a quest to destroy it. In Herman Hesse's book Siddhartha the main character, Siddhartha, becomes weary of his way of life and decides he must venture away from his accustomed life in order to attain spiritual enlightenment. Most Buddhist myths describe the Buddha as becoming bored with his royal life and venturing into the world. Other times, the hero is plunged into adventure by unforeseen events. In Homer's Odyssey, Odysseus is caught in the terrible winds of the angered god Poseidon and sent off to distant lands.

REFUSAL OF THE CALL

In some stories, the hero initially refuses the call to adventure. When this happens, the hero may suffer somehow, and may eventually choose to answer, or may continue to decline the call.

Campbell: Refusal of the Call-"Refusal of the summons converts the adventure into its negative. Walled in boredom, hard work, or 'culture,' the subject loses the power of significant affirmative action and becomes a victim to be saved" (Joseph Campbell, The Hero With A Thousand Faces, 59).

Modern Applications: In Star Wars, Luke is refused adventure by his uncle, a man who seeks to protect Luke from the inevitable dangers of fate. Subsequently, Luke's family is killed by stormtroopers. In The Matrix, Neo refuses to take the window washing scaffold to escape and is captured by the Agents.

Classic Examples: Myth and history are rife with examples of what happens to those who refuse the call too long or do not take it seriously. A Persian city was turned to stone, inhabitants and all, for refusing the call of Allah. Daphne was pursued by the Greek god Apollo (a herald), but refused his advances at all costs. She prayed to her father, Peneus, to take away her beauty to be rid of Apollo; Peneus turned the nymph into a tree, the only semblance left of her past self being her beauty. In Judeo-Christian mythology, Lot's wife is turned into a pillar of salt for looking back with longing to her old life when she had been summoned forth from her city by Yahweh. One of the clearest references to the refusal and its consequences comes in the voice of Yahweh in Proverbs 1:24-27 and 32:

Because I have called, and ye refused... I also will laugh at your calamity; I will mock when your fear cometh; when your fear cometh as desolation, and your destruction cometh as a whirlwind; when distress and anguish cometh upon you.... For the turning away of the simple shall slay them, and the prosperity of fools shall destroy them.

SUPERNATURAL AID

After the hero has accepted the call, he encounters a protective figure (often elderly) who provides special tools and advice for the adventure ahead, such as an amulet or a weapon.

Modern applications: In Star Wars, Luke encounters the Jedi Master Obi-Wan Kenobi who presents Luke with a lightsaber and teaches him the ways of the Force. In The Matrix Neo meets with The Oracle who gives him advice which proves invaluable in his journey.

In The Hitchhikers Guide to the Galaxy, Ford Prefect gives Arthur Dent the copy of the guide.

Classic example: In Greek mythology, Ariadne gives Theseus a ball of string and a sword before he enters the labyrinth to confront the minotaur.

THE CROSSING OF THE FIRST THRESHOLD

The hero must cross the threshold between the world he is familiar with and that which he is not. Often this involves facing a "threshold guardian", an entity that works to keep all within the protective confines of the world but must be encountered in order to enter the new zone of experience.

Modern applications: In Star Wars, the threshold is Mos Eisley, a spaceport that acts as a doorway between Luke's home planet and the wider universe; Luke must avoid capture by the threshold guardians, the Imperial stormtroopers. In The Matrix, Neo must choose the red pill to leave the Matrix and enter the real world.

Rebirth

The hero, rather than passing a threshold, passes into the new zone by means of rebirth. Appearing to have died by being swallowed or having their flesh scattered, the hero is transformed and becomes ready for the adventure ahead.

Biblical applications: In the gospels, John the Baptist baptizes Jesus before Jesus begins his public ministry.

Modern applications: In Star Wars, it is the Death Star, in which Luke is engulfed and in which he learns how to be a hero. In The Matrix, Neo finds himself waking up in a bio-electric cell where he is one of the humans being harvested by the machines.

INITIATION

The Road of Trials

Once past the threshold, the hero encounters a dream landscape of ambiguous and fluid forms. The hero is challenged to survive a succession of obstacles and, in so doing, amplifies his consciousness. The hero is helped covertly by the supernatural helper or may discover a benign power supporting him in his passage.

Marriage

The ultimate trial is often represented as a marriage between the hero and a queenlike, or mother-like figure. This represents the hero's mastery of life (represented by the feminine) as well as the totality of what can be known. When the hero is female, this becomes a male figure.

Modern Applications: In The Matrix, Neo confronts the Oracle. In The Matrix Reloaded, Neo takes Trinity as a lover.

Woman as Temptress

His awareness expanded, the hero may fixate on the disunity between truth and his subjective outlook, inherently tainted by the flesh. This is often represented with revulsion or rejection of a female figure.

Modern Applications: In The Matrix Reloaded, Persephone attempts to seduce Neo. In Star Wars, there is tension between Luke and Han Solo over their love for Princess Leia--this is resolved in Episode VI, Return of the Jedi when Luke finds out that Leia is actually his sister. Luke is also tempted by the dark side itself, as demonstrated by his vision in the cave on Dagobah.

Atonement with the Father

The hero reconciles the tyrant and merciful aspects of the father-like authority figure to understand himself as well as this figure.

Biblical Applications: In the gospels, Jesus wrestles with his impending death in the Garden of Gethsemane, before submitting to his Father's will.

Modern applications: In The Empire Strikes Back, Luke confronts Darth Vader and learns that he is his father and a former Jedi; in Return of the Jedi, he is reconciled with the reformed Vader. In The Matrix Revolutions, the Oracle explains to Neo that she and the Architect are two programs that work together to keep the Matrix working, the latter to "balance the equation" and the former to "unbalance" it.

APOTHEOSIS

The hero's ego is disintegrated in a breakthrough expansion of consciousness. Quite frequently the hero's idea of reality is changed; the hero may find an ability to do new things or to see a larger point of view, allowing the hero to sacrifice himself.

Modern applications: In The Empire Strikes Back, Luke sacrifices a part of himself (losing his hand) rather than turn to the dark side. In The Matrix, Neo faces off against Agent Smith resulting in his death and resurrection as the One.

THE ULTIMATE BOON

The hero is now ready to obtain that which he has set out, an item or new awareness that, once he returns, will benefit the society that he has left. Modern applications: In the climactic scene of Star Wars, Luke uses the Force to successfully destroy the Death Star by firing torpedoes down a narrow ventilation shaft of the Death Star.

RETURN

Refusal of the Return

Having found bliss and enlightenment in the other world, the hero may not want to return to the ordinary world to bestow the boon onto his fellow man.

Classic Examples: After obtaining Nirvana, Buddha doubted whether he could communicate the path to enlightenment. (Actually, some Buddhist traditions hold that this was only cunning politics by Buddha: by saying this he gave people the impression that he didn't want to teach them, which made them curious and eager to hear all about it).

The Magic Flight

When the boon's acquisition (or the hero's return to the world) comes against opposition, a chase or pursuit may ensue before the hero returns.

Classic Examples: In many fairy tales and folktales, it is literally a magic flight, with the hero or heroine transforming objects to stop the pursuit (The Master Maid, The Water Nixie) or transforming himself and any companions to hide themselves (Farmer Weathersky or Foundling-Bird).

Modern Examples: In the Metroid video game series, Samus Aran frequently has to outrun the destruction of a collapsing structure after defeating the final boss.

Rescue from Without

The hero may need to be rescued by forces from the ordinary world. This may be because the hero has refused to return or because he is successfully blocked from returning with the boon. The hero loses his ego.

Modern Application: In The Empire Strikes Back, Luke is rescued by the Millennium Falcon as he hangs on an antenna beneath Cloud City after a battle with Darth Vader. In The Matrix: Revolutions, Neo is physically trapped in the limbo-like Mobil Avenue subway station construct, and Morpheus and Trinity have to help him escape.

The Crossing of the Return Threshold

The hero returns to the world of common day and must accept it as real.

Master of Two Worlds

Because of the boon or due to his experience, the hero may now perceive both the divine and human worlds.

Modern Application: In Return of the Jedi, Luke becomes a Jedi. He has mastered the force and defeated the one true temptation, the Dark Side. In The Matrix Neo returns from death now able to see and control the world of The Matrix, stopping bullets and defeating the Agents. In The Matrix

Reloaded, Neo destroys several Sentinels in the real world using only his mind.

Classic Example: In the Christ story, Jesus is able to return to the ordinary world after resurrection.

Freedom to Live

The hero bestows the boon to his fellow man.

Modern Application: In "The Return of the Jedi" Luke has overcome the Empire and his rebellion is free to live and thrive, the ending scene establishes the peace restored by Luke's victory.

In The Matrix Revolutions, Neo realizes that machine life is as valid as human life and gives his own life in order to reconcile the worlds of man and machine.

According to the Gospels, Christ returns to the ordinary world after his resurrection, but not as an ordinary man. He can seem to be as others are and interact with them, but his body is a "glorified" body, capable of assuming visible and palpable form, but freed from the bonds of space and time; he is able to appear and disappear at will, for example.

Other traditional examples of something similar, are Elijah, Enoch, and Khidr, the "immortal prophet" of the Sufis.

Use of the Monomyth by the Men's Movement

Poet Robert Bly, Michael J. Meade, and others involved in the men's movement have applied and expanded the concept of the hero's journey and the monomyth as a metaphor for personal spiritual and psychological growth, particularly in the mythopoetic men's movement.

Characteristic of the mythopoetic men's movement is a tendency to retell fairy tales and engage in their exegesis as a tool for personal insight.

Using frequent references to archetypes as drawn from Jungian analytical psychology, the movement focuses on issues of gender role, gender identity and wellness for modern men. Advocates would often engage in storytelling with music, these acts being seen as a modern extension to a form of "new age shamanism" popularized by Michael Harner at approximately the same time.

Among its most famous advocates were the poet Robert Bly, whose book Iron John: A Book About Men was a best-seller, being an exegesis of the fairy tale "Iron John" by the Brothers Grimm.

The mythopoetic men's movement spawned a variety of groups and workshops, led by authors such as Bly and Robert L. Moore. Some serious academic work came out of this movement, including the creation of various magazines and non-profit organizations, such as the Mankind Project.

"The Hero's Journey"

The phrase, "the hero's journey," to describe Campbell's theories first entered into popular discourse through two documentaries. The first, released in 1987, The Hero's Journey: The World of Joseph Campbell was accompanied by a 1990 companion book, The Hero's Journey: Joseph Campbell on His Life and Work (with Phil Cousineau and Stuart Brown, eds.). The second was Bill Moyer's series of seminal interviews with Campbell, released in 1988 as the documentary (and companion book) The Power of Myth.

The phrase was then referenced in the title of a popular guidebook for screenwriters released in the 1990's, The Writer's Journey: Mythic Structure For Writers, by Christopher Vogler. Though they used the phrase in their works, Cousineau, Moyers, and Vogler, all attribute the phrase and the model of The Hero's Journey to Joseph Campbell.

Criticism

Thoughtless use of monomyth structure is often blamed for lack of originality and clichés in popular culture, especially big-budget Hollywood films. In addition to the popularity of Campbell-influenced guides such as The Writer's Journey, the influential book Screenplay by Syd Field also proposed an ideal three-act structure, which is easily compatible with modern screenwriters' attempts to craft a monomyth.

However, since the peak popularity of cinematic monomyth narratives in the 1990s, some would-be blockbuster movies that have been seen as conscious attempts to follow the structure have met with indifference from critics and often disappointing performance at the box office, as in the case of Cinderella Man and George Lucas' three Star Wars prequels.

THE HERO WITH A THOUSAND FACES

The Hero with a Thousand Faces (1949) is the seminal work of comparative mythologist Joseph Campbell. In this text Campbell discusses his theory of the journey of the archetypal hero found in world mythologies and religions.

Since publication of The Hero with a Thousand Faces, Campbell's theory has been consciously applied by a wide variety of modern writers and artists. The best known is perhaps George Lucas, who has acknowledged a debt to Campbell regarding the stories of the Star Wars films.

Summary

Campbell's insight was that important myths from around the world which have survived for thousands of years, all share a fundamental structure, which Campbell called the monomyth.

This fundamental structure contains a number of stages, which include: (1) a call to adventure, which the hero has to accept or decline, (2) a road of trials, regarding which the hero succeeds or fails, (3) achieving the goal or "boon," which often results in important self-knowledge, (4) a return to the ordinary world, again as to which the hero can succeed or fail, and finally, (5) application of the boon in which what the hero has gained can be used to improve the world.

In a well-known quote from the introduction to The Hero with a Thousand Faces, Campbell wrote:

> *"A hero ventures forth from the world of common day into a region of supernatural wonder: fabulous forces are there encountered and a decisive victory is won: the hero comes back from this mysterious adventure with the power to bestow boons on his fellow man."*

The classic examples of the monomyth relied upon by Campbell and other scholars include the Buddha, Moses, and Christ stories, although Campbell cites many other classic myths from many cultures which rely upon this basic structure.

While Campbell offers a discussion of the hero's journey by using the Freudian concepts popular in the 1940s and 1950s, the monomythic structure is not tied to these concepts. Similarly, Campbell uses a mixture of Jungian archetypes, unconscious forces, and Arnold van Gennep's structuring of rites of passage rituals to provide some illumination.

However, this pattern of the hero's journey influences artists and intellectuals worldwide, suggesting a basic usefulness for Campbell's insights not tied to academic categories and mid-20th century forms of analysis.

3

Fundamental Structure of the Monomyth

In the monomyth, the hero starts in the ordinary world, and receives a call to enter an unusual world of strange powers and events. If the hero accepts the call to enter this strange world, the hero must face tasks and trials, and may have to face these trials alone, or may have assistance. At its most intense, the hero must survive a severe challenge, often with help earned along the journey. If the hero survives, the hero may achieve a great gift or "boon." The hero must then decide whether to return to the ordinary world with this boon. If the hero does decide to return, the hero often faces challenges on the return journey. If the hero is successful in returning, the boon or gift may be used to improve the world. The stories of Osiris, Prometheus, Moses, Buddha, and Christ, for example, follow this structure very closely.

Campbell describes a number of stages or steps along this journey. Very few myths contain all of these stages-some myths contain many of the stages, while others contain only a few; some myths may have as a focus only one of the stages, while other myths may deal with the stages in a somewhat different order.

These stages may be organized in a number of ways, including division into three sections: Departure (sometimes called Separation), Initiation and Return. "Departure" deals with the hero venturing forth on the quest; "Initiation" deals with the hero's various adventures along the way; and "Return" deals with the hero's return home with knowledge and powers acquired on the journey.

ARTISTS INFLUENCED BY WORK

The Hero with a Thousand Faces has influenced a number of artists, musicians, poets, and filmmakers, including Bob Dylan and George Lucas. Mickey Hart, Bob Weir and Jerry Garcia of the Grateful Dead had long noted Campbell's influence and agreed to participate in a seminar with him in 1986 entitled From Ritual to Rapture.

George Lucas' deliberate use of Campbell's theory of the monomyth in the making of the Star Wars movies is well-documented. In addition to the extensive discussion between Campbell and Bill Moyers, broadcast in 1988 on PBS as The Power of Myth (filmed at "Skywalker Ranch"), on Campbell's influence on the Star Wars films, Lucas gave an extensive interview for the biography Joseph Campbell: A Fire in the Mind (Larsen and Larsen, 2002, pages 541-543) on this topic.

Christopher Vogler, a Hollywood film producer and writer, wrote the book The Writer's Journey: Mythic Structure For Writers, which became the basis for a number of successful Hollywood films and is believed to have been used in the development of the Matrix series.

Matthew Amerling, who had a severe case of writer's block, completed his first novel The Midknight after reading this book.

BACKGROUND

Campbell used the work of early 20th century theorists to develop his model of the hero (see also structuralism), including Freud (particularly the Oedipus complex), Carl Jung (archetypal figures and the collective unconscious), and Arnold Van Gennep (The three stages of The Rites of Passage, translated by Campbell into Departure, Separation, and Return). Campbell also looked to the work of ethnographers James Frazer and Franz Boas and psychologist Otto Rank.

Campbell called this journey of the hero, the monomyth. Campbell was a noted scholar of James Joyce (in 1944 he had authored A Skeleton Key to Finnegans Wake with Henry Morton Robinson), and Campbell borrowed the term Monomyth from Joyce's Finnegans Wake. In addition, Joyce's Ulysses was also highly influential in the structuring of The Hero with a Thousand Faces.

The Princeton University Press published all editions of this text. Originally issued in 1949, The Hero with a Thousand Faces has been reprinted a number of times. Reprints issued after the release of Star Wars Episode IV: A New Hope in 1977 used the image of Mark Hamill as Luke Skywalker on the cover. The 2004 Commemorative Edition has both a new introduction by Clarissa Pinkola Estés and a new cover.

Quotes

- "There are of course differences between the numerous mythologies and religions of mankind, but this is a book about similarities; and once they are understood the differences will be found to be much less great than is popularly (and politically) supposed. My hope is that a comparative elucidation may contribute to the perhaps not-quite disparate causes of those forces that are working in the present world for unification, not in the name of some ecclesiastical or political empire, but in the sense of human mutual understanding" (Third edition, page VIII).
- "As we are told in the Vedas: 'Truth is one, the sages speak of it by many names,' " (Third edition, page VII).

Criticism

- Clyde W. Ford (2000) was initially distressed by the opening lines of the prologue to The Hero with a Thousand Faces. He eventually returned to the text, in order to synthesize what was of value to him: "Several months passed before I mustered the courage to challenge Campbell again...I was rewarded for my persistence. Campbell's shortsightedness about Africa could not obliterate his immense contributions to mythology, and his omission gave me an opportunity to explore African mythology in a novel and meaningful way" (p. 12).
- Marc Manganaro (1992), argues that Campbell's theories violate the expectations of poststructuralism: "Campbell's

reading of mythology as text hardly aligns with post-structuralist notions of 'world as text,' as a realm of constantly shifting signifiers having no provable reference to a ground of signified meaning...on the contrary Campbell's trope of 'text'...functions as a shell that covers the true interior of the myth" (p. 159).

- Pearson and Pope (1981) claim that Campbell's model discounts the possibility of female heroes: "The great works on the hero--such as Joseph Campbell's The Hero With A Thousand Faces...all begin with the assumption that the hero is male" (p. vii).
- Novelist David Brin has been openly critical of his theories.
- Novelist David Foster Wallace in the short story Another Pioneer (part of the collection, Oblivion, 2004) critiques Campbell's journey of the hero.
- American novelist Kurt Vonnegut satirized Campbell's views on the monomyth as being excessively complicated by offering his interpretation, called the "In The Hole" theory; loosely defined as "The hero gets into trouble. The hero gets out of trouble."
- American philosopher John Shelton Lawrence and American religious scholar Robert Jewett have discussed an "American Monomyth" in many of their books, The American Monomyth, The Myth of the American Superhero, and Captain American and the Crusade of Zealous Nationalism.

STORYBOARD

Storyboards are graphic organizers such as a series of illustrations or images displayed in sequence for the purpose of previsualizing a motion graphic or interactive media sequence, including website interactivity.

ORIGINS

The storyboarding process, in the form it is known today, was developed at the Walt Disney studio during the early 1930s, after several years of similar processes being in use at

Walt Disney and other animation studios. In the biography of her father, The Story of Walt Disney (Henry Holt, 1956), Diane Disney Miller explains that the first complete storyboards were created for the Disney short the Three Little Pigs (film). According to John Canemaker, in Paper Dreams: The Art and Artists of Disney Storyboards (1999, Hyperion Press), the first storyboards at Disney evolved from comic-book like "story sketches" created in the 1920s to illustrate concepts for animated cartoon short subjects such as Plane Crazy and Academy Award winner Steamboat Willie.

According to Christopher Finch in The Art of Walt Disney (Abrams, 1973), Disney credited animator Webb Smith with creating the idea of drawing scenes on separate sheets of paper and pinning them up on a bulletin board to tell a story in sequence, thus creating the first storyboard.

One of the first live action films to be completely storyboarded was Gone with the Wind. William Cameron Menzies, the film's production designer, was hired by David Selznik to design every shot of the film. Many large budget silent films were also storyboarded but most of this material has been lost during the reduction of the studio archives during the 1970's.

Storyboarding became popular in live-action film production during the early 1940s, and grew into a standard medium for previsualization of films: "We can see the last half century... as the period in which production design was largely characterized by adoption of the storyboard," wrote curator Annette Michelson in a 1993 catalog for the Pace Gallery exhibit Drawing into Film: Director's Drawings, which featured storyboards of popular films. Storyboarding's most recent use is outlining websites and other interactive media projects during the design phase.

USAGE

Film

A film storyboard is essentially a large comic of the film or some section of the film produced beforehand to help film directors, cinematographers and television commercial advertising clients visualize the scenes and find potential problems before they occur. Often storyboards include arrows or instructions that indicate movement.

In creating a motion picture with any degree of fidelity to a script, a storyboard provides a visual layout of events as they are to be seen through the camera lens. And in the case of interactive media, it is the layout and sequence in which the user or viewer sees the content or information. In the storyboarding process, most technical details involved in crafting a film or interactive media project can be efficiently described either in picture, or in additional text.

Some live-action film directors, such as Joel and Ethan Coen, used storyboard extensively before taking the pitch to their funders, stating that it helps them get the figure they are looking for since they can show exactly where the money will be used. Other directors storyboard only certain scenes, or not at all. Animation directors are usually required to storyboard extensively, sometimes in place of doing a script.

Animatics

In animation and special effects work, the storyboarding stage may be followed by simplified mock-ups called "animatics" to give a better idea of how the scene will look and feel with motion and timing. At its simplest, an animatic is a series of still images edited together and displayed in sequence. More commonly, a rough dialogue and/or rough sound track is added to the sequence of still images (usually taken from a storyboard) to test whether the sound and images are working effectively together.

This allows the animators and directors to work out any screenplay, camera positioning, shot list and timing issues that may exist with the current storyboard. The storyboard and soundtrack are amended if necessary, and a new animatic may be created and reviewed with the director until the storyboard is perfected. Editing the film at the animatic stage can avoid animation of scenes that would be edited out of the film. Animation is usually an expensive process, so there should be a minimum "deleted scenes" if the film is to be completed within budget.

Often storyboards are animated with simple zooms and pans to simulate camera movement (using non-linear editing software). These animations can be combined with available animatics, sound effects and dialog to create a presentation of how a film could be shot and cut together. Some feature film DVD special features include production animatics.

Business

Storyboards were adapted from the film industry to business, purportedly by Howard Hughes of Hughes Aircraft. Today they are used by industry for planning ad campaigns, commercials, a proposal or other projects intended to convince or compel to action.

A "quality storyboard" is a tool to help facilitate the introduction of a quality improvement process into an organisation.

Design comics are a type of storyboard used to include a customer or other characters into a narrative. Design comics are most often used in designing web sites or illustrating product usage scenarios during design.

Interactive Media

More recently the term "storyboard" has been used in the fields of web development, software development and instructional design to present and describe interactive events as well as audio and motion, particularly on user interfaces, electronic pages and presentation screens. An interactive media storyboard may be used in the graphical user interface for the user experience design of a website or interactive project as well as a visual tool for planning the content. In contrast, a site map or flow chart may be better to plan the information architecture, navigation, links, organization and total user experience, especially when the sequence of events is less predictable or the audiovisual change between events is of little design importance.

Benefits

One advantage of using storyboards is that it allows (in film and business) the user to experiment with changes in the story-line to evoke stronger reaction or interest. Flashbacks, for instance, are often the result of sorting storyboards out of chronological order to help build suspense and interest.

The process of visual thinking and planning allows a group of people to brainstorm together, placing their ideas on storyboards and then arranging the storyboards on the wall. This fosters more ideas and generates consensus inside the group.

ANIMATION

Animation is the rapid display of a sequence of images of 2-D artwork or model positions in order to create an illusion of movement. It is an optical illusion of motion due to the phenomenon of persistence of vision. This could be anything from a flip book to a motion picture film.

Early Animation

There is no single person who can be considered the "creator" of the art of animation, as there were several people doing several projects which could be considered various types of animation all around the same time. (Short, hand-drawn animation scenes could be presented with the Phenakistoscope, the Zoetrope, and other optical "toys" already in the early 1800s.) The following is a brief listing on those who are often acknowledged as significant to the development of animation. Note that this list is by no means a comprehensive list of contributors to early animation.

Georges Méliès was a creator of special effect films, such as A Trip to the Moon. He used many techniques-one of which was to stop the camera rolling, change something in the scene, and then continue rolling the film. This is a very similar idea to that of stop-motion animation. Méliès accidentally happened upon the technique when his camera broke down while shooting a bus driving by. When the camera was fixed, a horse happened to be passing by just as Méliès continued to film. The result was that the bus appeared to change into a horse.

J. Stuart Blackton was possibly the first filmmaker in America to use the techniques of stop-motion and hand-drawn animation. Introduced to film-making by Edison, he pioneered these concepts at the turn of the 20th century, with his first copyrighted work dated 1900.

Émile Cohl began drawing cartoon strips and created a film in 1908 called Fantasmagorie. The film largely consisted of a stick figure moving about and encountering all manner of morphing objects, such as a wine bottle that transforms into a flower. There were also sections of live action where the animator's hands would enter the scene. The film was created by drawing each frame on paper and then shooting each frame onto negative film, which gave the picture a blackboard look.

Winsor McCay created detailed animations that required a team of artists and painstaking attention for detail. Each frame was drawn on paper, requiring backgrounds to be redrawn, as well characters to be animated. His films such as Gertie the Dinosaur (1914) and The Sinking of the Lusitania (1918) were of an impressive scale, although The Sinking of the Lusitania used cells.

Otto Messmer, in 1919, created the character of Felix the cat for Pat Sullivan's animation studios. The importance of Felix lies in the character's strong personality, created largely through gesture and actions.

Animation Techniques

Animation techniques are incredibly varied and difficult to categorize. Techniques are often related or combined. The following is a brief on common types of animation. Again, this list is by no means comprehensive.

Traditional Animation

Also called cel animation, the frames of a traditionally animated movie are hand-drawn. The drawings are traced or copied onto transparent acetate sheets called cels, which are then placed over a painted background and photographed one by one on a rostrum camera. Nowadays, the use of cels (and cameras) is mostly obsolete, since the drawings are scanned into computers, and digitally transferred directly to 35 mm film. The "look" of traditional cel animation is still preserved, and the character animator's work has remained essentially the same over the past 70 years. Because of the digital influence over modern cel animation, it is also known as tradigital animation.

Examples: The Lion King, Spirited Away, Les Triplettes de Belleville.

Full Animation

The most widely-known style in animation, known for its realistic and often very detailed art.

Examples: All Disney feature length animations, The Secret of NIMH, The Iron Giant

Limited Animation

A cheaper process of making animated cartoons that does not follow a "realistic" approach.

Examples: The Flintstones, Yellow Submarine

Rubber Hose

The characters are usually very "cartoony", and the animators have a lot of artistic freedom as rubber hose doesn't have to follow the laws of physics and anatomy to the same degree as the other main styles of animation.

Examples: Early Mickey Mouse cartoons, Popeye, Ren and Stimpy

Rotoscoping

A technique where animators trace live action movement, frame by frame, either by directly copying an actors outlines into an animated drawing (e.g. Ralph Bakshi), or use rotoscoped material as a basis and inspiration for a more fluid and expressive animation (e.g. Disney).

Examples: Snow White and the Seven Dwarfs, Gulliver's Travels, American Pop

Stop Motion

Stop-motion animation is any type of animation which requires the animator to physically alter the scene, shoot a frame, again alter the scene and shoot a frame and so on, to create the animation. There are many different types of stop-motion animation. Some notable examples are listed below.

Clay Animation

Often abbreviated to claymation, this is a type of stop-motion animation using figures made of clay or a similar malleable material. The figures may have an armature or wire frame inside of them, similar to puppet animation (below). Alternatively, the figures may be made entirely of clay, such as in the films of Bruce Bickford where clay creatures morph into a variety of different shapes.

Examples: Morph, Wallace and Gromit; Jan Svankmajer's Dimensions of Dialogue; The Amazing Mr. Bickford; The Trap Door

Cutout Animation

A type of stop-motion animation formed by moving 2-dimensional pieces of material such as paper or cloth.

Examples: Terry Gilliam's animated sequences of Monty Python's Flying Circus; Fantastic Planet; Tale of Tales; pilot episode of South Park

Silhouette Animation

A monochrome variant of cutout animation in which the characters are only visible as black silhouettes.

Example: The Adventures of Prince Achmed; Princes et princesses

Graphic Animation

Model animation: In this form of animation, model animated characters interact with, and are a part of, the live-action world.

Examples: The films of Ray Harryhausen (Jason and the Argonauts) and Willis O'Brien (King Kong)

Go motion
Object animation
Pixilation
Examples: Neighbours

Puppet Animation

Puppet animation typically involves puppet figures interacting with each other in a constructed environment, in contrast to the real-world interaction in model animation (above). The puppets generally have an armature inside of them to keep them still and steady as well as constraining them to move at particular joints.

Examples: The Tale of the Fox, the films of Jirí Trnka, The Nightmare Before Christmas, Robot Chicken

Brickfilm

Puppetoon

Computer Animation

Like stop motion, computer animation encompasses a variety of techniques, the unifying idea being that the animation is created digitally on a computer.

2D Animation: Figures are created and/or edited on the computer using 2D bitmap graphics or created and edited using 2D vector graphics. This includes automated computerized versions of traditional animation techniques such as of tweening, morphing, onion skinning and interpolated rotoscoping.

Examples: A Scanner Darkly, Jib Jab

- Analog computer animation
- Flash animation
- PowerPoint animation

3D Animation: Figures are created in the computer using polygons. To allow these meshes to move they are given a digital armature (sculpture). This process is called rigging. Various other techniques can be applied, such as mathematical functions (gravity), simulated fur or hair, effects such as fire and water and the use of motion capture to name but a few.

Examples: The Incredibles, Shrek, Finding Nemo.

- Cel-shaded animation
- Morph target animation
- Skeletal animation

- Motion capture
- Crowd simulation

Less Common Techniques

Drawn on Film Animation: A technique where footage is produced by creating the images directly on film stock.

Paint-on-glass Animation: A technique for making animated films by manipulating slow drying oil paints on sheets of glass.

Pinscreen Animation: Makes use of a screen filled with movable pins, which can be moved in or out by pressing an object onto the screen. The screen is lit from the side so that the pins cast shadows. The technique has been used to create animated films with a range of textural effects difficult to achieve with traditional cel animation.

Sand Animation: Sand is moved around on a backlighted or frontlighted piece of glass to create each frame for an animated film.

OTHER TECHNIQUES AND APPROACHES

Character Animation: Character animation is the animation of a character to create the illusion of life, usually as one aspect of a larger production, and often to complement voice acting. Character animation is artistically unique from other animation in that it involves the creation of apparent thought and emotion, in addition to physical action.

Historically, Winsor McCay's Gertie the Dinosaur, 1914, is often considered the very first example of true character animation. Otto Messmer imbued his Felix the Cat with an instantly recognizable personality during the 1920s. The following decade, Walt Disney made character animation a particular focus of his animation studio, best showcased in productions such as Three Little Pigs, Snow White and the Seven Dwarfs, Pinocchio, and Dumbo. Disney animation artists such as Bill Tytla, Grim Natwick, Fred Moore, Ward Kimball, Les Clark, John Sibley, Marc Davis, Wolfgang Reitherman, Hal King, Hamilton Luske, Norm Ferguson, Eric Larson, Johnny

Lounsbery, Milt Kahl, Frank Thomas and Ollie Johnston all became masters of the technique.

Other notable figures in character animation include the Termite Terrace/Warner Bros. directors (Tex Avery, Chuck Jones, Bob Clampett, Frank Tashlin, Robert McKimson, and Friz Freleng), independent animator Richard Williams, John Lasseter at Pixar, and latter-day Disney animators Andreas Deja and Glen Keane. Character animation is not limited to Hollywood studios, however. Some of the finest examples of character animation can be found in the work of Nick Park of Aardman Animations and Russian independent animator Yuri Norstein.

Character animation is augmented by special effects animation, which creates anything that is not a character; most commonly vehicles, machinery, and natural phenomena such as rain, snow, and water.

4

INDIAN CINEMA

Introduction to Indian Cinema

1896-1910

Cinema was introduced to India on July 7, 1896. It began with the Lumiere Brothers' Cinematography, unveiling six silent short films at the Watson Hotel in Bombay, namely Entry of Cinematographe, The Sea Bath, Arrival of a Train, A Demolition, Ladies & Soldiers on Wheels and Leaving the Factory. The Times of India carried details of the "Living Photographic Pictures in Life-Size Reproductions by Mssrs. Lumiere Brotheres". In the same year, the Madras Photographic Store advertised "animated photographs". Daily screenings of films commenced in Bombay in 1897 by Clifton and Co.'s Meadows Street Photography Studio.

In 1898, Hiralal Sen started filming scenes of theatre productions at the Classic Theatre in Calcutta, inspired by Professor Stevenson (who had brought to India the country's first bioscope)'s, film presentation alongside the stage production of The Flower Of Persia; his debut was a contribution to this presentation. He continued making similar films to complement theatrical productions, which were shown as added attractions during intermission, in private screenings for high society households or taken to distant venues where the stage performers could not reach.

Harischandra Sakharam Bhatavdekar (H. S. Bhatavdekar) alias Save Dada, who had attended the show, imported a cine-camera from London at a price of 21 guineas and filmed the first Indian documentary, a wrestling match in Hanging

Gardens, Bombay, in 1897. In 1901, he recorded the return from Cambridge of 'Wrangler' Ragunath P. Paranjpye, who had secured a distinction in mathematics from Cambridge University, and M M Bhownuggree, considered the first Indian news film.. He also filmed Lord Curzon (the Viceroy of India)'s Delhi Durbar that marked the enthronement of Edward VII in 1903.

The commercial potential of cinema was also tested during the time. F.B. Thanewala's "Grand Kinetoscope Newsreels" is one successful case. J.F. Madan was another highly successful film producer, who released hit films like Satyavadi Raja Harishchandra and Bilwamangal; also, he launched Madan Theatres Limited, which became India's largest film production-distribution-exhibition company and the biggest importer of American films after World War I. His films were marked by a high degree of technical sophistication, facilitated by his employment of experienced foreign directors like Eugenio De Liguoro and Camille Legrand. This expertise was complemented by grand sets and popular mythological storylines which ensured good returns.

Cinema houses were set up in major Indian cities in this period, like one in Madras (in 1900 by Major Warrick), the Novelty Cinema in Bombay (where newsreels from the Boer Wars were shown) and the Elphinstone Picture Palace in Calcutta (set up by J.F. Madan in 1907). Apart from these, a number of film shows were arranged in tents; examples are: shows arranged by two Italians, Colourello and Cornaglia, in tents at the Azad Maidan Bombay, J.F. Madan's tent cinema at the Calcutta Maidan. Another popular mode of broadcasting films was the touring cinema. In 1904, Manek Sethna started the Touring Cinema Co. in Bombay and a year later, Swamikannu Vincent, a draughtsman for the railways set up a touring cinema going around small towns and villages in the South of India. Pathe, the famous film production company set up an Indian Office in 1907.

1910-1920

The first feature film made in India was a narrative named Pundalik, by N.G. Chitre and R.G. Torney. The first full-length

Indian feature film was Raja Harishchandra (3700 feet as compared to 1500 for Pundalik), made in 1913 and released commercially in May that year, by Dadasaheb Phalke. Phalke had attended a screening of The Life of Christ at P.B. Mehta's American-Indian Cinema and was inspired to make films himself. He was convinced of the possibility of establishing an indigenous film industry by focussing on Indian themes. In this regard, he said Like the life of Christ, we shall make pictures on Rama and Krishna. The film was about an honest king who for the sake of his principles sacrifices his kingdom and family before the gods, who are impressed with his honesty and restore him to his former glory. The film was a success, and Phalke went on to make more mythological films till the advent of talkies, and commercialization of Indian films lessened his popularity.

In 1916, Universal Pictures set up Hollywood's first Indian agency (see Hollywood meets India, below). The first South Indian feature was Rangaswamy Nataraja Mudaliar's Keechaka Vadham, released in 1918. The following year, he made the film Draupadi Vastrapaharanam, featuring Anglo-Indian actress Marian Hill who played the role of Draupadi.

REGIONAL FILM INDUSTRIES

India is a large country where many languages are spoken. According to the 1991 Census of India there are about 10,400 'raw mother tongues' in India. If closely related and mutually comprehensible dialects are grouped, the number can be reduced to 1576 'rationalised' mother tongues, or with even more consolidation, 114 main languages. These 114 languages are the ones surveyed in the Indian census. Indian film producers have made films in thirty of the largest languages. However, only the very largest language groups support major regional industries. These are: Hindi, Bengali, Marathi, Kannada, Tamil, Telugu, Odiya, Malayalam. Official statistics categorise Indian films according to the languages in which they are distributed.

There is a great deal of mobility between the regional industries. Many workers in other regional industries, once their talent and popularity is established, move on to work in other film industries, nationally as well as internationally. For example, A. R. Rahman, one of the best known film music composers in Indian cinema, started his career in Tamil cinema in Chennai but has since worked in Bollywood, London, and New York. Similarly, films that succeed in one language are often remade or dubbed in others. Films like Padosan and Roja, for example, were re-made or dubbed from their original Bengali and Tamil versions respectively, into Hindi.

Bengali (Bangla) Film Industry

The Bengali film industry has long centred in the Tollygunge district of Kolkata (Calcutta). Its most famous film director is Satyajit Ray, who won an Oscar for lifetime achievement in cinema.

Hindi Film Industry

The Hindi film industry, based in Mumbai (formerly Bombay), is the largest branch of Indian cinema. Hindi film Industry is often called 'Bollywood' (a melding of Hollywood and Bombay). The word "Bollywood" is sometimes applied to Indian cinema as a whole, especially outside South Asia and the South Asian diaspora, but this usage is incorrect. Bollywood has been recently greatly criticized for what critics see as a violation of Indian cultural values and its discussion of controversial topics. It is considered the most liberal out of the Indian language film industries.

Regional movies are distinctively different from Bollywood (Hindi) movies, as the stories and themes of these movies portray the culture of the region from which they originate, while most Bollywood movies nowadays are greatly influenced by Western culture.

Although Bollywood does not distribute a lot of films, it can be considered to be largest in terms of viewers. It is believed that 95% of the Indian population watches Bollywood. It also has international recognition, especially in Western countries such as the UK, USA and Australia where there is a large South Asian community. Despite having the widest coverage, Bollywood movies fail to impress South Indians especially in Tamil Nadu & Kerala because of a very strong local film industry which arguably produces movies of much superior quality.

Kannada Film Industry

The Kannada film industry, based in Karnataka, is sometimes called 'Sandalwood', as Karnataka is known for its sandalwood; however, this term does not seem to be in widespread use. The Gubbi Veeranna Company, or Veeranna's Sri Chennabasaveshwara Krupa Poshita Nataka Sangha and other groups established themselves first as theatre troupes, and later went on to dominate kannada cinema into the 1960s. "They provided all its key directors like H.L.N. Simha, B. R. Panthulu and G. V. Iyer, its stars led by Rajkumar and Leelavathi and most of its early commercial hits: Bedara Kannappa (1953), for instance. The first big success in Kannada cinema adapted a Gubbi Company stage play written by G. V. Iyer to introduce the mythological adventure movie into that language.". Kannada films has become very popular after the recent hits like Jogi (2005) & Mungaru Male (2007).

Kashmiri Film Industry

The Kashmiri film industry, which had been lying dormant since the release of Habba Khatoon in 1967, was revived after a 39-year hiatus with the release of Akh Daleel Loolech in 2006. Cinema halls had been shut down for a long time in Kashmir, by militants protesting against the New Delhi based Government. There are few cinema halls and a handful of directors have been returning to shoot in the region. Though the region was favoured by many producers as a scenic locale in pre-militancy era Bollywood movies as a romantic backdrop, the regional industry was not very strong, due to lack of finances and infrastructure.

Malayalam Film Industry

The Malayalam film industry, based in Kerala. Malayalam movies are known for their artistic nature and they frequently figure in the national film awards. It is also currently known for being the most conservative out of the different film industries in India, despite the fact that it went through a liberal phase in the 80's. Notable personalities: filmmakers, Padmavibhushan Adoor Gopalakrishnan, Bharathan, Aravindan, Padmarajan, John Abraham; scriptwriter,

M.T. Vasudevan Nair, Sreenivasan; cinematographer, Azhagappan, Santhosh Sivan, Shaji; actors, Bharath Gopi, Tilakan, Padmabhushan Prem Nazeer, Satyan, Padmasree Bharath Mammootty, Padmasree Bharath Mohanlal, Padmasree Bharath Balachandra Menon; playback singers, Padmabhushan Dr. K.J Yesudas, Padmasree K.S. Chitra and Sujatha.

The first 3D film which has produced in India was in Malayalam. Its name is My Dear Kuttichatthan produced by Navodaya. Padayottam, the first 70MM film which has done its full work in India was in Malayalam which was also produced by Navodaya. The fist Cinemascope film in the world was produced in Malayalam. Chemmeen is the first film which bring a gold medal from the President in South India. Mohanlal's "Guru", directed by Rajiv Anchal, is the only malayalam film which is nominated for Oscar Award.

Malayalam film Industry has been nicknamed as Malluwood. Mohanlal's "Narasimham" has got the highest profit till 2005. Mammootty has got 3 times National Award for best actor with Kamal Hasan. The industry contributed many best directors, actors, writers etc. A.R. Rahman's first film which he give music was in Malayalam. Vanaprastham produced by Mohanlal is the first Indo-French production movie. It has been dubbed into English (International & Europe), French & German. Mohanlal's Kalapani tells the story about the life of people in Indian prison in Andaman.

Marathi Film Industry

The Marathi Film industry is based in Maharashtra. Marathi film industry is one of the oldest in India. Dadasaheb Falke was one of the pioneers of the films in Marathi. Every year there is an award given in the name of "Dadasaheb Falke Award" for exceptional contribution to India cinema. Marathi film industry is now a days overshadowed by presence of Bollywood, but is evolving due to some off-beat movies like Shwaas, Uttarayan, and so on.. Old marathi film songs are popular even today also. Old songs are remixed and presented now-a-days. Also actors like Dilip Prabhavalkar are making more difference in growing marathi film industry. Films like Chavkat Raja, Jhapatlele, Phachadlela, etc are excellent movies.

Tamil Film Industry

The Tamil film industry (Kollywood), based in the Kodambakkam area of Chennai is one of biggest film industries in India. Tamil films have enjoyed consistent popularity among Tamil speakers in India, Sri Lanka, Singapore, Malaysia and Mauritius.

In the Tamil film industry, directors such as K. Balachander, Shankar, Bharathiraja, Balu Mahendra, Santhana Bharathi, Cheran, and Mani Ratnam have achieved box-office success whilst producing films that balanced art and popular elements. The Tamil film industry accounts for approximately 1% of the gross domestic product of the state of Tamil Nadu. Costs of production have grown exponentially from just under Rs.4 million in 1980 to over Rs.110 million by 2005 for a typical star-studded big-budget film. Similarly, costs of processing per print have risen from just under Rs.2,500 in 1980 to nearly Rs.70,000 by 2005. There has been a growing presence of English in dialogue and songs as well. It is not uncommon to see movies that feature dialogue studded with English words and phrases, or even whole sentences. Some movies are also simultaneously released in two or three languages (either using subtitles or several soundtracks). Contemporary Tamil movies often feature Madras Bashai, a colloquial version of Tamil spoken in Madras.

Telugu Film Industry

The Telugu film industry is based in Andhra Pradesh's capital city, Hyderabad. After Bollywood, more movies are produced every year in Telugu than any other language. The state also has what is claimed to be the largest film studio in the world, Ramoji Film City. The first studio for Telugu talkies was Vel Pictures, constructed in 1934 by P.V. Das, located at Madras. The first film made here was Sita Kalyanam. The first film made by a Telugu person, R.S. Prakash, was Bhishma Pratigna (The Pledge of Bhishma, 1922). Another important Telugu personality of this era was Y.V. Rao (1903-1973), an actor and director, whose silent film (directing) credits include Pandava Nirvana (1930), Pandava Agnathavaas (1930) and Hari Maya (1932). The first big movies in Telugu were made by the Surabhi Theatres troupes. They produced the first Telugu talkie, Bhakta Prahlada, directed by Hanumappa Munioappa Reddy in 1931. In the first few years of Telugu talkies, films were all mythological stories, taken from the stage. In 1936, Krittiventi Nageswara Rao made the first Telugu film not based on mythology, Premavijayam. The film influenced other Telugu film-makers into making such films. Some popular themes of these films (often called 'social' films) were the feudal zamindari system (Raitu Bidda, 1939), untouchability (Maala pilla, 1938), and widow remarriage. Since then, there have been both social (contemporary) and mythological or folk stories in Telugu cinema.

Telugu films are released in Andhra Pradesh, Tamil Nadu, Karnataka, East Maharastra, Orissa and few parts of West Bengal. Telugu movies are released world wide in United States, Canada, parts of Europe, South Africa, Malaysia and Singapore.

The film Pokiri (Actor-Mahesh Babu) was released in 2006 collected 67 crores in India which is second heighest in India.

CONVENTIONS OF COMMERCIAL FILMS

The principal difference between American and Indian commercial cinema is that Indian films usually feature periodic song-and-dance routines which, in a good movie, are expected to move the story forward (in mediocre movies, they are poorly integrated into the story). The uniqueness of Indian Cinema is that songs in Indian films play a role. In generic films, they serve as fillers, often amusing distractions. In artistic commercial films, songs convey emotions and passions of the protagonist or of the situation-ranging from love and pathos to triumph and celebration. The lyrics in the latter type are usually well written and set to music with catchy tunes, that go on to become popular. Songs are sung by professionals play-back singers and lip-synched by dancing actors and actresses. Most non-Indians would consider the ordinary Indian film a musical, but this would be a mistake. The music and song industry associated with Indian Cinema is a major contender in determining box office hits.

Indian commercial films, in whatever regional centre they are made, tend to be long; they are usually two to three hours long, often with an intermission. They tend to be melodramatic, sentimental, and formulaic, but may also feature romance, comedy, action, suspense, and other generic elements. Unlike commercial Western films, there is almost no nudity at all in Indian films. Such scenes are classified as obscene in the Constitution of India and are usually removed by the Indian Censor Board.

ART CINEMA IN INDIA

In addition to commercial cinema, there is also Indian cinema that aspires to seriousness or art. This is known to film critics as "New Indian Cinema" or sometimes "the Indian New Wave" (see the Encyclopedia of Indian Cinema), but most people in India simply call such films "art films". These films deal with a wide range of subjects but many are in general explorations of complex human circumstances and relationships within an Indian setting.

From the 1960s through the 1980s, art films were subsidised by Indian governments: aspiring directors could get federal or state government grants to produce non-commercial films on Indian themes. Many of these directors were graduates of the government-supported Film and Television Institute of India. Their films were showcased at government film festivals and on the government-run TV station, Doordarshan. These films also had limited runs in art house theatres in India and overseas. Since the 1980s, Indian art cinema has to a great extent lost its government patronage. Today, it must be made as independent films on a shoestring budget by aspiring amateurs, much as in today's Western film industry.

The art directors of this period owed more to foreign influences, such as Italian neorealism or the French New Wave, than they did to the genre conventions of commercial Indian cinema. The best known New Cinema directors were Bengali: Satyajit Ray, Ritwik Ghatak, and Bimal Roy. Some well-known films of this movement include the Apu Trilogy by Ray (Bengali), Meghe Dhaka Tara by Ghatak (Bengali) and Do Bigha Zameen by Roy (Hindi).

Of these film-makers, Satyajit Ray was arguably the most well-known: his films obtained considerable international recognition during the mid-twentieth century. His prestige, however, did not translate into large-scale commercial success. His films played primarily to art-house audiences (students and intelligentsia) in the larger Indian cities, or to film buffs on the international art-house circuit in India and abroad.

Art cinema was also well-supported in the South Indian state of Kerala. Some outstanding Malayalam movie makers are Adoor Gopalakrishnan, G. Aravindan, T. V. Chandran, Shaji N. Karun, and M. T. Vasudevan Nair. Some of their films include National Film Award-winning Elippathayam, Piravi (which won the Camera d'Or at the Cannes Film Festival), Vaanaprastham and Nizhalkkuthu (a FIPRESCI-Prize winner).

Starting in the 1970s, Kannada film makers from Karnataka state produced a string of serious, low-budget films. Girish Kasaravalli is one of the few directors from that period who continues to make non-commercial films. He is the only Indian director after Satyajit Ray to win the Golden Lotus Awards four times.

From the 1970s onwards Hindi cinema produced a wave of art films. The foremost among the directors who produced such films is Shyam Benegal. Others in this genre include Govind Nihalani, Mani Kaul, Kumar Shahani, M.S. Sathyu.

Many cinematographers, technicians and actors began in art cinema and moved to commercial cinema. The actor Naseeruddin Shah is one notable example; he has never achieved matinee idol status, but has turned out a solid body of work as a supporting actor and a star in independent films such as Mira Nair's Monsoon Wedding.

GLOBALIZATION OF INDIAN CINEMA

Contact between Indian and Western cinemas was established in the early days of film in India itself. Dadasaheb Phalke was moved to make Raja Harishchandra after watching the film Life of Christ at P.B. Mehta's American-Indian Cinema. Similarly, some other early film directors were inspired by Western movies.

In India at least 80 percent of films shown in the late 1920s were American, even though twenty-one studios manufactured local films, eight or nine of them in regular production. American serials such as Perils of Pauline and Exploits of Elaine, and the spectacular sets of films like Quo Vadis and Cabira were popular and inspiring during the World War I era.

Universal Pictures set up an Indian agency in 1916, which went on to dominate the Indian distribution system. J. F. Madan's Elphinstone Bioscope Company at first focussed on distribution of foreign films and organization of their regular screenings Additionally, J.P. Madan, the prolific producer, employed Western directors for many of his films.

A number of Indian films have been accused of plagiarising from Hollywood Movies. Due to the long time taken by courts to decide a case, few cases relating to copyright violations are brought up.

One of the reasons Bollywood hesitates in purchasing rights is the assumption that these would run into millions of dollars, though according to some like screenwriter-director Anurag Kashyap, this is incorrect; He argues that while the films may cost millions of dollars in the west, the rights would be less expensive for Hindi remakes because the price would be based on the audience's buying power, the economy and the number of bidders.

In 2003, best-selling fiction writer Barbara Taylor Bradford brought a copyright infringement suit against Sahara Television for allegedly making a television series (Karishma: A miracle of destiny) out of her book, A Woman of Substance, without acquiring the legal rights to do so.

Today, Indian cinema is becoming increasingly westernised. This trend is most strongly apparent in Bollywood. Newer Bollywood movies sometimes include Western actors (such as Rachel Shelley in Lagaan), try to meet Western production standards, conduct filming overseas, adopt some English in their scripts or incorporate some elements of Western-style plots.

Bollywood also produces box-office hit like the films Dilwale Dulhaniya Le Jayenge and Kal Ho Naa Ho, both of which deal with the overseas Indian's experience.

However, the meeting between west and India is a two-way process: Western audiences mostly of Indian origin are becoming more interested in India, as evidenced by the mild success of Lagaan and Bride and Prejudice.

As Western audiences for Indian cinema grow, Western producers are funding maverick Indian filmmakers like Gurinder Chadha (Bride and Prejudice) and Mira Nair (Monsoon Wedding). Both Chadha and Nair are of Indian origin but do not live in India, and who made their names in Western independent films; they have now been funded to create films that "interpret" the Indian cinematic tradition for Westerners. A similar filmmaker is Deepa Mehta of Canada, whose films include the trilogy Fire, Earth and Water.

Indian cinema is also influencing the English and American musical; Baz Luhrmann's Moulin Rouge! (2001) incorporates a Bollywood-style dance sequence; The Guru and The 40-Year-Old Virgin feature Indian-style song-and-dance sequences; A. R. Rahman, a film composer, was recruited for Andrew Lloyd Webber's Bombay Dreams; and a musical version of Hum Aapke Hain Koun has played in London's West End.

AWARDS

The Filmfare Awards ceremony is one of the oldest and most prominent film events given for Hindi films in India and is sometimes referred to as the "Indian Oscars." The Filmfare awards were first introduced in 1954, the same year as the National Film Awards and gave awards to the best films of 1953. The ceremony was referred to as the Clare Awards after the magazine's editor. A dual voting system was developed in 1956. Under this system, "in contrast to the National Film Awards, which are decided by a panel appointed by Indian Government, the Filmfare Awards are voted for by both the public and a committee of experts."

Since 1973, the Indian government has sponsored the National Film Awards (which first began in 1954), awarded by the government run Directorate of Film Festivals (DFF). The DFF screens not only Bollywood films, but films from all the other regional movie industries and independent/art films. These awards are handed out at an annual ceremony presided over by the President of India.

Additional ceremonies held within India are:

- Stardust Awards
- Star Screen Awards

Ceremonies held overseas are:

- Bollywood Movie Awards-Long Island, New York, United States
- Global Indian Film Awards-(different country each year)
- IIFA Awards-(different country each year)
- Zee Cine Awards-(different country each year)

Most of these award ceremonies are lavishly staged spectacles, featuring singing, dancing, and lots of stars and starlets.

5

WRITING FOR RADIO

NEWSWRITING FOR RADIO

IMPROVING YOUR NEWSCASTS

The purpose of this website is to help radio journalists improve their skills as writers and anchors. Journalism education has greatly declined over the past two decades as colleges and universities have either closed journalism programs or transformed them into "Communications Departments." Radio journalism has been especially hard hit, with diminished teaching resources given over to television instruction because TV is the more attractive broadcast medium.

Consequently, many journalists starting out in radio lack basic knowledge on how to communicate effectively though the medium. In the past, much of that knowledge was learned on the job, but consolidations, cutbacks and downsizing in radio have reduced news staffs to the point where news directors can afford little time to training those new in the profession. In this sink-or-swim environment, far too many radio journalists have figured out only how to float. They haven't been introduced to the wide range of possibilities in preparing radio news and are often frustrated either by not being able to move up to a larger market or by not having the satisfaction of becoming respected journalists within their communities.

FEATURES

This discussion is intended for those who are early in their radio careers, whether in a first or second job or still in college or an internship. The pages assume some experience in radio, but visitors unfamiliar with some of the terminology may consult a small glossary. Although the Newswriting for Radio website has been extensively used in college journalism courses, the website is not meant to replace a broadcast newswriting textbook. The Newswriting for Radio website is a supplement to coursework, and especially to on-the-job experience.

The site is organized into four major sections. In The Basics, you learn fundamental lessons and characteristics of broadcast newswriting. Three different newscast formats are examined in The Styles. You'll examine some of the questions surrounding what deserves coverage in the section on News Judgment. Finally, The Newsroom teaches you about creating an organized environment that allows you to be better prepared for stories. There's also a collection of links to other radio journalism websites.

On several of the pages, sample news scripts are accompanied on the right side of the page by the speaker symbol (shown on the right side of this paragraph). The appearance of the symbol next to a script indicates that you can listen to a sound file (in the WAV format) containing the words of the script. Listening to these files will allow you to hear and practice the patterns of voice modulation regularly used in radio newscasts. Just click on the symbol to hear the script.

Here are some common terms in radio journalism used throughout the Newswriting for Radio website and their definitions:

Actuality: Recorded segment of a newsmaker speaking, generally lasting from 10 to 20 seconds; this is what people outside of radio journalism often call a "sound bite"

Clock: Schedule of a broadcast hour, with precise time in minutes and seconds allotted for the various programming segments; for example, a clock might begin "00:00-01:30--news," "01:30-02:30--spots," and so forth; often represented as a pie chart resembling an analog clock

Cut: Tape containing the recording of a voicer, wrap, actuality or nat sound; networks feed cuts to affiliates via satellite

Hourly: Network newscast beginning at the top of the hour; the cast generally contains a commercial break at two and a half or three minutes past the hour and resumes a minute or a minute and a half later; most hourlies conclude at five minutes past the hour

IQ: "in cue"--the first words recorded on a cut

Lead: First sentence of a news story, which should concisely reveal the story's basic events and provide an introduction to the details given in the rest of the story

Live Shot: Report introduced by an anchor that has not been recorded but is read live by another journalist, often at a news scene

Lockout: Final words of a report spoken by a journalist in which the journalist's name and station call letters or frequency are given, such as "Corrie Carpenter, 990 News"; often a location is given as well: "In Middleville, Corrie Carpenter, 990 News"

MOS: Abbreviation for "Man On the Street" interviews; that is, interviews of passers-by chosen at random in a public place and asked their opinions of events or people in the news

Nat or Natural or Raw Sound: A "raw sound" is recorded sound that is not of a newsmaker speaking, such as the sound of an airplane landing or a marching band playing or a crowd cheering; sometimes known as "natural sound" or "nat sound," especially when the source of the sound is from nature, such as frogs croaking or geese honking

OQ: "out cue"--the last words recorded on a cut

Reader: Script of a news story in which no actualities are to be played; this script is read live on the air by the anchor; the recording of a reader by a reporter is called a "voicer"

Script: Written-out version of a news story, the text of which is read on the air; a newscast is made up of a collection of scripts read by an anchor

Slug: Title of a script; used for reference purposes; wire-service stories are each given one

Sounder: Recorded tune used to introduce segments of the broadcast, such as at the beginning of a traffic report or sports; the networks use sounders at the beginning of the hourlies

Spot: Recorded commercial advertisement

Tease: Brief phrase spoken by the anchor immediately before playing a spot or going to traffic (or some other interruption of the newscast) to tell the listener about a story coming up later; the tease should intrigue the listener without either misrepresenting the story or revealing it entirely

Voicer: Recorded report containing only the journalist's voice--there is no actuality; can be understood as a recorded reader

Wrap: Recorded report in which a journalist's voice occurs at the beginning and end, and an actuality is played in between; the report is "wrapped around" the actuality

Zinger: Unusual and generally humorous feature story often placed at the end of a newscast

AVOIDING "COP TALK"

Many of the stories we report involve crimes and police attempts to apprehend those responsible. The importance of these stories to our listeners, as well as the often complex and uncertain nature of police investigations, can be quite intimidating for young reporters, with the result that they frequently repeat verbatim the description of a crime given to them by a police official.

DON'T "DO THE POLICE IN DIFFERENT VOICES"

Police officers are taught to describe their investigations in a way that provides specific details of events with the vaguest possible discussions about those whom police believe responsible. This "cop talk" developed from the legal requirements that enforcement officials need to meet in order to make arrests and gain convictions. But "cop talk" is inadequate for reporting on radio.

Here's an example of "cop talk," a story only slightly modified from what was broadcast on a small-market station:

- TWO MEN ARE UNDER ARREST FOR ROBBING A JEWELLERY STORE. POLICE SAY THE MEN ENTERED THE VILLAGE PAWN SHOP AT 1407 MAIN STREET AT APPROXIMATELY 10:15 YESTERDAY MORNING. AFTER WAITING INSIDE THE STORE FOR A FEW MINUTES, ONE OF THE MEN DISPLAYED A GUN AND ORDERED TWO EMPLOYEES TO PLACE INTO A DUFFEL BAG ALL THE CASH FROM THE REGISTER AS WELL AS SEVERAL ITEMS OF JEWELLERY. THERE WAS NO ONE ELSE IN THE STORE AT THE TIME. THE MEN LEFT THE STORE, AND ONE EMPLOYEE WAS ABLE TO SEE THE MEN DRIVE OFF IN A BLUE DODGE ARIES. THE EMPLOYEES NOTIFIED POLICE, AND AT APPROXIMATELY 11 O'CLOCK A VEHICLE MATCHING THE DESCRIPTION OF THE GETAWAY CAR WAS SPOTTED PARKED IN AN ALLEY IN BACK OF A HOUSE AT 684 WILLOW STREET. POLICE ENTERED THE HOUSE WHERE THEY FOUND TWO MEN, AN AMOUNT OF MONEY, AND ITEMS OF JEWELLERY LATER IDENTIFIED AS HAVING BEEN TAKEN FROM THE STORE. A COMPUTER CHECK OF THE VEHICLE DETERMINED THAT IT WAS STOLEN. THE MEN WERE IDENTIFIED AS 34-YEAR-OLD MILES STANDISH OF MIDDLEVILLE AND 28-YEAR-OLD JOHN ALDEN OF SMALLTOWN. THE MEN WILL FACE A VARIETY OF CHARGES.

CUT IRRELEVANT DETAILS

This script (which runs about 54 seconds) is far too long, with irrelevant details such as the make and model of the getaway car, while the identification of the suspects isn't revealed until the very end. It is obvious that the reporter merely repeated the words of a police officer or of a police press release. Here's a brief rewrite of the script (which now runs 31 seconds):

- TWO MEN ARE BEHIND BARS THIS MORNING AFTER AN ARMED ROBBERY OF A MIDDLEVILLE PAWN SHOP. POLICE SAY 34-YEAR-OLD MILES STANDISH OF MIDDLEVILLE AND 28-YEAR-OLD

JOHN ALDEN OF SMALLTOWN ROBBED THE VILLAGE PAWN SHOP ON MAIN STREET YESTERDAY, FORCING TWO WORKERS AT GUNPOINT TO STUFF A DUFFEL BAG WITH MONEY AND JEWELLERY. THE SUSPECTS WERE LATER ARRESTED IN A HOUSE ON WILLOW STREET AFTER POLICE SAY THEY SPOTTED THE GETAWAY CAR BEHIND THE HOME AND ITEMS TAKEN IN THE HEIST WERE FOUND INSIDE THE HOUSE. STANDISH AND ALDEN ARE EXPECTED TO FACE A VARIETY OF CHARGES.

The new version has the police making the allegations against the two suspects (as is legal and proper), but many details unnecessary to the main point of the story have been removed.

DON'T MAKE THE OPPOSITE MISTAKE OF BEING TOO INFORMAL

"Cop talk" is predominantly a problem in small-market stations in stories by inexperienced reporters, but the opposite extreme seems to be taking hold in larger markets. Big-city reporters are becoming exceedingly colloquial in their language when covering police stories. Here's an example that aired on a major-market station in New England. The story concerned a stolen minivan in which a mother had left two babies inside. In telling the story the reporter said:

- ...A WOMAN LEFT TWO INFANTS IN THE VAN WHILE SHE DROPPED OFF AN OLDER CHILD AT DAYCARE. THE VAN WAS STILL RUNNING, AND MEANWHILE SOME GUY MUST HAVE JUMPED IN AND DROVE OFF. WHEN HE REALIZED THERE WERE TWO INFANTS IN BACK, HE DITCHED THE VAN, AND POLICE ARE NOW SEARCHING FOR THE GUY IN SOME NEARBY WOODS.... BUT THANKFULLY THE KIDS ARE OKAY.

This script does not clearly report what police believe to have happened. In fact, the script seems to indicate that this version of events is merely speculation on the part of the reporter. There was no indication of any witness seeing who drove the minivan away. Perhaps the driver was a woman. Moreover, there is no evidence for the alleged motivation of this mystery driver to have abandoned the minivan. Maybe the driver saw the babies, maybe the driver didn't.

Just as troubling as the sloppiness with which this script was put together was the overly conversational tone. A suspect of unknown sex should be called a "suspect." If an unidentified suspect is a man, he should be called a "man"--not "some guy." Being too chatty damages the credibility of the reporter to be an authoritative source of information.

Radio reporters need to strike a balance in the language they use. Scripts cannot be ploddingly detailed and dull, yet being too colloquial may lead to sloppiness and lack of credibility.

Journalism instructors often state that broadcast newswriting is supposed to sound just like everyday speech. In essence, however, writing broadcast news is more akin to writing song lyrics. Both tasks involve constructing language in a visual form (writing) for communication in an oral form (speaking or singing). Like song lyrics, broadcast newswriting adheres to patterns of language use (such as appropriate vocabulary and formulaic sentence-structure) that the audience expects to hear and will use in interpreting the communication.

Even though commercial broadcasting has been around for less than a century, radio listeners have come to expect their newscasts to be written in a particular way. Learning about broadcast sentence-structure is one of the foundations for developing effective skills at radio newswriting.

KEEP IT SIMPLE

Grammarians distinguish between three types of sentences: simple, compound and complex. A simple sentence contains a subject and a verb. A compound sentence is composed of two simple sentences joined by a coordinating conjunction ("and," "but," "or," "nor"). A complex sentence is composed of two simple sentences joined by a subordinating conjunction (which may be temporal, such as "when"; causal, such as "because"; or concessive, such as "although"). You probably remember this lesson from elementary school, but the distinctions remain quite relevant to broadcast newswriting. In your scripts, simple sentences are best. You will, of course, regularly use compound and complex sentences, but the clarity achieved through the use of simple sentences can rarely be surpassed.

Linguists describe English as a highly asyndetic language--which means that clauses in the same train of thought do not always need to be connected by conjunctions or connecting particles. Such particles in English include the words "moreover," "furthermore," and "however," words that should be avoided in broadcast newswriting. Listeners are themselves capable of connecting the elements of a story if the story is presented clearly and concisely, and these listeners expect important news to be reported in simple sentences. This expectation is especially true of leads, which generally should be written as simple sentences. When a lead begins with a subordinating conjunction, listeners discount the story's urgency. This is why such leads almost always appear in feature stories or zingers.

AVOID YOUR RELATIVES

Relative clauses, which begin with a relative pronoun or adverb such as "who," "which" or "where," provide additional information about a noun in a sentence. Those relative clauses which interrupt the flow of the sentence should not be used in broadcast newswriting. In a text communicated visually, a reader has the words on a page or screen to help guide him back to the story after the detour of a relative clause. Listeners do not have such a guide and must rely on the speaker to provide information in readily understood clauses that are concise and uninterrupted. A sentence with an interrupting relative clause should be rewritten into two simple sentences. Take the following example:

- FRED GRANDY...WHO PLAYED "GOPHER" ON THE ORIGINAL "LOVEBOAT" T-V SERIES...LATER SPENT 8 YEARS AS A CONGRESSMAN FROM IOWA.

A clearer means of expressing the same information is through two simple sentences:

- FRED GRANDY PLAYED "GOPHER" ON THE ORIGINAL "LOVE BOAT" T-V SERIES. HE LATER SPENT 8 YEARS AS A CONGRESSMAN FROM IOWA.

Recognize that apposition--the placing of a noun or phrase after another noun and marked off only by commas or, in this very example, dashes--is like a relative clause without the relative pronoun. Long, interrupting oppositions, like interrupting relative clauses, should be avoided in broadcast newswriting.

Relative clauses and oppositions can be used at the end of a sentence. This placement is especially useful for clauses beginning with the adverb "where," as in

- FIRE DESTROYED THE HISTORIC HOME, WHERE GEORGE WASHINGTON ONCE SLEPT.

Clauses beginning with "who" or "which" are acceptable when placed at the end of a sentence, but sometimes it may be preferable to write two simple sentences instead. For example,

- SIMMONS IS SUING FOR RETURN OF THE "BARBIE"-DOLL COLLECTION, WHICH HE SAYS IS WORTH A QUARTER-OF-A-MILLION DOLLARS.

could also be written

- SIMMONS IS SUING FOR RETURN OF THE "BARBIE"-DOLL COLLECTION. HE SAYS THE COLLECTION'S WORTH A QUARTER-OF-A-MILLION DOLLARS.

BE ACTIVE

Finally, two very common writing faults made by beginning reporters also appear nowadays in all other types of English writing, namely the overuse both of the passive voice and of the existential "there is," "there are" construction. Use the active voice. Write sentences with subjects that are doing things and not subjects that are merely receiving actions upon them. Do not waste time stating an object's existence (this is what the "there is" construction shows). Describe that object doing something.

Simple sentences with active verbs form the basis of effective writing for radio. All other broadcast newswriting techniques are built upon the foundation laid by this type of sentence structure.

During the initial flurry of stories concerning President Clinton's relationship with former White House intern Monica Lewinsky, the late ABC-TV news anchor Peter Jennings interviewed humourist and social commentator P. J. O'Rourke. Jennings asked O'Rourke to discuss "the alleged age difference between the President and Ms. Lewinsky," to which O'Rourke wittily replied, "Yes, Peter, we haven't yet determined whether there actually is an age difference between President Clinton and Monica Lewinsky. There is only an alleged age difference."

Jennings smiled at the reply, realizing that he had misused the word "alleged." The word allows journalists to discuss claims that have not been proved, but it is a word easily open to abuse.

SAY, SAY, SAY

The best way to use the words "allege," "alleged" and "allegedly" is not to use them at all. Instead, have your scripts reveal who is making the claim by using phrases such as "police say" or "prosecutors say" followed by the substance of the allegation. For example, a story about a bank-robbery suspect that contains the sentence

- ...34-YEAR-OLD MILLARD FILLMORE ALLEGEDLY ROBBED THE "BANK NOW" BRANCH ON CHURCH STREET....

should be rewritten so that the sentence reads

- ...POLICE SAY 34-YEAR-OLD MILLARD FILLMORE ROBBED THE "BANK NOW" BRANCH ON CHURCH STREET....

As another example, if a sentence in a story about a local government official facing trial for corruption reads

- ...ZONING BOARD PRESIDENT DOLLY MADISON IS ALLEGED TO HAVE TAKEN BRIBES FROM DEVELOPERS....

rewrite the script into something like

- ...PROSECUTORS SAY ZONING BOARD PRESIDENT DOLLY MADISON TOOK BRIBES FROM DEVELOPERS....

Always use the verb "say" in such scripts. Avoid the temptation to employ other verbs (such as "claim," "state" or "charge") when reporting allegations. Other verbs bring connotations that will colour your reporting. For example, if your script has police claiming that an individual committed a crime, your listeners may well interpret the script as indicating that you the reporter do not believe the police. To speak of someone charging an allegation implies legal actions--charges--have been filed. To maintain as unbiased and accurate a report as possible, stay with the neutral verb "say."

J'ACCUSE

Learn the distinction between "accused" and "alleged." When legal charges have been filed against an individual, that individual becomes accused of the behaviour detailed in those charges. The individual can then be described as an "accused rapist," "accused murderer," "accused embezzler," and so forth. In scripts, the use of the adjective accused should be limited to one occurrence at or near the beginning of the script in order to describe a suspect quickly and efficiently. Notice the use of the word in this story about a homicide trial:

- ACCUSED MURDERER AARON BURR HAS BROKEN DOWN IN TEARS AT HIS TRIAL, TELLING JURORS THAT HE DID NOT KILL HIS FRIEND ALEX HAMILTON LAST JULY. TAKING THE STAND IN HIS OWN DEFENSE, BURR CRIED YESTERDAY AS HE WAS TALKING ABOUT HIS INITIAL INTERROGATION BY SHERIFF'S DEPUTIES. BURR SAID INTIMIDATING QUESTIONING CAUSED HIM TO GIVE CONFLICTING STORIES TO INVESTIGATORS. PROSECUTORS HAVE SAID THAT BURR KILLED HAMILTON AFTER AN ARGUMENT OVER MONEY IN HAMILTON'S MOHICAN SPRINGS APARTMENT. BURR IS EXPECTED TO FACE CROSS-EXAMINATION WHEN THE TRIAL RESUMES AT THE HANOVER COUNTY COURTHOUSE LATER TODAY.

In the above script, the adjective "accused" appears once and only once. Multiple use may lead listeners to believe that you the reporter want them to think a suspect is guilty because the adjective "accused" is weaker than the powerful nouns it regularly accompanies (such as "murderer" or "rapist").

CHARGED UP

As has already been mentioned, the verb "charge" implies that legal actions have been filed against an individual or company. The verb should be used only to describe the process of filing the action:

- POLICE HAVE CHARGED 32-YEAR-OLD LIZZIE BORDEN WITH TWO COUNTS OF FIRST-DEGREE MURDER FOR THE PICK-AXE SLAYINGS OF HER FATHER AND STEP-MOTHER....

The specific legal charge should also be named, such as the "two counts of first-degree murder" of the previous example. Pay careful attention to the specific charge. Prosecutors may say that an individual is a murderer and organized-crime boss but charge him with only tax evasion. The defendant could then be described as being "accused of tax evasion" but not as an "accused murderer and crime boss"--the murders and organized-crime connections are allegations, not charges.

PROPER ALLEGATIONS

Occasions do exist for the use of "allege," "alleged" or "allegedly." When claims are made concerning an individual but no legal charges have been publicly filed, and the source of the claims is complicated to identify, then "alleged" becomes an acceptable option for describing the individual and the claims. For example, a community group holds a press conference calling for the firing of the deputy chief of police. Earlier that week, three former civilian employees of the police department told a newspaper reporter that they have heard the deputy chief use racial slurs. The reporter was investigating a tip that the deputy chief had recently faced a closed-door, disciplinary hearing with the public safety director and the civil service commission.

The complex nature of the story can lead to extremely tortured syntax in your script. In this situation, a sentence such as:

- ...THE "TOGETHER COALITION" IS ANGRY OVER RACIST COMMENTS ALLEGEDLY MADE BY DEPUTY CHIEF FRANKLIN PIERCE....

might be the most efficient way of succinctly explaining the story. As with "accused," forms of "alleged" should be used only once in a given script.

Finally, remember the mistake of Peter Jennings and ensure that you place the word "alleged" in front of what is actually being alleged. Rewriting the previous script example to read

- ...THE "TOGETHER COALITION" IS ANGRY OVER ALLEGEDLY RACIST COMMENTS MADE BY DEPUTY CHIEF FRANKLIN PIERCE....

significantly changes the meaning of the sentence. Now the question is not whether the deputy chief made comments, but rather whether the particular words he used were racist. If, however, it has not yet been determined what, if anything, the deputy chief may have said, the allegations concern the making of the comment and not the sense of the comments themselves. The earlier version of the sentence is then the correct one.

Finally, until a judicial authority has rendered a decision, a suspect or defendant has not been proved guilty of the charges or allegations against him. Not only is it unethical to describe this individual as, say, a "murderer" or "embezzler" without the qualification of words like "accused" and "alleged," but such descriptions could turn you into a defendant yourself--for libel.

Getting listeners to keep their radios tuned to your entire newscast...that's the function of leads and teases. (Incidentally, the first phrase of the previous sentence is itself a tease.) Despite the importance of leads and teases, many radio journalists do not understand how to fashion effective "hooks" to keep listeners listening.

REPETITION IS THE MOST COMMON MISTAKE

Repetition is the most common mistake made in leads and teases. As you may have experienced when recognizing the identity of the first six words of the subhead with those at the beginning of this paragraph, repetition of words or ideas is tedious. Listeners understandably come to believe that there is far less news than meets the ear. Yet repetition is a far-too-frequent feature of news writing, especially between the lead-in to tape (be it voicer, wrap or actuality) and the first sentence on that tape. Here's one such example:

- EMBATTLED STATE LOTTERY DIRECTOR SAMANTHA WU HANDED IN HER RESIGNATION TO GOVERNOR FREDERICK DOUGLASS. REPORTER SUSAN STARR SAYS WU TOLD THE GOVERNOR THAT SHE HAD BECOME A POLITICAL DISTRACTION.
- IQ: "IN HER RESIGNATION LETTER TO THE GOVERNOR, WU SAID THAT SHE HAD BECOME A DISTRACTION...

The second sentence of the lead provides information that is immediately given again by the first sentence of the tape. This is not, however, the only problem with this lead.

KEEP IT FRESH

Tenses of the past should be avoided in leads and teases. The preterite, or simple past tense, must almost never be used. Any past action should be described in the perfect tense--"have/has" + past participle, which often ends in "-ed." The stative quality of the perfect tense can make it seem like the present.

Better still is the use of the present progressive tense--"am/are/is" + present participle ending in "-ing"--to describe an event that has just taken place. In the story above, it would have been better to write:

- EMBATTLED STATE LOTTERY DIRECTOR SAMANTHA WU IS CALLING IT QUITS. REPORTER SUSAN STARR SAYS WU FEARS THE CONTROVERSY SURROUNDING HER HUSBAND'S BUSINESS DEALINGS IS HARMING GOVERNOR DOUGLASS.
- IQ: "IN HER RESIGNATION LETTER TO THE GOVERNOR, WU SAID THAT SHE HAD BECOME A DISTRACTION...

Present tenses give immediacy and energy to news writing, allowing listeners to feel that they are hearing about the news as it is taking place. Moreover, in the course of the day leads should be advanced to freshen the story...even though the same tape is being used. In the example story given above, a later lead for the same tape could be as follows:

- GOVERNOR DOUGLASS MUST FIND A NEW LOTTERY DIRECTOR. REPORTER SUSAN STARR SAYS EMBATTLED CURRENT DIRECTOR SAMANTHA WU IS GIVING UP THE JOB.
- IQ: "IN HER RESIGNATION LETTER TO THE GOVERNOR, WU SAID THAT SHE HAD BECOME A DISTRACTION...

The changing lead shifts the emphasis of the story to a future event, the appointment of a new lottery director. The tape then functions as background information for this future event, and so the package of lead and tape together remain fresh.

ABSENT ANTECEDENT ALERT!

A frequent error in teases is the use of pronouns without any reference to identify the pronouns. The pronouns' antecedents are absent. This error leads to teases such as:

- HE WANTED TO DIE BUT THEY SAID NO. THE STORY NEXT ON 990 NEWS.

Who is "he"? Who are "they"? (The story concerns a convicted murderer who asked the jury to sentence him to death, but the jury decided instead on a sentence of life in prison without parole.) Some might claim that this lead has mystery, and this mystery will compel listeners to stay tuned. There certainly is mystery, but confusion seems the only result in the minds of listeners. A better tease gives listeners information, not a guessing game:

- LIFE WITHOUT PAROLE FOR CHILD-KILLER WALT THOMAS. THE DETAILS NEXT ON 990 NEWS.

Teases should not tell the entire story, but teases are only a sentence long. Even the most information-packed short sentence can rarely give all the necessary details to satisfy listeners. The tease whets the appetite of listeners, who will want the completeness of hearing the full script if they have an idea of what the story is about. Deliberately confusing or gimmicky teases only frustrate listeners and drive them away.

Radio reporters spend as much time rewriting scripts as writing them. Stories are rewritten from three types of sources: newspapers, press releases and other radio news scripts. The first two of these sources are not written in broadcast style, and radio reporters need to be aware of the differences between print and broadcast.

DIFFERENCES IN STYLE

One obvious difference involves numbers. In print style, numbers can be written out to exactitude, while on the radio numbers are reduced to two significant digits. Ages in the newspaper are written between commas after an individual's name; in broadcast style, ages are given as adjectival phrases preceding the name.

Newspaper stories also display a greater use of the past tense. Print is a distancing medium, separating events through the filter of the written word from the immediacy of their occurrence. Newspapers are also written hours before they are read, so the events described seem "old news." Radio, on the other hand, has an intimate, "you-are-there" quality that is enhanced by the use of the present tense. Newsmakers spoke to newspaper reporters ("Bush said...."); they speak to a radio audience ("BUSH SAYS....").

The Art of Condensing

The greatest difference involves story length and detail. Print reporters write hundreds, even thousands of words for a particular story. Few, if any, of your stories as a radio reporter should have even a hundred words. Rewriting newspaper stories becomes an art of condensing. Take the following example of a newspaper story from the imaginary Middleville Times:

- The crumbling Salt Creek bridge on Old Route 9, considered one of Middle County's most historically significant bridges, will receive a $200,000 grant for repairs from the state Department of Transportation, according to county engineer Squire Whipple.

The funding comes from the state's Transportation Enhancement Fund, Whipple said.

Built of sandstone in 1834, the bridge is a 285-foot span made up of three arches over Salt Creek on the old route from Middleville to Greenfield. Deterioration of the bridge in recent years has been a worry to local preservationists. The bridge was closed to traffic in 2002.

The $200,000 infusion will cover the estimated cost to stabilize the bridge until money can be found to restore it. Permanent repairs could cost as much as $1,750,000, Whipple said.

The example above is quite short by print standards, but it's far too long for radio. Remember, a radio story without an actuality (a "reader") should generally run about 20 seconds. Get to the heart of your story and leave the additional details out, as in the following 21-second rewrite:

- A CRUMBLING HISTORIC BRIDGE IS GETTING SOME LONG-NEEDED REPAIRS TO KEEP IT FROM COLLAPSING INTO SALT CREEK. THE MIDDLEVILLE TIMES REPORTS THE STATE WILL PROVIDE TWO HUNDRED THOUSAND DOLLARS TO PRESERVE THE OLD-ROUTE 9 BRIDGE BETWEEN MIDDLEVILLE AND GREENFIELD UNTIL MORE MONEY CAN BE FOUND FOR PERMANENT REPAIRS. THE 170-YEAR-OLD STONE BRIDGE HAS BEEN CLOSED FOR THREE YEARS.

Unless you have spoken to individuals involved in the story yourself, you must attribute your rewritten story to its newspaper source. The attribution generally begins the second sentence of the script ("THE MIDDLEVILLE TIMES REPORTS...."). Not only is it ethical to credit the news organization that discovered the story, but if the newspaper gets it wrong (a not infrequent occurrence), the error and any of its consequences will generally not fall on you or your station.

PLEASE RELEASE ME

Most of the press releases a newsroom receives concern community groups trying to gain publicity for themselves or their events. Usually these press releases are of minor news value. In smaller communities, however, listeners expect to be informed of such events, and program directors may well inform the newsroom that a story must be aired. Generally, though, if a news or program director believes a press release is worth a story, a reporter will make a phone call or visit an event, with the result that the reporting is original rather than a rewrite.

Businesses and organizations often use press releases...through mail though increasingly through the fax machine or PR Newswire...to tout promotions, reorganizations, mergers, hirings, layoffs and other activities. These press releases are the first, and sometimes the only official contact the business or organization will make with the media. Press releases are an essential aspect of business reporting. Let's say your fax machine spits out the following press release from an out-of-town bank announcing a deal for it to buy a local bank:

- Heron Bank, Inc., of Lyons, has entered into a definitive agreement to acquire the Middleville Savings Bank, Inc., of Middleville, in a cash transaction for $8,375,000.

Mary Gonzales, President and Chief Executive Officer of Heron Bank, announced, "We are very pleased with opportunities afforded by our prospective acquisition of Middleville Savings Bank. We are looking forward to serving the Middleville community."

The closing of the acquisition transaction is subject to the completion by Heron Bank of its due diligence investigation of Middleville Savings Bank, as well as regulatory approval by federal and state banking officials.

Middleville Savings Bank has assets of $65,000,000 and operates three branches, two in Middleville and the third in Smalltown.

Heron Bank operates in seven markets in two states and has assets of $1,880,000,000. Heron Bank provides a full range of banking services to individuals and small-to-medium businesses.

This press release is full of legalese and large numbers. Bring the story close to home for your listeners by referring to something that will directly affect their lives, as in the lead to this 16-second reader:

- YOU MAY SOON SEE A NEW SIGN OUTSIDE YOUR BANK. MIDDLEVILLE SAVINGS BANK IS ACCEPTING A BUYOUT OFFER FROM LYONS-BASED HERON BANK. THE EIGHT-POINT-FOUR MILLION DOLLAR DEAL WOULD ADD MIDDLEVILLE TO THE SEVEN OTHER CITIES SERVED BY HERON. THE DEAL STILL NEEDS THE OKAY FROM REGULATORS.

Remember that press releases are primary sources of information, like the tape from an interview. The information in a press release contains the bias of the organization that sent it out. Be aware of that bias and show the same prudence in dealing with press releases as you show with other forms of newsgathering.

Keep Stories Current

In the course of the day, stories you or other reporters have written need to be rewritten. Rewriting is essential not just because each time you tell a story it should sound different and fresh, but also because situations change. Keep the focus on what is current. An early-morning house fire will bring stories about the blaze, the firefighters and any injuries or fatalities. By midday, the lead concerns the amount of damage to the building. In the evening, the focus shifts to the family that might be homeless that night. The shifts in focus require rewriting the story several times in the course of the day.

Rewriting is an important aspect of radio journalism. Knowing how to adapt stories to your medium and to current situations will aid you in informing the public and gaining respect as a timely provider of news.

One of the catch-phrases in teaching broadcast newswriting is that scripts should be "just like speaking"--in other words, you should write the words and phrases you would use if you were talking to a friend. This is not quite correct. and it is especially not the case when it comes to numbers.

Not Exactly Like Speaking

Take ages, for example. Ages in broadcast scripts are given as adjectival phrases placed in front of the person's name or other identifying feature, such as "66-year-old Dick Cheney," or "the 66-year-old Vice President." This type of construction is not, of course, conversational. The purpose for it is to make the use of numbers in scripts as clear as possible to our listeners. This same desire for clarity should govern other appearances of numbers in our stories, such as in the following script on economic data:

- THE NATION'S HOMEBUILDERS ARE KEEPING BUSY. THE GOVERNMENT REPORTS HOUSING STARTS CLIMBED ONE-POINT-FOUR PERCENT IN AUGUST AFTER A THREE-POINT-FIVE PERCENT RISE THE PREVIOUS MONTH. ECONOMISTS WELCOME THE NEWS, SAYING IT'S ANOTHER SIGN OF STEADY YET SUSTAINABLE GROWTH.

This story is economic--so to speak--in its use of numbers. Only two numbers are given, the percentages of increase for the months of July and August. Listeners aren't faced with statistical overload, and the script ends with expert explanation of these numbers' significance.

TWO DIGITS ONLY

This story also follows the "two digits only" rule of newswriting: every number must be reduced to two significant digits. This involves rounding the numbers so that they don't end up taxing the short-term memories of listeners. For example, "six point eight three" becomes "six point eight," and "527" becomes "roughly 530." In addition, the descriptive words "half" and "quarter" are generally preferable to "point five" and "point two five." Here's a story that fails to follow the "two digits" rule:

- UNIONS REPRESENTING THE 1284 CLERICAL AND MAINTENANCE WORKERS AT MIDDLE STATE UNIVERSITY HAVE REJECTED PROPOSED CONTRACT CONCESSIONS. UNIVERSITY OFFICIALS WANTED THE UNIONS TO DELAY THEIR SCHEDULED THREE-POINT-SEVEN-FIVE-

PERCENT PAY RAISE TO HELP THE SCHOOL DEAL WITH ITS ESTIMATED FOUR-POINT-SIX-ONE-MILLION-DOLLAR DEFICIT. ALTHOUGH LAYOFFS HAVE BEEN THREATENED IF THE CONCESSIONS WERE NOT APPROVED, WORKERS VOTED AGAINST THE PROPOSAL 1090 TO 89, WITH 105 FAILING TO VOTE.

This script is quite bad in its use of numbers, which are too large and appear too often. A better approach is to simplify and follow the "two digits rule":

- UNIONS REPRESENTING NEARLY 13-HUNDRED CLERICAL AND MAINTENANCE WORKERS AT MIDDLE STATE UNIVERSITY HAVE REJECTED PROPOSED CONTRACT CONCESSIONS. UNIVERSITY OFFICIALS WANTED THE UNIONS TO DELAY A SCHEDULED PAY RAISE TO HELP THE SCHOOL DEAL WITH AN ESTIMATED FOUR-AND-A-HALF-MILLION-DOLLAR DEFICIT. ALTHOUGH LAYOFFS HAVE BEEN THREATENED IF THE CONCESSIONS WERE NOT APPROVED, WORKERS VOTED OVERWHELMINGLY AGAINST THE PROPOSAL.

Keeping track of numbers is a difficult task even for the most attentive of listeners. If your station broadcasts lottery results, you may already have discovered that the newsroom telephone rings immediately after the numbers have been read on the air, and on the other end of the line is a listener who became confused or was unable to remember the lottery numbers by the time he or she found paper and pencil to write them down. Our purpose as journalists is to impart information in a helpful manner. Being judicious in the use of numbers should allow listeners a clearer understanding of the events affecting their lives.

THREE STYLES OF RADIO NEWSWRITING

These pages provide hints on creating three different types of newscast through changes in writing. The topics include an in-depth style appropriate to many formats, a style similar to that heard on the network hourlies, and a vivid style that fits well with younger formats.

The In-Depth Style

Many stations run local news-talk during drive time, often with a longtime, well-respected, pillar-of-the-community talker--especially in morning drive.

The newsroom needs not only to inform listeners of the important events of the day, but also to give them...and the talker...something to talk about. Stories need to have enough detail to allow the talker to make cogent arguments and hold intelligent conversations with listeners. Here the in-depth style can help.

Asking and Answering Questions

We all remember the six essential questions a news story should answer: Who? What? When? Where? Why? and How? An in-depth story needs to pay special attention to the last two: the Why and the How...as in, Why is this politician proposing this plan? How will the plan work?, or Why is this researcher's work important? How will the research help people? When writing your stories, ensure that your script tries to provide some answers.

For example, a press release arrives from State University heralding better chickens. A researcher in the agriculture school says she's discovered that hens fed a special enzyme produce offspring less prone to disease. When you do your phone interview, ask about the implications for the person in the street in order to get tape that will be comprehensible to those listeners who are not poultry scientists. In your script, emphasize the general value of having healthier chickens while including a few details of the research with, say, a sentence like this:

- ...HENS GIVEN THE ENZYME TOBLERONE IN THEIR FEED PRODUCED LARGER CHICKENS LESS LIKELY TO PICK UP DISEASES THAT COULD BE PASSED ON TO HUMAN CONSUMERS IF THOSE CHICKENS AREN'T PROPERLY COOKED....

The story also gives your talker an issue, food safety. The talker can even extend the issue to question whether there's been too much manipulation of nature through all these research studies.

Thorough doesn't Mean Long

Story length in the in-depth style will be longer than in other styles, but not by that much. Stories without tape should run 25-30 seconds....stories with tape, 40-45. Shorter, 20-second stories should also be used both to increase story count (giving a wider sense of news coverage) and to provide listeners with some variety.

Since story count is relatively low, the in-depth style is not suitable for 90-second casts. This style is best suited for stations with a 5-minute news hole at the top of the hour and 3:30 at the bottom.

STORY PLACEMENT

Hierarchy is especially significant for the in-depth style. Length is often used by listeners to judge the importance of a story, but when many of the stories run at least half a minute, length no longer helps listeners figure out what's important. Story placement becomes the only means. The most important stories should come at the beginning of the cast....the less important stories towards the end.

You may want to end the cast with a zinger--a humorous or unusual piece that gives the talker something immediately to play with and helps the talker's phone lines light up. Use common sense, however, in choosing a zinger. A longtime, well-respected, pillar-of-the-community talker is not going to want to offend listeners. Also keep in mind that you're supposed to be a journalist, not a comedian.

The Network Style

Credibility can often be a problem in medium-sized markets, where communities are too large for listeners to be personally familiar with most of the people or places making news, yet the resources of the station rarely allow for a newsroom staff of more than half a dozen reporter/anchors (if that)--and this small staff often means few stories are produced and listeners perceive a "reporting gap."

One way to restore station credibility is to make the cast resemble the network hourlies, regardless of whether your station replaces the hourly with a local cast or does a 90-second local after the hourly.

High Story Count

The hallmark of the network style is high story count. Listen to a network hourly and notice how many different events are related. This variety gives listeners a sense of completeness....they feel they know all the major stories. This feeling helps build trust between your listeners and the station, and it gives your newsroom credibility.

A 90-second cast should aim for seven stories. You might be wondering, "My staff is so small to begin with, how am I to get seven different stories?" Odds are you're already taking some of your stories from press releases and the local newspaper. The two or three stories you've taken haven't exhausted their source....there are still plenty of press releases on your desk and dozens of pages left in the newspaper. Certainly there are stories your listeners want to know about.

Short Story Length

Of course high story count means short story length. A 90-second cast with seven stories works out to an average of 13 seconds per story. This doesn't mean every story should be 13 seconds....rather, important stories should be given adequate time (20-25 seconds, though certainly no more), but less important stories need only a sentence or two. For example, let's say city council has been in a dispute with the mayor over cuts in the police budget. This story has been in the news on and off for a couple of weeks, and today at City Hall council members are holding a special meeting with the mayor to reach some sort of compromise. Here's all you need (and it runs roughly 7 seconds):

- MIDDLEVILLE CITY COUNCIL MEMBERS ARE HUDDLING WITH MAYOR JANE SMITH TODAY, WITH BOTH SIDES HOPING TO RESOLVE THEIR DISPUTE OVER POLICE CUTS.

There should be some variation in story length throughout the cast...don't give listeners five 7-second stories followed by three 20-second ones. But there should be some progression, with the more important, longer stories at the beginning of the cast and the shorter, less important stories towards the end. One way of producing variation is to stick a 20-second-long humorous or feature story near or at the end of the cast.

Tape and the Network Style

You might think it impossible to incorporate much tape into a cast with such a high story count, but listen to the hourlies, which often have half a dozen or more tape pieces (both actualities and voicers/wraps). There's little difference in editing actualities for the network style. Keep them under 15 seconds or so, as you probably would for a more discursive style. The difference is in the copy surrounding the act. Two sentences in front, one sentence at the most (and quite often none at all) after.

For example, let's say the governor is proposing eliminating parole for those convicted of using a firearm when committing a crime. Your State News Network has fed you a 9-second cut, which runs as follows:

- IF YOU USE A GUN WHEN COMMITTING A CRIME, YOU SHOULD DO THE TIME...AND THAT MEANS ALL THE TIME...BEFORE YOU ARE ALLOWED BACK IN SOCIETY.

Here's a script to make the cut fit within your time constraints:

- PAROLE COULD BE A THING OF THE PAST FOR CONVICTS WHO USED A GUN IN THEIR CRIMES....THAT'S IF GOVERNOR DOUGLASS GETS HIS WAY.
- Douglass act...OQ: "IN SOCIETY."
- LEGISLATORS WOULD HAVE TO APPROVE DOUGLASS'S PLAN.

This entire story runs 18 seconds. In summary fashion it includes the important facts: the concept behind the governor's proposal, an actuality, and that the legislature would have to pass a bill for the proposal to become reality. For voicers and wraps, station reporters should be instructed to keep stories short (though reporters often have difficulty with the concept of limiting the time their voices are on the air). For voicers in general...and network tape in particular...edit the cut down to 20-25 seconds. Start either from the beginning or, even better so long as the story remains coherent, with the second sentence of the piece, and continue for 20 seconds or so until there's a natural break (which there usually is). Leave off the lockout. In other words, transform the tape into what's often called a "correspondent's" cut.

If you leave out the first sentence of the original report, the information should be incorporated into your lead-in. You do not need to identify the reporter at the front....the differences in the sound of the voice will tell listeners there's a new reporter. When the cut ends, get out of the story only through identifying the reporter, such as:

- ABC'S SUSAN STARR.

Cutting down wraps is far more difficult, and often wraps can't be coherently reduced under 30 seconds (especially if they contain a 20-second-long actuality). Nonetheless by editing voicers and wraps down to 20-25 seconds, you'll be able to include several pieces of tape into your network style cast.

THE NETWORK STYLE

Two popular radio formats are political talk and the FM Zoo. In political talk, the talker spends time generally warning listeners that Armageddon is upon us. Many political talkers are syndicated, but there are plenty of local versions as well.

The FM Zoo is a morning drive format on FM stations that during other dayparts play various shades of popular music (contemporary hit radio, adult contemporary, hot country, oldies, and so forth). In morning drive there is some music played, but much of the time is spent in sophomoric banter (often of a sexual nature) among the hosts, a traffic reporter, a sports reporter and a news anchor. You may recognize that the so-called "shock jocks" are merely the Zoo without music.

Tedium is fatal to these formats, and news anchors must employ a vivid writing style to keep listeners engaged.

Choosing Stories

Story selection differs wildly between political talk and the FM Zoo. Violent crime, natural disasters and, of course, politics are the mainstay of the political talk newscast. The FM Zoo prefers stories about celebrities (which often include politicians) and about the humorous or unusual. Generally the news in the FM Zoo format should give listeners an excuse to be happy. The news in political talk gives listeners an excuse to be unhappy. In both formats, however, the same vivid style of newswriting applies.

Content, Sentence Structure, Word Choice

Vivid writing brings out unusual elements in everyday stories. For example, contract negotiations between the city and its workers have made little progress. A strike is possible, though the current contract still has a few weeks to run and no strike vote has been taken. The mayor has repeatedly said that any pay increase would lead to layoffs. The unions say the pay raise can be met by cutting fat in the city administration.

At the biweekly city council meeting, union leaders make a presentation. One council member tells the leaders in a matter-of-fact style, "I think it's a shame the way you've been treated. I want you to know that I support your efforts to improve your standard to living, and I support your right to strike. I hope it doesn't come to this, but shut down the city if you must. It's the mayor who's the only city worker who ought to be losing her job."

A standard reader on the story, lasting 18 seconds, might run like this:

- CITY WORKERS IN MIDDLEVILLE HAVE TAKEN THEIR CONTRACT DISPUTE TO CITY COUNCIL. UNION LEADERS GOT A SYMPATHETIC HEARING AT LAST NIGHT'S COUNCIL MEETING IN THEIR ATTEMPTS FOR A PAY RAISE AND JOB GUARANTEES. MAYOR JANE SMITH HAS SAID THERE'S NO MONEY IN THE BUDGET FOR A PAY INCREASE, AND CONTRACT TALKS SO FAR HAVE MADE LITTLE PROGRESS.

The vivid writer notices that a city council member has told the unions, albeit conditionally, to "shut down the city." This becomes the lead of a more vivid reader lasting 21 seconds:

- "SHUT DOWN THE CITY"--THAT'S WHAT ONE MIDDLEVILLE CITY COUNCILMAN IS ADVISING CITY WORKERS IN THEIR SIMMERING CONTRACT DISPUTE WITH MAYOR JANE SMITH. DON JONES TOLD UNION LEADERS AT LAST NIGHT'S CITY COUNCIL MEETING THAT HE SUPPORTS THEIR RIGHT TO STRIKE FOR BETTER PAY AND JOB SECURITY, ADDING THAT IF ANY CITY WORKER'S TO LOSE A JOB, IT OUGHT TO BE THE MAYOR.

Content isn't the only difference between these two readers. The vivid reader is more conversational in sentence structure, beginning with a quotation that is back-referenced and ending with a conditional ("if...then") clause. The standard reader is prosaic, with simple sentence followed by simple sentence. There are also differences in word choice. The standard reader contains the bland adjective "sympathetic," in contrast to the vigorous "simmering" of the vivid reader. Notice also that "better pay" has a stronger sound than "pay increase."

Short and Spare

Don't confuse vividness with verbosity. The vivid style is generally spare, with few adjectives ever used. Readers should run about 20 seconds. Wraps should last about 30 seconds. Far too often reporters fall in love with their own cleverness and give newscasts that sound like second-rate Victorian novels. The fault is especially evident in reporting violent crime, when we hear of "city sidewalks drenched with crimson stains from tepid pools of blood," or of "the languid evening interrupted by the sudden patter of semi-automatic weapons."

Violent crime is usually dramatic enough as it is. A simple telling of the event will be far more powerful than any re-creation compiled with the assistance of Roget's Thesaurus.

NEWS JUDGMENT

These pages allow you to grow as a journalist by getting you to think about how to cover events and what sorts of events should be covered. The topics involve reporting public meetings, analyzing polls and studies, how and whether to broadcast profane speech, as well as tips on avoiding bias, and on becoming an enterprise reporter who finds the stories other reporters miss.

Avoiding Bias

As politics has become more polarized and the radio audience more fragmented, listeners are now quite sensitive to perceived biases in broadcast journalism. Radio talk-show hosts are frequently highly partisan in their comments on current events, and program directors may choose to promote controversial talkers in order to attract a particular demographic for a particular station. With media consolidation, many markets are now dominated by a single ownership group, which programs deliberately distinct formats and political viewpoints on the different frequencies in that market under the group's management.

Reporters must take particular care to ensure that their stories are free from bias. Of course, journalists are expected to discover the truth about events in their communities and report that information to their audience. Journalists are not supposed to be politicians or entertainers. Under the rules of classical rhetoric, the three tasks of the public speaker are to inform, to entertain and to persuade. Let your talk-show host concentrate on the final two tasks. You are responsible for the first task: to inform. This is especially true if your reports are used on multiple stations with different formats and demographics.

SIGNIFICANCE OF THE STORY

Story selection is one area where listeners are quick to perceive bias. From my own experience, I remember criticisms I received from listeners upset at the attempts by a mayor to fire the city's police chief. Supporters of the police chief complained that the media highlighted negative news about the police department but gave little attention when the police successfully solved cases. One example brought up by these supporters was the greater prominence given to the story that a city police officer had been expelled from a statewide drug-enforcement task force because of drunken behaviour at an out-of-state convention, than what was given to the capture of a local burglary ring and the recovery of many of the items stolen from several homes.

Listeners argued that the burglary ring affected far more members of the community than did the out-of-town antics of a single police officer who was not acting under the police chief's direct supervision. Although the disgraced officer's story had merit as news and did reveal aspects of the management of the police department--a central issue in the mayor's desire to replace the chief--these listeners were correct in the underlying rationale that should always govern the choice and placement of news stories: the greater the impact on your listeners, the more significant coverage of the event should be. Bias is often perceived when listeners believe that significant stories are given diminished coverage in favour of sensational, salacious and scandalous news that has little real impact on their daily lives.

Play it Straight

The popularity of sarcastic political talkers has infected some reporters who perhaps aspire to talk-show careers. I recently heard a story on a station in a midsized market about a downtown antidrug rally involving elementary-school students. The reporter affected a sarcastic tone in his voicer, which began

- NANCY REAGAN SAID, "JUST SAY NO TO DRUGS." WELL, WITH THE WAY THESE KIDS ARE RUNNING AROUND AT TODAY'S RALLY, THEY CLEARLY DIDN'T SAY NO TO SUGAR.....

Aside from being an ineffective lead that fails to provide listeners with basic information about the rally, this script seems merely a lame attempt by a smarmy reporter to make himself appear clever. It demeans the children who participated in the rally. Furthermore, the sarcasm implies that the rally was a waste of time. The reporter should not have been making social commentary on how children are being raised and on the efficacy of antidrug rallies. Listeners easily could have perceived bias on the part of the reporter, harming the credibility of station's news department as an accurate source of information.

Keep the tone of scripts informational, without partisanship or sarcasm. And give stories the proper amount of coverage, neither too little nor too much. These steps will help ensure that you become a trusted source of information in your community, and that your listeners will not ignore, or worse, turn off the radio during your newscasts.

BE ENTERPRISING

Enterprise reporting is a term that has become unfamiliar to far too many radio journalists. Enterprise reporting refers to stories generated by a reporter on his or her own, as opposed both to stories assigned by the news director and to breaking news (such as police and fire department activity).

What Neighbours are Talking About

Investigative journalism (of, say, the Watergate or Whitewater variety) is one type of enterprise reporting, and important political stories have been generated by reporters rather than news directors. Most enterprise reporting, however, is rarely that glamorous and involves bringing stories active within a small subset of the community out to a wider audience.

For example, residents of a working-class neighbourhood complain that an unoccupied house is the site of illegal drug sales and prostitution, and those neighbours want the house torn down. The owner, who lives in another part of the city, is an architect who says the building has historic value and that she eventually intends to restore the house. The neighbours blame the owner for leaving the property in disrepair, which they say invites criminals. The owner blames the neighbours for allowing criminal activity in their neighbourhood, activity that she says hinders her plans to restore the building.

This story does not belong at the top of a newscast, but it brings up a variety of important issues: public safety, preserving historic buildings, absentee owners, and disputes among differing groups about urban planning and city priorities. It may well be the most talked about story in the neighbourhood at that time, and because the issues it raises reverberate in neighbourhoods throughout the listening area, it is worth reporting on the air. But the story hasn't made the daily newspaper, nor has it appeared on television. How does the enterprise reporter find out about it?

Paying Attention

Here's where young reporters have to learn to pay attention to what concerns ordinary listeners. When you're in line at the bank, the post office, the grocery store, you may hear about all sorts of events going on in various neighbourhoods. Some of these stories may deserve a wider audience. Barbers and hairdressers often have a wealth of information gleaned from their clientele. When you're getting your hair cut, think about whether that information might be of interest to your radio audience. Organization mailings and community newspapers often provide valuable leads to stories you might otherwise miss.

Cyberspace can also provide you with story ideas from farther away. E-mail lists and on-line forums contain postings that reveal the concerns of ordinary individuals. Sign up for a few of the lists or forums that cover your hobbies or interests (but be judicious; your e-mail box might get overloaded with junk). Although most of the postings will not generate stories, some will.

For example, on an e-mail list dealing with religion, a parent in Texas posted a message about a new book in the high-school library that the parent found inappropriate for his 14-year-old daughter. The novel was written for early teen readers and had been recommended by the school librarian. In learning about the novel from his daughter, the parent was offended by one particular scene in the book, and he sent an e-mail message to the list for advice on what to do. After reading this e-mail message, the enterprise reporter will want to investigate whether the book has generated any controversy at schools in the station's listening area.

Don't forget your own curiosity as you go about your daily life. I remember a former news director of mine a dozen or so years ago was furious with himself one day. On this particular day, the front page of the feature section of the daily newspaper had a large story about the sudden popularity of car air-fresheners shaped like little crowns. Not a major story, to be sure, but the news director said, "I must have seen these crowns inside a dozen or so cars, and I always wondered what they were. But I forgot that others might also be wondering, which made it a story worth investigating." Now that the newspaper had explained the mystery of the crowns, there was no longer a story to report.

Gaining Respect as a News Source

This episode gets to an important aspect of enterprise stories: they distinguish your version of the news from that available on other radio stations, on television or in the newspaper. By reporting the stories no one else has...or has yet...you give your station added stature as a primary source for information. Listeners will perceive when TV stations and the newspaper are following your lead. (They also know when you are following them.)

Enterprise stories require a little more time than stories whose basic facts are already known to listeners. While it may be difficult to fit a wrap from such a story under 45 seconds, having an enterprise story should never be a license to go long (that is, more than 55 seconds). Condensing the story to its basic elements also forces the reporter to gauge how important the story really is and how interesting the station's listeners will find it.

You won't get any additional pay for enterprise stories--after all, most of the discovery will have to be done on your own time--but you will gain a satisfaction far greater than that from reporting assigned stories. You will also be developing news judgment and journalist's instincts, which will serve you well in your career ahead.

DEALING WITH PROFANITIES

Language changes over time, and each generation understands words in a slightly different way. In addition, diverse ethnic, religious and social groups have distinct usages and interpretations of everyday speech. Language that is acceptable to some may be offensive to others, and often newsmakers will...both deliberately and inadvertently...use words that offend some listeners. Journalists need to take care when preparing reports that may contain a profanity.

Is it News?

First and foremost is the issue of whether to report the profanity at all. As we all know, there are many causes for "cussing." Minor self-injury is one of them, and such a cause is generally not newsworthy.

For example, a local minister is hammering a ceremonial "first nail" as part of a volunteer project to renovate low-income housing. The minister sends the hammer down on his own thumb and then screams several choice words, to the great surprise of his congregants. While this is undoubtedly embarrassing to the minister and quite possibly amusing to the congregants, the episode is irrelevant to the story of the volunteer effort to fix up the housing.

Another example demonstrates that sometimes a profanity should be reported. At a public hearing concerning controversial behaviour by members of the police department, the mayor faces criticism from community activists and rival politicians concerning his administration. After listening to the angry...but not generally offensive...words of a city council member and potential mayoral candidate, the mayor becomes visibly irritated and utters a profanity-laced reply.

Here we have a public official using a public forum to discuss public events. It is newsworthy that a mayor would utter a profanity in such a context because the utterance demonstrates how the mayor interacts with the public and with other city officials.

Private Emotions in Public View

Another reason for profane speech is sudden, deep emotion, such as grief at the loss of a loved one. It has become fashionable for some stations to broadcast profanities spoken in these situations because the language reveals the strong emotions felt by the speakers.

In contrast, I believe that these sorts of actualities should not generally be aired. The people involved are usually private individuals thrust into the news because of the catastrophe that has just enveloped their lives. They are not prepared to make public statements, and they may well be embarrassed in the days to come concerning their words and behaviour at this moment of intense emotion. A good reporter should have enough sound to prepare pieces that adequately reveal the emotional state of a victim's relatives and friends without resorting to replaying their profanities.

To Bleep or not to Bleep

If news judgment dictates playing an actuality containing a profanity, the further question arises whether to broadcast the cut unedited or whether to insert a tone to replace the offensive word. Altering an actuality should never be done without serious deliberation about the degree to which the meaning of and impression left by the cut will be changed. Some words are less profane than others and can be broadcast. Most profanities--including racial, ethnic and sexual slurs--are, however, best replaced in the actuality by a tone that extends from immediately after the offensive word's first phoneme to immediately before the word's last phoneme. This will allow listeners to figure out what the word is without actually having to be confronted by it.

To give one example, it's probably okay to broadcast the word "bastard," but not okay to broadcast "f*ck."

Finally, a warning on racial, ethnic and sexual slurs, though this warning also holds true for other types of profanity. When the utterance of such slurs by a newsmaker is worth reporting, care must be taken in the script to ensure that listeners are well prepared if an actuality...even (probably, preferably) a bleeped actuality...is played. Before the cart is played the anchor or reporter should say that

- THE FOLLOWING TAPE CONTAINS LANGUAGE THAT YOU MAY FIND OFFENSIVE

to give listeners the opportunity to avoid listening to the profanity themselves or to prevent children from listening.

Profanities...especially slurs...lend themselves all too easily to sensationalism, particularly when reporters in their eagerness to relate the story fail to provide adequate context for the utterance or adequate warning to listeners who may not wish to be confronted by offensive speech.

POLLS, SURVEYS AND STUDIES

Polls, surveys and studies have increasingly become a newscast staple. Nearly every day we seem to be bombarded by a poll, survey or study indicating, or seeming to indicate, how everything from a disease to a politician (if the two are distinct) might be faring among the public. It's always a good idea to figure out beforehand the types of poll and study results you plan to tell your listeners and why.

Get an Expert

Polling data are among the most misunderstood and misused information with which we deal. It helps to have an expert available to explain to our listeners...AND TO US...what a poll's results can mean. Usually there's an expert on polling at a nearby college or university. Get in contact with that person and try to build a working relationship. Both you and your listeners will be grateful. Polls are conducted by various groups--polling organizations, news operations, colleges and universities, businesses and interest groups, as well as political consulting firms. These groups will generally provide some information on how any given survey was taken, such as how many people were interviewed, how those people were chosen, and how they were interviewed. There are advantages and disadvantages to various polling techniques, and your expert should enlighten you on how trustworthy the results may be.

The Numbers Game

Care must be given when providing poll results to our listeners. On the one hand, a simplifying vagueness about the results can be deceptive. To say

- SENATOR ALISON WILLIAMS IS LEADING IN HER RE-ELECTION BID OVER CHALLENGER MARC ANTONY IN THE LATEST MIDDLEVILLE TIMES/ CHANNEL 8 POLL.

and to leave it like that gives listeners no impression on how close the race may be. Something must be said about the size of the lead, keeping in mind how the the method of sampling used affects the margin of error and other aspects of result reliability.

Another presentation problem involves tossing ALL of the numbers from a poll to our listeners:

- SENATOR ALISON WILLIAMS HAS A 9-POINT LEAD...42 TO 33...IN HER RE-ELECTION BID OVER CHALLENGER MARC ANTONY IN THE LATEST MIDDLEVILLE TIMES/CHANNEL 8 POLL. 25 PERCENT OF THE 607 PEOPLE SURVEYED STILL HAVEN'T MADE UP THEIR MINDS, AND THE POLL HAS A MARGIN OF ERROR OF PLUS OR MINUS 4 POINTS, SO WILLIAMS COULD BE AHEAD AS MUCH AS 46 TO 29 OR ONLY 38 TO 37.

Aside from not being a particularly helpful interpretation of the polling data, this story throws so many numbers that listeners might think they're hearing sports scores or the lottery results. Numbers are, of course, necessary to this story, but they should be included judiciously, and hypothetical results created by manipulating the margin of error should not be included.

Whose Study is It?

Reporters who take great care to reveal the source and accuracy of political polling data may be cavalier about surveys and studies that do not directly address political issues. This carelessness is especially apparent in the reporting of lifestyle surveys, medical studies, environmental-impact studies, and surveys of economic activity. As an example, the American Automobile Association released a study that said most pollution in the air came from factory smokestacks rather than from automobile exhausts. One major-market, clear-channel station told the story this way. First the anchor read the sentence,

- ARE CARS THE BIGGEST POLLUTERS OF OUR AIR?

Then followed a buzzing noise such as is heard when a wrong answer is given on "Family Feud" or some other TV gameshow. The anchor continued:

- WRONG! FACTORIES ARE THE NUMBER-ONE POLLUTERS ACCORDING TO TRIPLE-A....

Aside from the gimmicky (and credibility-destroying) presentation, this story gives undue credence to Triple-A's study. Triple-A is an interest-group for drivers of passenger vehicles, and the link between Triple-A and the study must be prominently reported. Stating the report's conclusions as fact at the beginning of the story provides too much bias and may prevent listeners from acquiring a critical understanding of the report.

It ain't over 'till it's Over

Political polling provides a measure of how well a campaign is doing at a particular point in time. Surveys are useful in reporting on the progress (or lack thereof) of a campaign and on any changes that may take place in the campaign as a result of this feedback. But, as we all know, they are not official election returns, and while they may reflect upon the substantive issues in a campaign, poll results do not themselves represent a substantive issue worthy of extensive coverage. In other words, don't spend your time covering the polls instead of covering the election.

Public Meetings

For many radio journalists, their first "beat" involves covering regular meetings of a governmental board such as a city council or school board. Properly reporting board meetings demands a significant investment of time and effort, but that effort will be richly rewarded through informing the public about their government and developing a sense of judgment about what makes news.

Know thy Board Members

Make sure you know who the board members are. Study up on their backgrounds, careers, the neighbourhoods they represent, their political experience and political affiliation. You are coming to these meetings as an outsider, and only by demonstrating familiarity with the people and issues involved will you gain the respect and trust you need to do a proper job as a reporter. Being present at the meeting is only part of your job. While you should try to record all of the meeting's activities from the call to order to adjournment, rarely do the public deliberations provide compelling actualities. Your best opportunities for sound will come after the meeting has ended, through interviews with individual board members and members of the public. Ask them for reactions to the decisions taken, remembering to get reactions from both sides. Moreover, do not "play favourites" by interviewing the same board member meeting after meeting. Sometimes political caucuses designate one board member to speak on their behalf, but that's a decision for the caucus to make, not for you. By demonstrating knowledge and fairness, you'll readily be granted the interviews you need.

An Agenda for Reporting

Board meetings follow an agenda that is usually available at least a day and perhaps even a week in advance. Some boards will oblige news organizations by mailing or faxing the agenda to them, though others may treat reporters like any other member of the public and require them to stop by the board's offices or city hall to pick up a copy. Get the agenda and study it before the meeting. Not only will you know what issues will be coming before the board, but you will also have the opportunity to do a preview piece ("Should skateboarding be banned from downtown? City council will take up the issue at tonight's meeting....") to air the day of the meeting.

Keep Your Focus

Far too many news directors view board meetings as inherently dull, even though these meetings demonstrate the workings of government. Reporters only reinforce this view by failing to write interesting scripts. Perhaps this is because so many meetings go on...and on...and on for hours, and reporters lose focus on what the important issues were. Countless stories end up sounding like the following, slightly modified from what I heard on a small-market station:

- THE MIDDLEVILLE SCHOOL BOARD HEARD A REPORT AT LAST NIGHT'S MEETING. THE REPORT WAS PREPARED BY ASSISTANT SUPERINTEN-

DENT CHESTER ARTHUR. ARTHUR FOUND THAT STUDENTS COMMITTED 12 ACTS OF VIOLENCE LAST YEAR IN THE MIDDLEVILLE SCHOOLS, UP FROM FIVE THE YEAR BEFORE. ARTHUR TOLD THE BOARD THAT GREATER COOPERATION WAS NEEDED WITH POLICE BUT THAT THERE WAS NO NEED TO HAVE OFFICERS ASSIGNED TO THE SCHOOLS AT THIS TIME.

This 21-second reader misses the story. The lead should not be that the school board heard a report, but rather that violence was on the rise in city schools. There are a number of ways to bring the real story--violence in the schools--to the fore. Here's an example using a question lead:

- SHOULD POLICE OFFICERS PATROL MIDDLE-VILLE SCHOOLS? ASSISTANT SUPERINTENDENT CHESTER ARTHUR DOESN'T THINK SO...AT LEAST NOT YET. DESPITE A DOUBLING LAST YEAR OF THE NUMBER OF VIOLENT ACTS COMMITTED BY STUDENTS ON SCHOOL PROPERTY, ARTHUR IS TELLING SCHOOL BOARD MEMBERS A DIRECT POLICE PRESENCE IN THE SCHOOLS IS NOT NECESSARY.

Remember that even though you may have sat through a meeting lasting 4 or 5 hours, you are condensing that meeting into a 20-, 30-or 40-second story. The issues facing the community provide you with your subject matter. With those issues forefront, you should be able to craft interesting stories that inform your listeners about their government and their community.

IMPROVING NEWSROOM OPERATIONS

These pages address organization, preparation and performance. The goal of these lessons is to turn your newsroom into an efficient and credible source of information for your audience. The topics in this section deal with handling equipment failure, making your newscast distinct from your competitors, presenting a more professional sound and preparing for cyclical stories about schools and weather.

Improving On-Air Delivery

Although the Newswriting for Radio website is devoted, as the name suggests, to improving the writing of radio news, many visitors have requested tips on speaking and vocalization. This page will address two of the most common faults in newsreading: monotonous delivery and slow reading.

Follow the Pattern

The reading of news on the radio is expected to conform to a pattern of musical pitches or notes. If you were to speak to your friends using this exaggerated pitch pattern, your conversation would seem a bit too much like "sing-song." The pitch pattern--which is present in all speech--does not need to be as noticeable in direct conversation because the listener can pick up visual cues (such as facial expressions or hand gestures) that aid in interpreting the words spoken.

Radio--unlike television--must rely solely on vocal quality to convey this additional information, information that may include the length of a story, the story's seriousness and the credibility of sources. The pitch pattern is especially helpful in informing listeners when stories begin and when they end.

Pitch should be considered in relative terms as "high" or "low" based on the range used in normal conversation. Listeners hear the modulation between "high" and "low" pitch and interpret those changes, even though most listeners are unaware of the pattern. They become aware only when the pattern is not properly followed, at which point they become confused or bored by the story.

Change Pitches

Stories begin on a "high" pitch and end on a "low" pitch. In between the pitch modulates from one clause or sentence to the next. Within a clause or sentence, the pitch falls slightly from beginning to end, except in questions, where the pitch rises at the end.

For example, in a standard, four-sentence script, the pitch begins "high," falling slightly at the end of the first sentence. The second sentence begins at a lower pitch than the end of the first sentence. The third sentence begins at a higher pitch than the beginning of the second sentence. The final sentence, like the second sentence, begins at a "low" pitch and gently falls towards the end of the script.

When news directors, program directors or general managers complain about monotonous delivery, they are referring to readers who remain on the same pitch throughout the script. The easiest way to gain an understanding of pitch is to listen to the pitch patterns of other anchors and reporters, and to practice, practice, practice. With time, the pattern will become automatic when you're on the air.

Speed it Up

The other common fault in newsreading concerns speed. Most beginning radio journalists read and speak too slowly. Perhaps we remember all too well when, in speech and debate class in junior high school, the teacher chastised us for being nervous and speaking too quickly. Radio, however, cannot provide the additional, visual information that exists when speaking in public or on television. With only one mode of information-retrieval available, the radio listener prefers to process speech at a faster rate. Normal conversational speed is generally too slow for reading radio news.

Some reporters and anchors--notably those on public radio--seem to want to make an art form out of speaking VERY SLOWLY. Colleagues in public radio claim that their listeners prefer the news to be read slowly. I suspect this preference has more to do with aesthetics than with cognition, but in any case, choosing to read slowly because of the wishes of a public-radio news director may limit a reporter's subsequent career.

Many young journalists find their first jobs with public radio stations. Higher pay and greater opportunities may be found at commercial stations, but commercial-radio news directors often balk at hiring a reporter whose demo tape reveals slow reading. Even if your news director demands slow reading, use examples from the commercial network hourlies (e.g., ABC, AP, CBS, CNN) to set the speed for reading the news on your demo tape.

Monotonous delivery and slow reading are very common among beginning radio journalists. Understanding the causes of these faults can lead to their correction.

R.I.P. "RIP 'N' READ"

A news director at a radio station in New England once complained to me that whenever he chats with folks at an area store or bank, he finds that these listeners often confuse his station's newscasts with those of his AM rival. Much of his audience cannot seem to tell one station's news from another. While there are plenty of cosmetic changes that will make a newscast distinct--such as expensive sounders, employing announcers with unusual voices, or rearranging the clock to, say, stick traffic in the middle of the cast--often the most neglected aspect of the cast is the easiest and least expensive to correct: the actual words spoken by the anchor. The primary reason the newscasts of so many stations sound the same is that these casts are using identical scripts, scripts written by wire news services. This is the practice known as "rip 'n' read." The name comes from the days when wire-service stories came into the newsroom on a bulky, teletype machine that spat out the stories onto a large roll of paper. An anchor would rip the story off the roll and read it on the air.

"Rip 'n' read" was a necessary evil in those days due to the lack of time that often existed between when the story finished printing and when the anchor had to go on the air. Even then, however, it was expected that anchors would rewrite wire copy if time was available. The reasons for rewriting are manifold: to emphasize elements of the story that are particularly relevant to the station's audience; to create a newscast in which stories flow seamlessly one into another; to avoid repetition of the same wording in subsequent newscasts; and even to correct errors and faults of style in the wire copy itself. These reasons are just as important today, when many newsrooms have the wires fed directly into personal computers on which stories can be edited before being sent to a printer.

How to Destroy your Credibility

News directors should demand that wire copy be rewritten whenever time allows. This would, however, require leadership by example, and far too many news directors themselves partake of "rip 'n' read." I was reminded of this fact through a recent scan of the airwaves while I was in my car during morning drive, when many news directors have their anchor shifts.

I turned the dial to an AM news-talk station to hear the lead story, which concerned the decision of an area school district to require students at certain schools to wear uniforms. I knew the story quite well, for I had already heard the identical script read five minutes earlier during the news segment of an FM morning-zoo show. I heard the script again that morning on another AM station and another FM station.

The credibility of news operations in music-heavy formats is not particularly high to begin with, but credibility is fundamental to all-news and news-talk formats. Listeners quickly perceive when stories sound the same, not only between newscasts on one particular station, but also between the news reports on different stations as these listeners punch the buttons on their car radios. When listeners face the same words telling the same story over and over again, they come to believe that there's no news on the radio, and so there's no need to listen to news-based formats.

"Rip 'n' read" can be deadly to a radio news operation. Kill "rip 'n' read" at your station before "rip 'n' read" kills you.

School and Weather Stories

Education and the weather may be the most important issues to your audience. This is especially true of AM stations with news-heavy formats, which regularly gain listeners in the fall and winter with the beginning of the school year and the arrival of unsettled weather. Reporters and news directors need to be prepared to cover school stories and weather emergencies that inevitably appear every year.

Be Prepared for the Start of School

Keep a timetable in the newsroom of when school districts in your area come back into session. As schools open, you should have at least brief readers in your morning casts informing listeners that "It's the first day of classes in Middleville," or "Kids are heading back to school in Small town." If you have a separate traffic reporter, that person should also have a copy of the list of school openings and should remind drivers to watch out for children going to and from school. If you don't have a traffic reporter, make the reminder yourself in the final sentence of your readers on the start of school. Kids and traffic safety is an obvious story idea, and usually a state Triple-A official (who has probably sent you a press release) is available for interview.

Keep Stories Interesting and Current

Other obvious story ideas may need careful attention to make sure they remain interesting. Back-to-school shopping is an example. Doing MOS of mothers buying notebook paper is dull, dull, dull. Examine store ads and look for the unusual. If you have school-age kids, you may already have been badgered to buy all sorts of nonsense--and if one of those requests strikes you as particularly wacky, it may strike your listeners as interesting, too! (If you don't have school-age kids, there's bound to be someone at the station who does.)

While there is a certain timelessness about the annual return of children to school, your stories should be firmly rooted in the present. For example, instead of a generic story about buying clothes for the kids, look at the more current topic of school uniforms (would uniforms end up being less expensive for parents? what do children think about having to wear the same clothes to school every day?). Another recent controversy involves "low-riding" pants, which some school districts have banned.

Prep for School Closings

Your station probably already has a procedure for receiving and announcing school closings. All reporters should be familiar with this procedure, regardless of whether or not the newsroom actually takes the phone calls from nervous superintendents cancelling school. Knowing how the lists of school closings are prepared and then make their way into the studio allows everyone to assist in ensuring that school closings are announced in a timely fashion. In addition, when listeners call the newsroom asking whether a particular school is closed, the reporter on the other end of the line will be able either to find the answer for the caller or to tell the caller when the school-closing list will next be aired.

The list of closed schools should be organized in logical fashion so that listeners may easily discover when their school should be announced. In small markets, alphabetical listings may be adequate. In medium-sized and larger markets, a combination of alphabetical and geographic organization (such as alphabetical listings within a list of counties) might be preferable.

On the Road

Bad weather is often the cause of school closings, but when the schools are closed many worksites remain open. Listeners who have to make their way to work want to know about road conditions. Even if your station relies upon a commercial traffic-reporting service, there may well be several occasions during the year (such as the sudden arrival of storms) when you want to have a reporter on the roads. Reporters need little more than a cellular telephone, a tape recorder and a good timepiece. The reporter might drive along the major roads in the listening area, pulling onto exit ramps or into parking lots at set intervals to provide live reports. Reporters can also interview stranded motorists, or try to interview busy automobile towing and repair shop employees. It goes without saying that reporters should not become stories themselves by being stranded or involved in accidents, so use common sense when reporting from the road.

Don't Shovel Tired Features

Weather-related stories can enlighten listeners, though care must be given to avoid the tired and trite. A few years ago we heard far too many stories about "El Nino"--the unusually strong warming of the waters of the Pacific off the coast of South America--that were sensational rather than informational. (I fear we are in for a similar barrage of bad journalism with the newly emerging El Nino.) Stories typically overdone during the winter include sales reports on shovels and snowblowers, features on the workday of a road-salting crew, and travel agents discussing where locals are heading to escape the weather.

A better approach for generating stories takes issues already of community concern and adds a seasonal aspect. For example, many communities have school buildings that are in poor condition. How are those buildings affected by winter weather? As another example, use of road salt is declining in some areas out of concern for the environment. What has been the effect on driver safety, and if safety has diminished, is the trade-off for a cleaner environment worth it?

Coordinate your Efforts

In the news-talk format, cooperation with your talker can generate deeper discussion of the issues and help both of you in your separate tasks. For example, let's say your station has some midmorning or midday local talk, and the talker has scheduled a psychologist to discuss a child's first day at school. You can assume that the psychologist will talk about separation anxiety, so don't do that story in the morning. Instead, pick a different topic, such as school violence. Your talker now has a different subject to bounce off her guest, who will discuss separation anxiety and the psychological trauma violence inflicts on a young child.

Take a few cuts from the talk-show interview, and you now have a different story for afternoon drive. You will, of course, credit your talker ("...as psychologist Elizabeth Linden-Rahway told News-Talk 990 midday host Sarah Barnes..."), giving the sort of cross-promotion that warms the heart of any program director or general manager.

TECHNICAL DIFFICULTIES

Two of the most dreaded words in broadcast news are "technical difficulties." Equipment problems can never be entirely eliminated. There will always be carts that malfunction, phone lines that go dead, and computer terminals that freeze up. With a little preparation and organization, you'll be able to handle those "technical difficulties" and get through your cast with minimal disruption.

Prevention is the Best Medicine

Many on-air snafus are due to the carelessness that accompanies haste. Perhaps the most prevalent mistake involves playing the wrong cut. At stations that still use tape, this problem is easily prevented by properly labelling and stacking your carts I was always amazed when visiting newsrooms at how often I saw carts lying around with only the tiniest of illegible scrawls to identify them. Carts should be marked with the name of the speaker (the newsmaker for an actuality, the reporter for a voicer or wrap), the number of seconds the cut runs, a slug (story title) that matches a story title on the script, and perhaps even the outcue and a further identifying number that matches a number written at the top of the script.

For example, you have a 10-second actuality of Middleville Mayor Jane Smith discussing plans for the city to build a downtown parking garage. The cut runs as follows:

- IT'S NOT WASTING TAX MONEY. IT'S SAVING DOWNTOWN. IT'S EXPENSIVE BUT IT'S MONEY WELL SPENT. THIS IS THE ONLY WAY TO KEEP BUSINESSES DOWNTOWN.

The label you put on the cart might read like this:

#4	PARKING	0:10
SMITH	OQ:"...DOWNTOWN."	

Similar information should also appear on the hard copy of the script. The script should have a line break to indicate when a cart is to be played, and information on the speaker, the outcue and the duration should be given. Here's an example of what the script accompanying the previous cut might look like:

- .... CRITICS SAY THE PROPOSAL IS A WASTE OF TAX MONEY, BUT SMITH DISAGREES.

  #4 PARKING

  OQ: "...DOWNTOWN."

  CART RUNS 0:10

  CITY COUNCIL WILL DISCUSS THE MAYOR'S PLAN AT TONIGHT'S MEETING.

Having this information on the cart label and in your script will help ensure you play the right cart at the right time.

SOUND IDEAS FOR THE DIGITAL NEWSROOM

Many newsrooms are now tapeless, using digital sound files for actualities, voicers and wraps. Most computer audio-editing programs automatically assign a file number to each sound file, but the file still requires a slug for further identification. The slug should contain a word immediately followed by a number indicating which particular story uses that file.

For the story about the proposed parking garage, let's say this actuality is the second of three actualities taken from the interview with the mayor.

One of the actualities will be used by the reporter in a wrap, the other two in scripts to be read by an anchor. So there are three scripts to be created from this story, and this particular script and its accompanying actuality should be slugged parking02 to distinguish it from the other scripts and sound files (which would be slugged parking01 and parking03).

Computer programs may allow further identifying information, such as outcue and length of cut, to mark each sound file. The more information in your script, the better. This will help ensure that the sound file you select to accompany the story is the correct one.

CART-ASTROPHIES AND OTHER GLITCHES

Another common snafu in newsrooms that still use tape involves not having the cart properly cued. This often happens during the second airing of a cut. The anchor during the first airing may have had to stop the cart immediately after the actuality or wrap finished (and before the cart could recue) because the cart machine was needed to play another cart during that cast.

It is the responsibility of the anchor about to go on the air, or the anchor's producer, that carts be properly cued prior to broadcast. Carts should be played in the newsroom before the next airing to ensure the carts are cued. (Anchors between broadcasts should be playing and listening to these carts anyway to aid in the rewriting of the accompanying scripts.)

If a cart is not properly cued, or if the cart machine malfunctions (such as playing the actuality very s l o w l y), stop the cart and say a sentence that summarizes to listeners what they would have heard without the "technical difficulties." Then return to your script and finish the story.

When I worked as a writer in Detroit, I was expected to type a few bare phrases summarizing a cart's contents, and that summary appeared at the bottom of the script, separated from the on-air story by a double line.

This summary was provided in case problems arose playing the cart. The anchors (who, in an all-news format, had 5-hour air shifts and may not have heard the tape before it was brought into the studio) needed that summary to ad lib when the cart failed.

In the tapeless newsroom, anchors often read their stories off computer screens. If the computers fail, neither the scripts nor the sound files will be available. It is crucial that a printout of all the scripts for the cast be taken into the studio. A frozen computer screen won't then lead to a frozen newscast.

SNAP, CRACKLE, POP

Telephone connections also fail, or the quality of the connection may be too poor for broadcast. Poor quality connections are becoming more prevalent as more and more stations send reporters out with cellular telephones, whose quirks can at times be maddening.

If you in the studio have a hard time understanding the words of the speaker on the other end of the line (be it a newsmaker or a reporter in a live shot), your listeners...many of whom are in automobiles...won't fare any better. End the telephone interview or report immediately with a graceful apology to the listeners about sound quality and "technical difficulties," and move on to the next story. No matter how important the story may be, if the sound is incomprehensible, the value for radio news is worthless.

The possibility of "technical difficulties" in a cast should remind anchors always to bring into the studio more stories than they would normally need.

If you're giving a cast that runs 3:30, bring in 5 minutes of copy and sound. If you have a 5-minute cast, bring in 8. A problem with a computer screen, cart machine or telephone line could easily cut a full minute or two from your cast.

You need to be prepared to get through the cast in a professional manner, and it is far more professional to complete with confidence a variety of different news stories than to try to return to a tape or a phone report that failed the first time around.

6

Principles of Writing Radio Drama

INTRODUCTION

First of all, the way you choose to present your script is really important if you want the reader to enjoy your play and to concentrate fully on it. Here are a few things which can make reading difficult:

- Plays presented on brightly coloured paper
- Plays printed with expiring cartridges so that the type is so faint you have to squint at it
- Plays printed on continuous listing paper with the content of each page dropping down on to the next one (one of our readers likened this to reading a toilet roll)
- Plays typed in unusual fonts which are really difficult to read, or typed in very large or very small fonts
- Plays typed in such a way that there's no differentiation between character names, sound effects and dialogue
- Plays hand written in pencil

A common mistake is to abbreviate characters' names down to a single initial so the reader has to keep stopping to think who's speaking. The best way to present a script is not so that it will stand out from the competition, but just the opposite- if it's neatly typed, double-spaced, with the characters' names in capitals down the left margin and sound effects or music described in italics, it'll be so easy to read, the reader will find it effortless. Then they can really concentrate on the content of the play.

As for the content of the play-radio drama is very different from theatre and television. We often get scripts which say 'written for the stage but I thought it might do for radio' on the front cover. It usually doesn't. Stage directions like 'puts glasses on' or 'bends over and picks up a piece of paper' aren't going to be easy to get across to a radio audience. It has to be in the dialogue or sound effects, otherwise it will be lost. Stage plays can be adapted for radio, but not without a great deal of attention to detail.

There are no limits on the imaginative potential of the dramatist and there are no limits on how the radio dramatist can express that potential. The sound medium is free of all the physical and practical limitations of the stage and film set. A radio play can move through any dimension of time. It can move to any location. It can voice metaphysical, surrealist and subconscious feelings and images.

The radio dramatist needs a creative interaction with the listener, and the ability of the radio dramatist to create a unique world in the listener's imagination is a special quality generally denied to TV viewers or theatre-goers. Theatre, film and TV plays paint the colours for the audience, whereas the pictures in the mind of the radio listener are individual to that person alone. This gives radio a special intimacy.

Radio is very good at dramatising what people are thinking. The contrast between what people say and what they think can be shown very effectively on radio. 'Interior thought' is a convention which is special to the radio medium. In radio the listener can be instantly transported inside the head of a character and can hear those secret, private thoughts that are often better left unsaid. Radio drama has been described as 'The Theatre of the Mind'. The potential conflict between exterior dialogue and speech and interior thought creates a special ground of conflict which is a fertile area for the creative radio playwright.

The key to writing successful plays for radio is to realise that the listener can only understand what is going on by what he or she hears. The physical environment and the appearance of the characters depends on what they say and the images created in the listener's imagination by words and sounds and/

or music. Radio drama has only one chance to be successful. A dissatisfied listener only has to twiddle the radio dial, or turn the switch off altogether and the playwright has lost the audience. It's important to bear in mind that a radio playwright can't afford to bore or confuse the listener.

All good writing requires a strong element of honesty and integrity from the writer. The great dramatists strive to express a truth about human experience or human nature. This means that superticiality, pretentiousness and ostentation are quickly recognised by the listener and will normally lead to failure when the listener switches off.

SOME HORRIBLE TRUTHS

Most radio drama is very badly written. Radio drama is an endangered species. It has never taken a hold of mainstream programming on commercial radio in the UK. It used to be the mainstream in the States and Australia but lost out to TV in the middle to late fifties.

It is under threat within public radio services including the BBC because of the pressure of monetarist ideology and the fact that authors and radio drama directors have been too complacent. IRDP is a significant oasis and continues to support the principle of the original play.

GROUND RULES

The Beginning: The beginning is everything. If this part of it does not work you are 'up shit creek without a paddle'. Your listeners will desert you. You have failed. You do not exist as a dramatist. Booo!

The Moment of Arrival: This is how you drop your listeners into the story. Don't give them a warm bed with comfortable pillows and a hot water bottle. The background and sub-text of previous histories is better explored through revelation in dramatic action. So parachute your listener into a top dramatic moment. Not the climax. That would be premature. Find the MOMENT to join the story. Avoid the slow snail's explicatory route. Kick 'em into a high energy trip and whoosh them through the rapids.

Structure: Set up...struggle...resolution. You can reverse this if the set-up is more dramatic and explosive than the resolution. Regard your play as a series of phases

The Plot: This is the story with lots of twists and turns. The more the merrier. Most listeners like good exciting plots. Without a good plot you're eating a souffle that has gone flat. You need plot, more plot and more plot. Run at least two story lines.

Two sub plots would be interesting. Keep the plots linked logically within the same play. The best system is a major and a minor story-line linked to one another. Get them to come together at the end.

Surprise: People are hungry for entertainment. If they wanted boredom they would be filling out their tax returns instead of listening to your radio play. Make people afraid, but also excited.

Character: Your main character must have the sympathy of the audience. Your audience has to identify with your main character. If this does not happen you have created a failure. Booo!

Conflict: Drama = conflict = audience. There has to be an emotional, financial, human, moral, physical struggle so your listeners can laugh or cry. Yes, you want your listeners to laugh or cry or laugh and cry. If you don't, give up.

Polarities or Extremes: The art of story telling is exploring the extreme limits of our psychological or physical existence. To pitch one polarity against another.

The Climax: I apologize for the sexual metaphor. But there is something in this. The better sex has foreplay, development, sustained excitement, surprise and affection, nay love followed by an explosion of ecstasy. Good radio drama is not all that different. If you don't use it, you lose it.

Dialogue: This is how we engage dramatically with the world. Characters inform, argue, amuse, outrage, argue through the ebb and flow of dialogue. When we do we talk and that is how great radio plays are made.....by talking in dramatic dialogue.

Atmosphere / Ambience: This sets the emotional spirit of the play. It determines whether your listeners believe in the world that you have created. Worlds are not created by dramatic dialogue alone. There is attitude and atmosphere. This is determined by detail and relevant detail. It could be in a sound effect. It could be in the writing. It could be in the music. It could be in everything. But the result is that the fifth dimension of radio writing-the imagination of the listener-is stimulated to become a picture palace of the mind.

Emotion: Got to be there. You have to generate an emotional response from the audience....preferably to the main character....also not so strongly in relation to the other characters. Emotion = love, hate, admiration. Never mind about the type of emotion.....concentrate on whether it is there or not. Emotional connection between the writing and the listener = good radio drama.

Balance Character and Plot: You have to have both. You cannot trade. One can predominate over the other. Where they are balanced equally....it can only work if characterisation relates to plot development. If your main plot is character intensive, make sure that your minor plot is plot intensive.

Purpose: Crook's golden rule is that every word, every line, every scene must serve a dramatic purpose in terms of characterisation and plot development. Drop anything that does not have a dramatic purpose.

Tension and Humour: To stop the listener dropping off or switching off, maintain the tension always and throw in the humour. Tension, humour, tension, humour, tension humour...like the foxtrot..Make the emotional rhythm of the play dance on the listener's heart and mind. Charm and alarm, charm and alarm. But they've got to be linked. Your character uses humour to react to the tension in the scene or play. Keep one character who uses humour to deal with difficult situations. Make sure the humour is verbal. Slapstick belongs to a different type of play or entertainment. Make sure you do not have characters taking it in turns to be funny. This is not stand up comedy or sitcom. Make sure that the character who uses humour has a consistent sense of humour.

Get your listener inside the world of your play. How?

a. Sympathy or empathy with the main character.

b. A bloody good set up.

c. A big, nasty antagonist or villain.

d. Great Plot...Great Story....twists and turns.

e. Crisis at the beginning is dramatic and a great start.

f. Emotional intensity. Hit some high points.

g. Escalating conflict so the structure climbs with tension and humour.

h. Strike the colours with detail so there's an atmosphere, mood...ambience.

I. Modulate charm with alarm...humour with tension...tension with humour...funny policeman nasty policeman.

j. Surprise, surprise...that's what you do to the listener, through the plot.

The principle of developing scenes

1. Introduction.
2. Character one...goal and objective.
3. Character two...goal and objective.
4. Purpose of scene in overall plot.
5. One of the characters achieves a goal.
6. Link to the next scene by introducing or pointing to location of next scene or presence of character in next scene.

Question marks in the mind of the listener. Always keep one, better two or three

THE PRINCIPLE OF CHARACTER

1. Believable and recognisable.
2. Purpose within the plot.
3. Characters have to have function. Character has to be consistent with function.

4. Characters have to be intentional.
5. Start with a stereotype to ensure rapid recognition, then twist the stereotype. Challenge the homily that there is nothing new under the sun by making it new under the moon.
6. Give each character a dominant physical or behavioural characteristic. Make the dominant characteristic purposeful. Make it extreme.
7. Your main character must be active.
8. Active character / urgent plot. The character's energy has to fight the urgency of the plot and the urgency of the plot makes the character more energetic.

THE PRINCIPLE OF HERO / HEROINE

1. Listeners look up to main characters, want to admire them because we all want heroes and heroines in our lives. Life's eternal fantasy that transcendent people and transcendent moments conquer adversity.
2. If you are very clever you can transfer the hero from the obvious to the humble and make great the inferior or character who has greater potential for human dignity.
3. Charisma. Characters need intensity and conviction. They may not be perfect but they are attractive. You cannot identify with people who are unlike ourselves...too perfect, no beliefs...take themselves too seriously...lack a sense of humour..
4. Give your characters private moments when they drop their guards and allow us into their minds and hearts. Make the listener privileged. Use this moment for revelation.
5. The main character has to change and has to be changed by the plot.
6. You must have a main character and secondary characters. Your main character changes. Your secondary characters are probably more singular in their characteristics. Your secondary characters are already committed. Your main character is still weighing up the options.

7. You must have characters who are extreme in relation to each other...characters that are different make drama.

Where are we now?

Well, we should be here....

a. The main character is in the middle of the story.

b. You've used dominant characteristics.

c. The listener likes the main character.

d. The listener cares what happens to the main character.

e. The listener hates the antagonist.

f. The main character is developing.

PRINCIPLES OF DIALOGUE

a. Dialogue must be a response to a situation, plot or action.

b. Dialogue must be a response to each character in the scene.

c. Dialogue must be comic relief.

d. Dialogue must connect to the next scene.

e. Avoid reflective, passive and neutral. Go for active, and direct and emotional.

f. Dialogue must be believable by being specific...by being specific to the character's background and emotional state.

g. If dialogue is reacting to action or situation then it must be dramatic and poised on polarities. The goals of the characters in each scene should be different.

h. Dialogue should be continuous. Tip...characters often take a tag by repeating the last word spoken by the first character.

i. Dialogue must relate to function.

j. You can mix direct with indirect between two characters because they have different goals.

k. Humorous dialogue is not a character telling a joke but a line or lines responding to the dramatic situation.

1. Heightened dialogue vs naturalistic dialogue. Heightened language is the language of the theatre...high octane communication...poetic, philosophical... charged..the expression of the playwright...It serves not only the development of the plot and character, but it also presents the view of the writer. Works well in radio. But there is now a tendency for more naturalism. Radio producers like to go out on location and explore realism. In these situations you must stick to natural dialogue.

PRINCIPLES PECULIAR TO RADIO

1. The inner existence.
2. The tension and conflict between the interior and exterior.
3. More psychological.
4. Easier to explore the real and the surreal and to delineate the line between the two.
5. Have to work in the fifth dimension...the energy of the listener's imaginative participation.
6. The interior existence offers exploration of personal thoughts, fantasies, emotions and conflicts.
7. All levels of external conflict can be explored.
8. The precipitating event through plot has to threaten the inner life of the main character. This is the kick-off in radio drama.
9. The end or resolution in radio drama is more deeply rooted in the emotional equilibrium and insight of the main character. Changes are internal as well as external.
10. Time transposition and translocation are faster and more rapid and more complicated. Flashbacks... flashforwards... different ages.
11. Radio requires less rather than more characters. Characterisation needs to be strong and fascinating.
12. Maintain the focus of the main character and plot.

13. Economy of words underlines subtextual surprise and engagement with the listener's imagination.
14. Wit is vital because language is so important... cleverness with words...energy with words..humour with words...Wit is advanced by surprising the listener...being aggressive with the listener..being fast, short and clever with the listener.
15. Irony is pathos and bathos. It's conflict between the inner life and outer action.

WHAT MAKES RADIO DRAMA DIFFERENT?

So what makes a radio play different from one for theatre or television? What follows here are a few quick pointers to help you in the right direction. These points are explored further by Craig Warner, a successful radio drama writer.

Everyone knows the cliche about how radio "stretches the imagination". This suggests radio is hard work for the listener. You can't doze off in front of a radio play and expect to pick up the story again when you wake up. Good radio drama therefore, is not easy to write. To create the world of the play in the mind of the listener, you, the writer have to think as an impresario, sometimes acting as your own producer, director, set designer and dialogue coach.

In radio, there are no limits to the imaginative potential of the dramatist and to how the radio dramatist can express that potential. The sound medium is free of all the physical and practical limitations of the stage and film set. A radio play can move through any dimension of time and to any location. A radio play can voice metaphysical, surrealist and subconscious motivations and images.

The radio dramatist needs a creative intimacy with the listener to conjure a unique world in his or her imagination. Radio is very good at dramatising the contrast between what people say and what they think. Indeed, radio drama has been called the "theatre of the mind". "Interior thought" is a convention that is special to the radio medium; the listener is instantly transported inside the head of a character and can hear those secret, private thoughts that are often left unsaid.

The medium liberates the scope of imaginative recall, providing a perfect opportunity to explore consciousness and dramatise all the voices that motivate different aspects of experience. Moving beyond the bounds of naturalism, radio drama can also give animals a voice, invest inanimate objects with character and give emotion to all aspects of nature.

THE WRITER: CRAIG WARNER

"I remember once when I was rehearsing a staged reading of a play in New York, I brought along a tape recorder so that I could tape the run-through of the play. When I got home I cued the tape up to a particular scene I wanted to hear, and played it. I was amazed. The whole scene seemed transformed. Suddenly there was not the three actors saying the lines in a dingy church hall-just the mystery of words and voices on their own, a kind of pure music from which there seemed torn away a thousand limitations that my sight had imposed. The dialogue seemed bigger, broader, more magical; this was my first experience of what radio drama might be like.

The first play I sent to the BBC was a stage play I wanted to adapt for the radio. The producer who read it liked it, but he said it was firmly rooted in the stage, and would not make a good radio play. He suggested I write something for the radio directly, something more 'radiophonic'. But what did this mean? I tried to conceive of the play by imagining someone in a room with nothing in it but a box with sounds and voices coming out of it. The producer was right: imagining the telling of a story in this way not only changed the conventions I wanted to use, but actually the story itself. I came up with the idea of a young man who could not speak. Everyone at his work and his home would treat him as though he was intellectually inferior; but the audience of this play would be able to hear his thoughts; they would be able to hear that he was extremely sensitive and highly intelligent, making it all the more moving that the other people in the play never took the time to discover this. This device was a successful one, and it made the play work in a way it could never have worked in any other medium.

It could almost be said that the medium's limitations are also it strengths. Spectacle is out of the question-but for this reason you can furnish a room with a word, clothe and equip and mount an army with a phrase. Vegetables and trees can speak. And the unimaginable and the contradictory can be used without difficulty-for instance, if one of your characters is a woman so beautiful that men instantly die when they set eyes on her, the role would be impossible to cast in any other medium but not on radio. Equally, in the radio world there can be round squares, objects that are all black and all white simultaneously, buildings so tall that their roofs hit the bottom of the earth. You cannot see the frown on an actress's face, but this is little payment to make in exchange for the freedom the medium allows.

Besides, a frown on an actress's face can always be embedded in the dialogue. Often people writing plays will provide emotional clues for the actors to help them interpret lines, like 'angrily' or 'happily'. But, although these may sometimes be helpful to the actor, it is unwise to expect them to say the lines 'angrily' in exactly the same way you hear it in your head. Their idea of anger might be different from yours. But they will be expected to say the lines as you wrote them, so for this reason it's always better to avoid emotional cues at first and to try to make the line an angry line instead. This is particularly true on radio, when the actor's facial expressions cannot be seen, nor can their postures or movements; emotions and all other clues about a character's inner life are portrayed entirely by the vocal delivery.

The other main instrument you have at your disposal in telling a story on radio is sound, and there are several different uses of sound on the radio. One is music. Music can be used as part of a story-for instance, when one character plays a song to another on his record player-or as a score, when the music is not 'heard' by the characters, only the audience, and is used to enhance a scene, for instance to make it more romantic or suspenseful. Many writers and producers use pre-recorded music to score a play-rock, jazz, classical, or any other kind of music that might be appropriate-or a composer can be asked to write original music.

Another use of sound in radio plays is the collection of sounds used to create an atmosphere. If a scene takes place in a crowded restaurant, on a beach, at a football game, or in an airport lounge, you will want the acoustic and the other background sounds associated with whatever location you've chosen. The BBC has almost every imaginable setting already recorded for use in radio plays, and occasionally plays are even recorded in actual locations rather in a studio.

A third use of sound is the use of sound effects. Sometimes these could be additions to the background sounds-for instance, if the scene takes place in a car driving through the city, and suddenly the car has to swerve to avoid hitting another car or there could be distinct sounds that carry the action of your story a bit further, like someone knocking on the door, a siren approaching, or sudden thunder. I find it more satisfying to limit the sounds I use as much as possible, so that each sound will stand out as a clear step in advancing the story, rather than as contributing to a confusion of sounds, which can make them less potent or ultimately meaningless. For this reason, each sound should be carefully considered so that it will be given the proper weight in your play-neither too much nor too little.

The most important thing when writing a radio play is to hear it in your head as you write it. But never let it become too perfect in your head. The drama is a collaborative art form, and the director and the actors, as well as the technicians, will all have creative ideas that will help to take the play out of your head and onto the airwaves."

APPROACHES TO WRITING FOR RADIO DRAMA-KEY POINTS

The key, therefore, to writing successful plays for radio is to realise that the listener can only understand what is going on by what the listener hears. The physical environment and the appearance of the characters depend on what they say and the images they create in the listeners' imagination by words and sounds.

A radio drama play has only one chance to be successful. Dissatisfied listeners only have to twiddle their dial, or hit the off switch and the playwright has lost the audience. It is important to remember that a radio playwright cannot afford to bore or confuse the listener. Radio drama is capable of capturing the imaginations of the listener with very fine strokes of sound and much can be achieved with a subtle use of effects. Silence in radio drama can be as dramatic as the spoken word or a devastating sound effect. Entire plays have been constructed without a single word of dialogue. BBC Radio has transmitted a radio play which consisted solely of the sounds of a man being chased.

But of course speech will normally be the dominant element. It is in the dialogue that the writer will provide most of the essential information, but this should not sound explicit or it won't seem natural. It follows that the art of dialogue on radio is, at its best, extremely sophisticated. In order to convey information without sounding artificial or stilted the writer must consider the structure of scenes and of individual lines with great precision. It is not a matter of stringing together conversations. A radio play may predominantly consist of dialogue but a radio that was "all talk" in a static conversational sense would be very boring.

A variety of sound is essential for holding the listener's attention and engaging their imagination. This variety can be achieved by altering the lengths of sequence, number of people speaking, pace of dialogue, volume of sound, background acoustics and location of the action. On radio, one room sounds very like another if they're about the same size, but the difference between an interior and an exterior acoustic is considerable.

There are five technical features which make a good radio play stand out

1. Quality of characterisation. Can the listener imagine the experience of the character through the script? Is the character immediate to the listener and can they empathise with her or him? Do the characters undergo some significant change through the course of the drama and does that change encompass conflict?
2. Quality and Originality of Sound Design. Is your script uniquely suited to the radio medium? Have you created a sound atmosphere and 'sound set' that enhances and complements the mood of the writing, the characters

and the plot? Is sound used symbolically, ironically, surrealistically, or satirically and does it form part of the texture and artistic fabric of the play?

3. Quality and Originality of Dialogue. Are the characters created by the idiom and speech rhythms of their lines? Are characters developed by effective and revelatory dialogue? Is there a sense of reality in the speeches? If you are writing about real people do they sound like them?
4. Quality and Originality of the Plot. Are you able to keep the listener on tenterhooks? Do you leave the listener determined to hear the play to the very end? How logical and believable is the story? Is the listener sure of what is happening in each of the developing scenes?
5. Effectiveness of the beginning of the play in making the listener want to continue listening. Remember some drama producers insist that the writer has only a minute to engage the listener before they are liable to turn off!

THE WRITER: ANGELA TURVEY

"Radio can take you anywhere-from the top of Mount Everest to a submarine at the bottom of the sea. You can crawl inside somebody's head and listen to their thoughts, cross continents or travel through time. The setting for radio drama is just as flexible-your imagination is free to go wherever it wants to without being held back by financial or practical limitations.

The lack of visuals is a powerful advantage in radio-it allows the audience to create their own mind pictures which are invariably more realistic than any special effects on screen or stage. Listening to a radio play is therefore, not a passive exercise: the listener's mind works with your words to create a dramatic experience. The intimacy of radio is also important in this, as your aim is ultimately to elicit a response in your audience.

A lot of my work is set in London and here, radio's unique ability to evoke mood and atmosphere come in to play. The desolation and eerie silence of London's Docklands inspired me to write 'Splendid Isolation', a story about a young woman establishing her independence for the first time. The location need not be exotic. My own rule is that wherever I set a play, I must make it real for the listener and entice them into hearing my story.

Obviously, radio also has it limitations. Everything you want to communicate to your audience must be done verbally or with sound effects whereas in a visual medium, one action may be enough to reveal character or show the audience something vital. Successfully conveying information without being clumsy or stilted is part of the skill of writing for radio and is something which will improve with practice and by listening to as many plays as possible.

Listening to radio drama, if you are familiar with it, is perhaps the first step in beginning to write for radio. Decide what you think works and what doesn't and bear these points in mind when coming up with ideas and writing dialogue. If you are unsure what to write about, my own advice would be to write the kind of play you would like to hear. When I first started to write for radio, I made the mistake of writing what I thought other people wanted to hear. Once I started to write about subjects and characters that genuinely interested me, I was more successful. Always remember the medium you're writing for and ideally, your play should rely on the strengths I have already mentioned.

Assuming you've got the most important elements in place and a director likes your idea, he or she will probably invite you for a chat about your script and perhaps suggest some rewriting. My first play was rewritten three times and each draft was a considerable improvement on the previous one. Eventually, I was offered a contract. I had to wait a few months for the studio recording which I found very exciting. I became more aware of the technical possibilities and kept this information in mind when writing subsequent plays.

Radio is sometimes well-known for producing a particular type of play which some sections of our society may well find interesting, but not particularly relevant to their own lives, experience or history. Barring certain radio-festivals, I had rarely heard a play on the radio with black actors in the leading roles or plays which reflected our multi-cultural society. So why don't I write one, I thought? If you listen to radio and likewise feel there is no voice to speak for you, why don't you become that voice?

I would say that directors are only too happy to receive scripts from all sections of the community, writing about subjects which concern them. What is important is that you wrap your theme in a good story with strong characters and exploit the advantages of radio. As a writer who is also black, I have had the pleasure of working with actors and directors from various cultural backgrounds to produce drama that is popular and accessible to everybody. Because of the number of original plays broadcast on radio every year, it is an excellent medium for allowing many different voices to have their say on air. So what are you waiting for? Pick up that pen and get writing"

SCRIPT LAYOUT-A FORMAT FOR PRESENTATION

When submitting a script to a radio producer, it must be presented in a particular format. A list of recommendations follows and we advise wherever possible that you follow these.

1. Scripts must be typed or printed. Hand-written scripts will be returned unread. The script should be double spaced with a clear, 12 point font. Do not send scripts printed or photocopied so faintly that they are difficult to read.
2. Please use A4 sized white paper, and use one side of the paper only.
3. Names of characters should be clearly separated from the speech and should be given in full throughout. You know who Mrs B. is but the reader might not.
4. Sound Effects, and other technical information should also be clearly differentiated from the speech.
5. Always attach a synopsis of the play, even with a completed script, together with a full cast list and brief notes on the main characters.
6. Always keep a copy of your script.
7. Make sure that all pages are firmly fastened and numbered consecutively. (Rehearsal scripts number each

speech, starting afresh at the top of each page, but this is not necessary when first submitting.)

8. If you want your manuscript returned, enclose a stamped addressed envelope.
9. Please remember, you may have to wait some time, often several months, before you get a response.

SPECIMEN LAYOUT

(INTERIOR. SMALL BEDROOM ACOUSTIC. CLOSE TO MIC MUFFLED BREATHING SUGGESTS THAT THE SLEEPER HAS HIS HEAD UNDER THE BLANKETS. WHICH HE HAS. HIS THOUGHTS ARE AWAKE HOWEVER. AND OCCUPY A LIMBO. INDICATED BY A SLIGHT ECHO.)

1. PREBBLE: (thoughts) I must say in concluding, Mr. Chairman-to conclude, that is, the preamble to my preliminary thoughts on this matter. Or, to put it more succinctly-the summation, as it were, of our serious thinking during our anticipatory study.....
2. CHAIRMAN: (thought acoustic) Get on with it, Prebble.
3. PREBBLE: I must seek the Board's indulgence if I go-briefly, I may add, briefly through the points which seem to me to lie-
4. CHAIRMAN: One minute, Prebble, I warn you. You know what'll happen.
5. PREBBLE: No, please, Mr. Chairman. I'm going as fast as I can-
6. CHAIRMAN: Ten seconds.
7. PREBBLE: No! You're counting too fast.
8. CHAIRMAN: Too late. Bring in the gong.
9. PREBBLE: No. (pleading) Not the gong. I tried. I tried. (A LOUD. DEEP-TONED GONG. SOUNDS RHYTHMICALLY. LIKE A GIANT CLOCK STRIKING.)
10. PREBBLE: (moaning) Oh, no. No. Stop. Please. I can't-I can't bear-

    (AT THE LAST TRIUMPHANT GONG. THE SOUND TURNS INTO A CHEAP ALARM CLOCK. RINGING IN THE BEDROOM.)

11. PREBBLE: (normal voice, waking up) Hmm? Oh-what time is it?
12. MRS HANDS: (approaching) Morning Mr. Prebble. I've brought you tea. But you'll have to be quick. It's the board meeting this morning and you never set you alarm right, did you?

    (CUT TO INTERIOR LARGE LIMOUSINE. TRAFFIC PASSING.)
13. CHAUFFEUR: Thought I'd come this way, Mr. Prebble. Can't get round Hyde Park Corner. Protest March.

7

Skills for Radio Journalists

INTRODUCTION

This module covers the basics of radio journalism:

- Skills and responsibilities
- Writing for radio
- Presentation
- Interviews

Module Objectives: At the end of this module, you should be able to:

- Recognize techniques that are used by radio journalists
- Understand writing techniques used for radio
- Identify key practices for effective radio presentation
- Identify different techniques used for radio interviews
- Discuss how writing and presentation play a role in radio interviews

Throughout the module, examples and exercises will help you practice what you are learning. In order to master the skills presented, you should practice the techniques and ask for feedback from experienced radio journalists.

SKILLS AND RESPONSIBILITIES FOR RADIO

Radio stations have many people with different skills and responsibilities. There are those who voices are heard on the air, like talk show hosts and reporters, and there are also people who work behind the scenes like sound engineers, producers, marketing managers, researchers and call-screeners.

Sometimes one person may take on several roles. In smaller radio stations, a talk show host may also do research or a news reader may file reports from the field. Even at larger stations, producers are often involved in research and booking guests. Whatever the structure or size of the station, remember that successful radio depends on teamwork and all roles are equally important.

This module focuses on the responsibilities and fundamental skills that a radio journalist needs to do her job.

Responsibilities: Professional journalists, whether they work in radio, television or print, are expected to adhere to basic principles. Journalists should be:

Accountable

Balanced

Independent

Journalism associations or unions in many countries have established codes of ethics for the practice of journalism. Many media companies have also established their own ethical standards. Find out more about codes of ethics from these websites:

- EthicNet-European Codes of Journalism Ethics
- International Journalists' Network
- Society of Professional Journalists
- Guiding Principles for the Journalist-Bob Steele, The Poynter Institute

Skills: This module explains three core skills of radio:

- Writing
- Presenting
- Conducting interviews

These skills can be used in different ways, depending to the kind of program being scripted or presented. For example, the style used to present a news bulletin is different from the style used in a late-night music show. Understanding the core principles of writing, presenting and interviewing for radio will help you adapt these principles for different programs.

WHAT TO SAY: FINDING THE ANGLE

The first step in developing a news story is to find the angle, or the main point of the story. One way to find the angle is to clarify the facts and then ask the question, "So what?"

To answer the "so what?" question, you need to understand who the listeners are. What news interests them? What information is relevant to their daily lives? What are they worried about? What do they feel strongly about?

The answer to "so what?" will lead to the story angle.

The Necessity of an Angle: The angle is what makes listeners say, "Oh, that's important," or "That's interesting."

Identifying the angle helps to sharpen focus for the story and leads to clearer writing. A story without an angle that covers every aspect of an issue will be confusing and lose listeners.

Finding the Angle: While researching a story, ask:

- What is happening or what has been happening?
- Why is the story important?
- Why will listeners care about this story?
- What will listeners want to know?

Think about:

- Listeners
    - Who are they?
    - What will make them identify with the story and find it relevant and interesting?
    - What do they already know or think about the issue?
    - What other questions would they like to have answered?
- The story from all its perspectives
    - Why did the event occur?

* What do people think about the event that occurred?
* Who is involved in the event and why?
* Will something happen in the future as a result of the news event?

WHAT TO SAY: WRITING FOR LISTENERS

Writing for radio is different than writing for print media. Keep these differences in mind:

Reading	Listening
• Readers usually focus only on what they are reading. They are usually not doing something else at the same time.	• Listeners are usually doing something else while listening to the radio, so their focus may be divided unless they are interested.
• Readers can go back to what was written before and re-read it to make sense or to clarify.	• Listeners hear words and sounds once and then they are gone. They only have one opportunity to understand and make sense of a story.

WRITING FOR THE EAR

Writing for radio means writing the way people speak. Keep the following tips in mind:

- Break the rules of grammar when necessary. Clarity is the goal.
- Say aloud what you've written to make sure it makes sense.
- Imagine that someone is listening while you are writing and pretend you are talking to that listener.
- Keep it simple by using just one idea per sentence and avoiding long words.

WHAT TO SAY: TIPS FOR SCRIPTING

Like other kinds of writing, scripting involves several steps:

- Researching • Creating a structure • Writing

Research: Research is the foundation of any story. Consider these sources:

- News events related to the topic
- Stories previously written or aired about the topic
- People who can talk about the topic (interviews)
- Organizations involved in the story

Use a combination of research methods. Start with these basic research tools:

- The Internet. Use search engines to research a topic, find organizations or resources related to stories and locate archives of earlier stories. Some of the most popular search engines are AlltheWeb, Google and Yahoo.
- Publications. Newspapers, magazines and books can provide ideas and resources for stories.
- Contacts. Talk with colleagues and friends to find out what they think about a topic. They may be able to suggest people to interview.

Script Structure: The structure of a script depends on its purpose. Is it a news report? Is the purpose to entertain? To persuade? Or to share something important? Be clear about how the script will flow. What pieces of information will be included? In what order? While a news story requires a more formal style and approach, these tips can be useful for scripting:

- Imagine talking to a friend. What questions does the friend ask? Answering these questions one-by-one will help you write with the listener in mind.
- Draft a rough outline based on the "talking to a friend" exercise above. Decide whether to tell it chronologically, with the most important facts first or some other way.
- Start with an arresting sentence--called a "hook"--at the beginning to attract and hold the listener's interest.
- End the story by satisfying listeners that all important questions have been answered.

Content: Use the following tips to write for the ear. Remember that these general tips will need to be adapted accordingly when writing news stories.

- Write in short phrases. Keep it short, punchy and direct. Use only one idea per sentence.

Write in short, punchy and direct phrases. Use only one idea per sentence.

This version is grammatically correct, but it's not written for radio: We are going to hear a song by one of South Africa's best-known voices--Sibongile Khumalo--a woman who is equally skillful at performing opera, jazz and traditional music, and she will be singing a song called "Mountain Shade" which was composed by a young local composer called Moses Molelekwa.

Try rewriting it.

- Keep it short, punchy and direct.
- Make sure there is only one idea per sentence.

Take a look at one rewritten version. Do you see why it works better? Now here's a well-known voice. Sibongile Khumalo. Someone who's equally at home singing opera, jazz, traditional music, you name it. And the song? "Mountain Shade"--composed by another local talent. Moses Molelekwa.

Round off complicated numbers and write them in words. Round off complicated numbers and write them in words.

For example, rather than:

- Authorities spent $3,589.50 on the system.

Try:

- Authorities spent about four thousand dollars on the system.
- Try to humanize statistics, facts and figures.
- Use verbal signposts such as "and," "but" and "so" to show structure in longer chunks of talk and to help listeners know where they are.
- Paint pictures with words. Remember, listeners have to use imagination to visualize what is happening.
- Write as if talking to only one person and create a connection with listeners by using personal words like "you" or "we."

- Use contractions like "can't," "won't" and "we'll." They will make the story sound more natural.

Here's an exercise to help you think about writing for radio.

Tone: Getting the content right is not enough. The tone, or voice, is equally important. Listeners should not be insulted or embarrassed by an inappropriate tone.

The tone for news writing should be:

- Unemotional.
- Direct and dynamic, but not sensational.

In other kinds of radio programs, such as talk shows or magazine programs:

- Be warm, friendly and enthusiastic.
- Treat listeners with respect. Don't patronize them.
- Talk to listeners but don't lecture them.

Creativity: All good writing springs from creativity, including news reporting even though it is more formal in style than other programs.

Creativity involves:

- Selecting specific details that paint pictures and allow the listener to imagine what is being described.
- Avoiding generalizations and adjectives such as beautiful, nice and lovely. Describe the scene in detail and let the listener decide whether it is truly beautiful.

What to Say: What not to Say

Part of being a good radio host or presenter is knowing what not to say. If listeners are insulted or embarrassed, they won't want to listen any more. Being a good radio host requires cultural sensitivity and accurate knowledge about an audience, from what style of program listeners prefer to what topics interest them. Experienced radio professionals know what offends listeners.

Radio hosts should not:

- Make listeners feel like just part of a crowd.

- Use sexist or patronizing language.
- Talk unprofessionally or make amateurish requests.
- Send private messages to friends.
- Alert listeners to commercials so that they will want to turn off the radio.

These examples of actual phrases heard on the radio illustrate how listeners might respond.

What was said:	**Possible listener reaction:**	**Why this shouldn't be said:**
Hello to all of you out there in listener land!	Well, I don't live in "listener land!" And I'm NOT "all of you!"	Makes listeners feel like part of a crowd
And thanks to our lovely newsreader, Angela. She's looking drop-dead gorgeous today!	Angela's a professional. Isn't that what you're supposed to be? Such comments are sexist and patronizing.	Sexist
Whoops! Finger trouble again -- we've just got a new computer in the studio--so do bear with me!	Why should I? I expect YOU to do your job. I've got problems of my own!	Unprofessional and amateurish
Well, I seem to have run out of time again. Join me again tomorrow.	WHY have you run out of time? Shouldn't you be watching the clock?	Amateurish
And here's a special song for my boyfriend, Sipho. He'll know why it's special.	Why should I be excluded just because you want to send a private message to what's-his-name?	Private message
Well, let's go off to the marketplace for a few messages from our sponsors.	Oh, commercials. I'll go and make a cup of coffee. Maybe I'll just switch off.	Commercial alert

REVIEW: WRITING FOR RADIO

Before moving on to the next section, let's review what's been covered so far. Choose the best answer for each of the questions below.

(1) What is the key to keep in mind when writing for radio?

a. Callers can ask a radio announcer to repeat messages.

b. Listeners often are paying full attention to the radio program.

c. The ear can process a picture of the words better than the eye can.

d. Listeners have only one chance to make sense of what they hear on radio.

(2) When writing for radio:

a. Always be careful to use correct grammar.

b. Use long words rather than simple ones.

c. Imagine talking to one listener.

d. Try to fit as many ideas into one sentence as possible.

HOW TO SAY IT: TALKING TO ONE LISTENER

A good script is the beginning of a good radio show. Presentation--the sound or tone of the presenter--is next. Whether reading a script or speaking spontaneously, on radio how you say something is just as important as what you say.

Effective presentation depends on:

- Understanding the audience
- Understanding your own voice and body

Audience: One Listener

In the section on writing scripts, you read about the idea of talking to only one listener. This principle is also the basis of all radio presentation, even news reporting. This practice will help you create intimacy and listeners will be drawn into the program.

Because people listen to the radio almost everywhere (in their bedrooms, in their cars, while they are working) radio provides the opportunity to be close to the audience in a way that other media do not.

Respecting listeners-talking to them as equals, friends and colleague-is an important aspect to this relationship. Listeners should not feel preached to or patronized. By visualizing this closeness with listeners, the right tone will come naturally.

Choice of tone is also influenced by:

- *Type of Program:* The tone of a youth show announcer is different from that of a news reader. The presenter of a gender talk show will have a different tone than the host of a music program.
- *Time of Day:* Early morning programs require a lively, high-energy tone to get listeners going. News programs require announcers to use a formal tone. Talk show hosts try to come across as friendly and more casual.

How to Say It: Body and Voice: In addition to imagining one listener when talking, three other factors are key to effective radio presentation:

- Tension and stress
- Body positioning and gesturing
- Voice and speech

Tension and Stress: If a radio presenter is stressed, listeners will hear it in her voice, they won't focus on what she is actually saying. Tension ties the body's muscles in knots and can cause the voice to sound thin, strained, irritated or bored.

Before going on the air it is important to release the tension that stress, anxiety or other emotions can cause. Relaxation exercises, such as the ones listed to the right, can relieve stress by releasing tension from the body and calming emotions. Releasing tension opens the diaphragm, which promotes deeper breathing. This, in turn, helps the voice to sound more open and confident. During times of political turmoil or conflict, it is even more important for radio presenters and reporters to manage their personal tension.

"Radio should be a sane, comforting voice in times of tension or difficulty. Like a friend, your local station should tell you the truth in a calm, unemotional way--and help you to focus on solving the problem."

Indonesian Radio Presenter: Feeling anxious, angry, sad or depressed can make it difficult to sound sane, comforting or calm. But that is what radio presenters need to do for the sake of their listeners. Here' an example of how this all comes togetner in a tense reporting situation. Read how to keep your cool.

POSTURE, GESTURING AND FACIAL EXPRESSIONS

Posture: Tension, as noted above, can cause the body to tie itself up in knots. Good body positioning, or posture, promotes confidence and allows for both a physical and psychological opening-up. Keep these tips in mind:

- Sit in a position that allows easy breathing and body movement.
- Never sit in a hunched or doubled-over position. Bad posture makes breathing more difficult and leads to a voice that sounds tense and uncomfortable.
- Good posture also involves
  * Allowing the back to open and lengthen
  * Allowing the neck and shoulders to be free
  * Sensing the support of the floor or chair

Gesturing: Gesturing is a natural part of conversation. A presenter who gestures naturally as she talks will communicate more clearly. Listeners will notice the difference even if they can't see the gestures.

Facial Expression: Facial expressions are critical to the scund of a voice. If this seems hard to believe, imagine talking to someone on a telephone. Often, a person's voice indicates whether she is frowning or smiling. Listen to the radio and decide by tone if the announcer is smiling or has a serious expression. On radio a smile is the equivalent of making eye contact. A smile, even if no one sees it, makes a person sound more inviting, confident and fresh. Of course, a smile is not always appropriate.

For example, news reports on serious subjects are seldom delivered with a smile, unless a lighter story is included at the end.

Also, think about the fact that there are many different kinds of smiles. In addition to smiles of happiness, there are smiles that indicate understanding, sympathy or comfort. Think about how and when a smile during the following programs might be used.

- Talk shows
- Shows that give advice or support to the community
- Human interest stories or interviews
- Music request shows

Practice what it feels like to read a script while smiling. Then read a news script with a more serious expression. Listen for the difference. Try listening to the radio to "hear" the expression on the presenter's face.

Voice: The best voice for radio is natural and relaxed. The more comfortable you are with yourself and your voice, the clearer your voice will be. Voice exercises can help build confidence and promote speaking clearly.

Listen to someone who mumbles or someone who lowers the volume of her voice at the end of her sentences and notice how hard it is to understand what she is saying. Since listeners can't interrupt the radio to ask what was said, radio presenters must take extra care to be clear. Here are some tips:

- Before you go on air, do some exercises (included in the link above) to free up your jaw and tongue.
- If you are planning to read from a script, practice aloud until you feel confident. Pay special attention to difficult words and foreign names.
- Practice your pace and rhythm. Are you speaking too fast or too slow? Remember to pause and breathe naturally. Ask someone to give you feedback.

HOW TO SAY IT: PRESENTATION TIPS

Before going on the air:

- Avoid stressful situations.
  - * Get plenty of rest to feel free and alert.
  - * Allow plenty of time to prepare.
  - * Check for necessary items, such as script, reading glasses, water, etc.
  - * Wear loose, comfortable clothing.
  - * Use the relaxation exercises from the previous page.
- Prepare the voice.
  - * Avoid fizzy drinks and milky liquids. They can cause a film on the throat, which causes throat clearing.
  - * Don't eat sweets or chocolate. Sugar thickens saliva.
  - * Allow time for voice warm-ups and breathing exercises, like those reviewed on the previous page.
- Prepare your body and posture.
  - * Take a minute to relax your neck and shoulders. Do deep breathing to focus your mind and body. Breathe from the diaphragm.
  - * Check your posture and make sure the microphone is in a good position.
  - * Focus your thoughts and regulate your breathing.
  - * Remember to gesture.
  - * Finally, remind yourself that you are ready. Try saying to yourself:
- I'm going to talk to one listener, just beyond the microphone.
- I'm exactly where I want to be.
- I'm well-prepared.

On the air:

- Equipment and materials

headphones over one ear so you can monitor
'ou sound and still be alert to what is happening
e studio.

ys have pen and paper ready.

iscipline

repared with cues. A cue is the introduction
a studio presenter gives to a pre-recorded story
live interview. A good cue will lead the listener
rally into whatever follows.

id giving long lists of what's coming up. Nobody
l remember and lists are boring anyway.

* B fore announcing the time, make sure it's correct.
* Give frequent station IDs and throw aheads.

- Professional discipline
  * Don't take personal phone calls.
  * Listeners are the first priority, even when visitors are in the studio.
- Scripts
  * Use these guidelines for reading scripts:
- Prepare. Unless there's a real emergency, never read anything on air that hasn't been practiced aloud. Tongue-twisters are not always apparent until they are spoken aloud.
- Understand. Never read anything that could be confusing to your listener. Your voice will reflect it. Take the time to re-write the script before reading.
- Mark the script. Underline key words, mark pauses (with "/" or another symbol), write phonetic pronunciations for foreign words.
- Choose the appropriate tone of voice. How much emotion/feeling should be conveyed? Should the tone be light-hearted or serious?
- Look ahead. Don't look at the script word by word. Train yourself to take in whole blocks of words.

- Handle mistakes professionally If you ma mistake, don't panic. If it's a big error--one tha ld cause confusion or misunderstanding--apologiz d correct it. Otherwise, take a breath and carry o on't draw attention to stumbles.

REVIEW: PRESENTATION ON THE RADIO

Before moving on to the next section, let's revie what was just covered. Choose the best answer for each of th questions below.

(1) Why should you smile when your audience can't see you?

  * Because presenting on the radio is always a happy occasion.
  * On radio (or on the tel phone), a smile is the equivalent of making eye contact.
  * It helps with breathing.
  * Smiling lifts your voice and makes you sound more confident and fresh.
  * b and d

(2) Radio is about connecting at the human level, reaching the listener. What technique helps do this?

  * Talking to all the listeners.
  * Writing down what to say.
  * Imagining that you are talking to one listener.
  * Sounding energized and enthusiastic.

RADIO INTERVIEWS

Types of Interviews

It can take a lifetime to become a good radio interviewer. Every interview is different, with its own special challenges. In a program, an interview can run for several minutes or it it might end up as a brief, edited comment.

It's also helpful to keep in mind that people being interviewed might have different motivations for speaking to you. Sometimes people have a duty to speak because they are public officials. In other cases the interviewee does not have any obligation to talk, but chooses to do so because she has been persuaded that her experience is worth sharing.

This section explains two kinds of interviews: opening up and pinning down. Remember that the differences are not always clear cut and that interviews may have elements of both.

Opening up Interviews: An opening up interview ourages a person to share a story or experience. It is usually ducted in a relaxed and friendly way.

Opening up interviews include:

1. Human interest interviews
   * Examples
     - A chat with the leader of a youth choir who's just taken the group to perform at the International Choir Festival in Tokyo. How was the experience?
     - An interview with a former drug dealer who now runs a youth center for teenagers who have been involved in street gangs. What led to the change in his life?
2. Personal profiles
   * Examples
     - An interview with the first woman to be put in charge of the South African Prison Service. What kind of person is she?
     - An interview with a former Olympic swimmer who is now running for parliament. What prompted her interest in politics?
3. Highly sensitive interviews
   * Examples
     - An interview with a survivor of child abuse who now wants to tell her story for the sake of others who may be in the same position.

- An interview with a Burmese woman who was abducted from her village and forced to become a sex worker in Thailand.

Pinning Down Interviews: A pinning down interview is used to get answers to questions in the news. Radio reporters use this type of interview when they need to ask tough questions of people who are accountable to listeners, for example, an elected official or a company spokesperson. Asking revealing or hard-hitting questions without sounding aggressive can be a challenge. Use these tips:

- Do not raise the tone of your voice
- Do not speak louder than the person you are interviewing
- If you need to interrupt, and you often do, wait until the person you are interviewing takes a breath and then slide in with your question.
- Make sure you have your facts straight!

Examples of pinning down interviews can include:

- Talking with the minister of health about a series of tainted vaccinations. What can she tell listeners about the vaccinations?
- Interviewing a company spokesperson about the sudden recall of a popular children's toy. What is he able to say about the safety of the product?
- Speaking with a company president about the embezzlement charges he is facing. What is his side of the story?

Radio Interviews: Preparing to do an Interview: Conducting an interview is a fascinating, complex and uncertain art. The interviewer never knows what might happen.

Preparation is key under such uncertain circumstances. Consider these important questions when preparing to do an interview.

Questions to Think About

Who
- Who will be interviewed?
- Who will be the interviewer?

Why	• Why is this person being interviewed? • Does this person have a story to tell? • Is the interview part of a bigger story or report? Or is the interview the story?
What	• What is the subject or focus of the interview? • What questions will be asked? • What needs to be done to convince the interview subject to participate? • What permission, if any, will be needed? • What, if any, ethical issues might the interview raise? How will you deal with them?
Where	• Will this interview be conducted on the street or in a studio or someplace else (e.g., a public cafe or private home)? • Is the situation likely to be dangerous? • Will there be an audience?
When	• When will the interview be conducted? Morning, afternoon, night? • When will the interview be aired? Morning, afternoon, night? • Will it be before, during or after an emotional or disturbing event, a happy, exciting event or neither?
How	• Will it be live or will it be taped and edited later? • How will the interview subject be prepared for the interview? • How much will the interview subject know about the focus of the interview beforehand? • Will callers be allowed to ask questions?

The next section, Tips for Interviews, gives additional guidance for preparing for interviews.

TIPS FOR INTERVIEWS

Use this checklist to thoroughly prepare for an interview.

The Interviewer: An interviewer:

- Is a great listener
- Knows when, and how, to ask follow-up questions

- Has good communications skills
- Has the ability to be flexible in the interview
- Understands that there is an order in which interview questions should be asked
- Knows how and when to ask "why?"

It's important to consider gender with respect to interviewing. For example, a woman who has survived rape may not feel comfortable being interviewed by a male journalist. On the other hand, women journalists have sometimes encountered difficulties when interviewing men, especially when the man is powerful. Sometimes this can take the form of sexual harassment. Like any kind of intimidation, sexual harassment must be taken seriously. It's not just a "women's issue" and should be openly discussed in newsrooms so support systems can be put in place.

What should you do if you encounter sexual harassment in the course of your work?

- Trust your instinct. If you are uncomfortable about a suggested venue or time for the interview, make an alternative arrangement. If this is not possible, take a colleague. At the very least make sure your news editor knows where you are going and what time you expect to be back. Take your mobile phone. Remember: no interview is worth putting yourself at risk. If it doesn't feel right, don't go at all.
- If the interviewee is making you uncomfortable with remarks or actions, make it clear that your station takes sexual harassment of its employees very seriously. If the interviewee does not heed this warning, leave. Make a note of what happened and inform your boss immediately so you can discuss what action to take.

The Interview Subject: Deciding who to interview also takes some consideration. When selecting interview subjects, these tips can help:

- Make sure the interview subject is confident and articulate. This is especially important if you are looking for more than a short clip or comment.

- Be gender-aware. Don't stereotype people according to their sex. Not all nurses are women and not all soldiers are men. Also, if a woman's husband or father does not "give permission" for her to be interviewed, how will you deal with this? Will you just give up or take time to discuss possible solutions with her?
- Think beyond the obvious. A person doesn't need to have a university degree to be an expert. For example, a market seller may give you a more interesting view on the economy than a university professor.
- Keep an eye and ear out for people who have a story to tell and an interesting way of telling it.

It is important to find out as much as possible about an interview subject.

- What are her credentials?
- Why is she the right person to interview?
- What is her background?
- What will she bring to the interview?
- Will she be lively?
- Will she offer a unique perspective?

Interviewing someone soon after she has experienced a traumatic or emotional event requires special skills. Here are some suggestions for these kinds of interviews.

Asking for the Interview: Use these tips to prepare before picking up the telephone to request an interview:

- First, decide:
  * Why you want to interview the person.
  * When you want to do the interview (time and date).
  * How to get in touch with the person (have a list of possible contacts).
- Before calling:
  * Rehearse the call. To keep from being nervous or forgetting something, write rough notes on what you want to say.

  * Be ready to suggest calling back later if the person isn't available now.

- During the call:
  * If it feels appropriate, smile to sound more assertive, confident and friendly.
  * Remember that this call is the only chance to get the person to say yes.
  * Be prepared to explain why the interview is important to listeners or to the story.
  * Be ready to counter comments like: "I'll need a list of your questions first." (See the information below for what to do when someone asks for questions in advance.)
- Remember to:
  * Be polite, positive, friendly and clear.

Once the person has agreed to the interview, she may want to see the questions up front. It is important to find out why she wants to see the questions and try to resolve those reasons without giving her the questions. Perhaps you can explain that you don't provide questions in advance but that you can go over the areas you plan to cover.

Providing a list of questions beforehand can create issues with:

- Follow up. If you agree only to ask approved questions, you will probably have difficulty asking any follow-up questions. If this happens, you won't be doing your job as an interviewer.
- Balance. The interview will be unbalanced if you are not able to follow up.
- Sounding rehearsed. If the interview subject knows exactly what you are going to ask, the interview will probably sound boring or rehearsed.

Use these preparation tips just before the interview.

Interview Questions: Brainstorming is a helpful process for coming up with an initial list of questions. This is often done with the program's producer or other colleagues.

Questions should:

- Explore the story or topic. What is the purpose of the story? What does the audience need to know? What will listeners be interested in knowing?
- Add dimension to the obvious. "Why" questions are important. They open up room for exploration and can delve into what is not obvious.
- Provide different perspectives. Coming up with the list of interview questions may uncover a need to interview more than one person. For some interviews and stories, more than one perspective is needed.
- Paint the picture. Questions that ask the interview subject for description are important. They help listeners "see" the story or message.
- Ensure the listeners are not left hanging. Wrap-up questions close loose ends and answer anything that is still unclear.
- Be simple and clear. Questions should be short, simple and clear. For guidance, review the writing tips covered in "What to Say." Multi-layered questions should never be part of an interview. They confuse the interview subject and the listeners.

Questions should follow a logical order. Consider these guidelines:

- The first question shouldn't be too deep, complex or broad because you run the risk of losing focus or control of the interview.
- Core questions do not necessarily have to follow the chronology of events. You won't have time to cover everything, so focus your questions according to the key issues you want to address.
- Follow-up questions are used when the interviewer wants the subject to elaborate.

  * Magic question:

- "Why?"

  * Opening up questions might start with:

- "Tell me more"
- "Take me back to the first time you..."
- "What was going through your mind when"
  - * Pinning down questions might start with:
- "What do you mean when you say...?"
- "Let's be more specific. Are you saying?"
- "To recap...do you mean that?"
  - * Closing questions wrap up the interview.
- "What's your message to..." (this works especially well for a profile or "soft" interview.)

Interview Location

The type of program often dictates where the interview is conducted. For example, if the interview subject is a guest on a talk show, the interview will probably be in the studio. If the interview is part of a live news report, the interview is likely to be live from the scene.

At other times, where the interview is done depends on the topic of the interview and the interview subject. Think about:

- The interview subject's time schedule. If she's busy and her comments are needed for the story, the interview may have to take place at her location, possibly her office, home or some other place.
- Whether the interview subject can travel to the studio. If the distance is too great, the interview could be done by phone.
- What other factors may affect the interview location.
- Whether background noise will add to the interview. For instance, an interview with a fishing captain may benefit from the noise of the ocean in the background.

Doing an interview on location means that all the recording equipment has to be taken along. Make a list of what will be needed and check the items off the list before leaving.

Well-managed background sound is a great way to give context to the interview, but remember that it can also ruin your recording if you're not careful. These recording tips offer ideas to ensure good technical quality in the field.

CONDUCTING AN INTERVIEW

Formal and informal interviews use the same skills:

- Listening
- Asking effective questions
- Sticking to the focus

These skills are part of everyday communication. This section will show how to polish these naturally learned skills and use them more consciously.

During the Interview: Remember the presentation tips that were presented in an earlier section. For example:

- Talk one-on-one.
- Smile appropriately.
- Relax and breathe naturally.
- Speak at a natural pace, not too fast, not too slow and pause appropriately.

Use written questions to help stay focused and on track:

- Ask open-ended questions--beginning with how, what, why--to encourage an interview subject to open up.
- Keep the questions short and simple. Never ask multi layered questions that the interview subject struggles to understand.
- Ask questions to which there are only yes/no or one-word answers to pin down or focus the interview subject. (If she can't stop talking, for example!) A good follow up for many one-answer questions is "why?".
- Invite the interview subject to give specific examples, experiences and stories. For example, "Take us back to the first time you performed in public. What happened?".
- Keep thinking of the listeners. What would they want to ask?

During the interview:

- Show attention by using eye contact, body language and repeating key bits of information. ("You say you first started composing at the age of six. How did you start so young?") But be careful not to give too much audible feedback-like "mmm" or "OK." They sound irritating on radio and they'll cause you problems later if you have to edit the interview.
- Remember to help the interview subject come alive as a person and tell her story. An interviewer should be responsive but does not steal the spotlight or use the interview to show how clever she is.
- If it is necessary to interrupt the interviewee, do it with a smile as she takes a breath. Try not to raise the volume--or pitch--of your voice. Do not talk over what she is saying. It sounds aggressive.
- Listen carefully.
- Ask follow-up questions.

Track progress:

- Watch the clock and keep the interview paced to cover everything.
- Know when to start bringing the conversation to a close. Do it as naturally as possible. Don't say "Well, I'm afraid we have to stop there. We've run out of time." The interviewee and the listeners will feel cheated. And you'll sound unprofessional.
- Thank the person you interviewed simply. Don't go overboard.

Remember that interviewing a guest or talking to callers by telephone requires distinct skills. Check out these tips for telephone interviews.

Telephone Tips: The telephone is an indispensable tool for radio. It's used for news sound bites, live interviews and phone-in contributions from listeners. But the telephone also offers special challenges. When using the telephone to conduct an interview or to talk with listeners, remember to:

- Speak more slowly than usual.
- Speak into the microphone/mouthpiece of the telephone.
- Make an extra effort to be clear.
- Let the caller know you're still at the other end by giving occasional verbal feedback: Mm-hmm, Right, I understand, Go ahead.
- Smile.
- Watch the voice levels on your equipment and be prepared to adjust them.
- Be extra alert about your control buttons. You don't want to accidentally cut someone off in mid-thought!

Problems will crop up on telephone chat shows. Use these suggestions to handle the most common ones.

Problem	Suggestion
How do I handle the caller who won't shut up?	**Smile** and interrupt. For example, say, "Thanks for your point." Then move the discussion forward.
How do I handle a very upset or angry caller?	**Show** that you understand why she is upset by: • Using her name when you respond. • Not raising your voice. Be polite, friendly and professional. • Resisting the temptation to counsel her over the phone. You're not a psychotherapist. (Consider having the contact number of your local helpline at hand.)
What if the caller is making a great point, but the line is bad?	**Apologize** and cut the call. No matter how good the point is, if listeners can't understand or hear it, it's useless. If possible, ask the caller to call back and hope for a better line.

REVIEW: INTERVIEWING

Before we close out this module, let's review the material we just covered.

True/False:

(1) Always give the interview subject the questions up front.

T ❑ F ❑

(2) Use closed questions to get someone to answer yes or no.

T ❑ F ❑

(3) The interviewer should never deviate from the list of prepared questions.

T ☐ F ☐

(4) In a longer interview, invite the person you are interviewing to give specific examples, experiences, stories.

T ☐ F ☐

MODULE SUMMARY

At the start of this module we indicated that you should be able to

Recognize techniques used by radio practitioners.

- The module described three techniques: writing, presenting and interviewing.

Understand writing techniques associated with the radio.

- The key is to write as you speak.
- Keep things simple and short.
- The module also covered story structure, sentence content, tone and word choice.

Identify key practices for effective radio presentation.

- The module covered two presentation principles.
  * Talk as if addressing one listener.
- It also addressed the importance of body position and gesturing.
- Finally, the module described how voice and body are interconnected and gave tips for making the voice sound its best.

Identify different techniques used for radio interviews

- Interviewing is a primary way people interact on radio. This course covered two types of interviews:
  * The opening up interview
  * The pinning down interview
- The module covered some basic techniques for preparing and conducting interviews.

Discuss how writing and presentation play a role in radio interviews.

- Both writing and presentation skills are needed to successfully conduct an interview.

Additional Resources: To help you think about what you've learned about radio presentation, ask yourself:

- Who is your favourite radio presenter? What do you specifically like about this person? Is it her style, her presentation, her voice?
- As a listener, what do you find irritating in a radio presenter? Why?
- When you've listed what you like and what you don't like, write a description of the elements of a successful radio presentation.

8

WRITING FCR RADIO: THE BASICS

STRUCTURE OF A RADIO NEWS STORY

Sound: Generally, radio news stories split their time evenly between narration and sound bites. You want soundbites to be 30 seconds or less, but you want to use them often to break up your narration--if you read for much more than a minute uninterrupted, your listeners will start to get lost in the drone.

Conflict: Most stories, in fiction and news alike, build their narrative around a central conflict. Protesters versus police. Workers versus management. Community organizers versus government officials. Even more "human interest" stories have conflicts driving the narrative-a homeless person's struggle to stay warm, a poor mother's struggle to get healthy food for her kids. When you're conceptualizing your story, trying to figure out what the central conflict is--it will make it much easier to decide who you need to interview, and how you need to write it.

A typical three-minute radio story will be built around three 30-second soundbytes: one from each side of the immediate conflict, and one from an expert or analyst who's able to either arbitrate or put the conflict in a larger context. The lead is the most important part of your story. It needs to grab the listener's attention and make them want to listen to everything that follows. You can either: 1) do a quick summary of the who, what, when, where, and why of your story, 2) throw out a provocative piece of information that you'll then go on to explain, 3) pose a question the story will try to answer.

The lead must give the listener a sense of what the rest of the story will be about, and make them want to listen. Here's a tip: after you've finished writing your story, go back and rewrite your lead. You'll often find the story took you somewhere you didn't expect to be when you started it. The end is the best place to give your listeners information about what comes next-are there more demonstrations planned? Will there be an appeal? When does the new law take effect? Process for composing a radio story:

1. *Research Your Story*: Check out the web sites of the players involved. Look for recent news clippings on related issues. Make a note of who other reporters have spoken to---you may want to use the same sources. Make a list of the questions you need answered to do the story well, then try to figure out who has the answers and set up interviews.
2. *Gather Sound*: Record the interviews and other audio (e.g. ambient sound) you'll use. Take notes and mark times during the interviews-it will make it easier to go back and pull soundbytes later.
3. *Log Audio/pull Soundbytes*: Mark the cuts you think you'll use for your story. If you have time, transcribe them.
4. *Write*: Decide what cuts you'll us, put them in order, and then write your script around them.
5. *Check your Facts*: Go through the script and see if you can independently confirm the facts and figures your sources gave you.
6. *Re-write*: See if you can get someone with a fresh set of eyeballs to read your script and give you feedback. Then, do any structural changes you need to. Next, clean up your sentences. Finally, re-write your lead.
7. Record your narration and mix your audio.

BROADCAST WRITING

Writing for radio is different from writing for print. First, you have less "space" for information, so you will have to prioritize and summarize carefully. Second, your listeners can't reread sentences they didn't understand the first time--you have to keep your writing simple and clear. Finally, the ultimate product is not what's on the page, but what comes out of your mouth--it's okay to break some writing rules, as long as the result is smooth and easily-understood. With that in mind, here are some tips.

Write Short Sentences: Take a close look at long, complex sentences: chances are you can break them up into two or three smaller ones. Don't try to pack in more than one idea per sentence. Grammarians take note: broadcast writing should minimize the use of dependent clauses, relative clauses, parenthetical remarks, and compound structures. You can almost always come out with a clean sentence by putting the subject first, and the verb second.

Before	After
As a delegation of over 30 workers and community members stormed through the employee entrance of the 350-room Hilton hotel in downtown Glendale, hotel security could do little more than grasp their radios and call for backup.	30 workers and community members stormed into the downtown Glendale Hilton.
Followed by a barrage of hotel managers, curious on-duty employees and about half a dozen security guards, the workers made their way through the winding corridors of the employee area and into the offices of the hotel's executive committee, where the concerned Hilton employees addressed their need for a union and insisted that management not interfere with their efforts to organize.	The hotel has 350 rooms. The delegation bypassed security by using the employee entrance. Security guards called for backup. The delegation made its way to the offices of the hotel's executive committee. Managers, guards, and curious employees followed. The workers said they need a union They also told management not to interfere with their organizing efforts.

Summarize and Prioritize: There are less words in radio stories than print stories. Think carefully about what information is essential, and which details can be summarized. Here's how you might pare down the sentences we just broke out:

Before	After
Thirty workers and community members stormed into the downtown Glendale Hilton. The hotel has 350 rooms. The delegation bypassed security by using the employee entrance. Security guards called for backup. The delegation made its way to the offices of the hotel's executive committee. Managers, guards, and curious employees followed. The workers said they need a union They also told management not to interfere with their organizing efforts.	Thirty workers and community members stormed into the downtown Glendale Hilton. The delegation evaded security and confronted the hotel's executives in their offices. The workers said they need a union. They also told management not to interfere with their organizing efforts.

Be Conversational: It's okay to be less formal when you're writing for broadcast--do what it takes to make your copy easy to listen to. Here's how you might smooth out the flow of what we just summarized:

Before	After
Thirty workers and community members stormed into the downtown Glendale Hilton. The workers evaded security and confronted the hotel's executives in their offices. The workers said they need a union. They also told management not to interfere with their organizing efforts.	Workers at the downtown Glendale Hilton are organizing a union, and they say they don't want management to interfere. So today dozens of them stormed the building and confronted the hotel's executives in their offices.

Use Statistics Sparingly: It is easy to lose your listeners when you put too many numbers in a story. If the precise number isn't that important to the story, use words like "most," "more," "relatively few," etc. When you do use numbers, round them-*i.e.*, substitute "about 5 million" for "4,850,326." When you're comparing numbers, try to use a plain-language fraction or multiple rather than giving two numbers:

Before	After
Today, just 11% of americans get lung cancer—twenty years ago, that number was 22%	Lung cancer rates have dropped by half since smoking was outlawed

Put Attribution First: You listeners need to know who they're hearing from.

Before	After
"The attacks on Karl Rove are unjustified and immoral," said President Bush.	President Bush said, "The attacks on Karl Rove are unjustified and immoral."

Minimize Direct Quotations: Paraphrase what people have said, unless the exact wording is important to your story.

Before	After
President Bush said, "The attacks on Karl Rove are unjustified and immoral."	President Bush lashed out against the attacks on Karl Rove, calling them "immoral."

Read it Out Loud: If what you've written doesn't feel natural coming out of your mouth, then there's something wrong with it.

Read it to someone else. This is the best way to find out if your story is missing information your listeners will need to understand it.

In general, the principles of clean writing apply the same as always-here are some time-tested guidelines:

- Kill adjectives and adverbs. They don't usually do any work.
- Use active phrasing-*i.e.* "management locked out the workers," NOT "the workers were locked out"
- Show, don't tell. "he pounded the table with his fist" NOT "he was very angry."

- Use non-judgmental language. Present the facts and let your listeners make up their own minds. For instance, don't tell them a policy is "racist"--show them how it impacts Latinos differently than Anglos.

HOW WRITING A RADIO AD WILL IMPROVE YOUR COPYWRITING

Knowing how to write, and write well, is a skill that will come in handy in all sorts of situations. And if you combine good writing skills with the persuasive selling tactics found in, say, copywriting, you'll be that much more ahead of your competition.

Of all the different types of writing I've done in my life (and believe me, I've tried practically all of them) writing radio has made one of the bigger impacts on my writing style.

Below are three ways writing radio can help strengthen your writing style. (Oh, and these tips will also help you write better radio copy too.)

1. Follow the rules.

Sometimes rules are good. Especially rules that force you to write a certain way. (Think poetry--mastering those rules can have an amazing effect on your writing style.) Rules require you to slow down and think, to analyze your word, sentence, grammar, punctuation, etc., choices. And that can be very beneficial to your development as a writer.

Radio is short. You have to write something that fits into a 30-or 60-second slot. Not a lot of time or a lot of words. In that 30 or 60 seconds, you need to capture the listener's attention, explain why they should be interested in buying what you're selling, then let them know what you'd like their next step to be. Oh, and did I mention you need to have the business name in there at least twice and probably a tag line as well? And don't forget about music. Or sound effects.

Now the beauty of this is once you've mastered radio rules, you can apply it to all sorts of things. A 30-second pitch for your business you can tell people at networking events. A 15-second introduction before a speech. A quick product spiel for your voice mail. A 15-second pitch for your novel to spit out at agents and editors at writers' conferences. The possibilities are endless.

2. Forces you to write tight.

Remember, radio is short. Yet, there's still a lot you have to shove into it. So what's the solution? Absolutely no extra words allowed.

Be brutal. Cut out anything you don't need. In fact, radio is where I first learned to start cutting "that" out. Most "thats" you don't need, and nothing shows you this like radio.

Here's how I write radio. I start with a first draft. I read it over. I think it's pretty good--I have all the salient points in there. I read it out loud.

Now the fun begins.

Usually it's too long. You see, I time myself reading. So I have to start chopping words.

When you have to make a script fit into a certain time frame, it's amazing how many words you suddenly discover can be deleted. Or replaced with simpler, shorter words. Or how many sentences can be trimmed. Or phrases made more concise.

As you can imagine, writing radio has really honed my editing skills.

3. Writing for the ear.

Writing for the ear is different than writing for the eye. The eye is far more forgiving. Oh that sentence is a bit too long, but it's okay. Hmm, yes I do see that awkward phrase, but I'm fine with it.

Not the ear. The ear is brutal. It's like one of those headmasters from a Dickens' novel, standing in front of the classroom with a stick and banging it every time a student stutters on an answer.

The ear catches everything--sentences that are too long and don't allow you to take a breath; sentences that don't flow properly; long, complicated five-dollar words that twist the tongue in a knot and much, much more. Focus on writing shorter sentences. Simpler sentences. Vary your sentences.

Use simple words. And that's just plain good old writing advice no matter what you happen to be writing.

First, choose something you want the ad to be about. Maybe one of your products or services. But choose only one. More than one and you're just asking for trouble. (Rule of thumb--one message per ad. No more. Otherwise you run the risk of losing your target market. Pick one message and make it very simple and very clear.)

Now do what I do. Write the ad. Start by keeping it under a general word count--100 words for a 30-second ad and 190 words for a 60-second spot.

Finished your first draft? Great. Now read it. And time yourself. (Those clocks on the computer desktop are great for this.)

What, you went over your limit? Better start cutting. See how many words you can take out and sentences you can tighten. Or replace words and phrases with something shorter.

Now read it again. Still too long? Or maybe now it's too awkward. See previous paragraph. Keep repeating until you end up with something that sounds smooth and fits in the allotted time.

Martin Esslin said, "The almost telepathic transference of images from mind to mind is the beauty and the glory of the radio play."

Also George Bernard Shaw once said about radio drama that "It provides the maximum of temptation with the maximum of opportunity." Well, he actually said it about marriage but let's not be pedantic. In radio almost anything is possible.

By far the most important piece of advice for anyone wanting to write for radio is to listen to as much as possible. Radio is a distinctive means of communication with its own limitations and possibilities and its own particular techniques and anyone who seriously wishes to sell their work to radio must make themself familiar with its existing output.

As with any other type of freelance writing, the writer must study the market. There is for instance, no single type of radio play, for the BBC's large output is broken down into distinctive series, each with their own characteristics. A play will have a far better chance of acceptance if the writer decides in the beginning if they are writing for a Radio 3 or Radio 4 audience such a Saturday night theatre or the Monday play.

The reality is the market is always right. You aren't writing for the general public, you're writing for a small handful of people whose sole opinion will decide whether your work gets produced. You don't have to know what the public wants but what a producer considers they want. But how can you find that out? One way is to buy the Radio Times, look at the radio drama listings, listen to the plays and keep a record. A record may have the following elements: date; slot; title; length; how many characters; producer; region; theme; category; plot. The purpose is to identify trends and identify producers who you feel will respond to your work favourably.

The BBC isn't afraid to tackle difficult issues these days, it's not as po-faced as it used to be. They're quite happy to broadcast difficult material. While you can get away with the odd non-sexual swearing in daytime, sexual swearwords are still referable though to the head of drama. Somebody somewhere along the line makes a decision about those words and how often and when they may be used. While the BBC isn't afraid of reflecting English as its spoken, they're not interested in gratuitously rubbing the audience up the wrong way.

These days the BBC are very concerned about people switching over. I learnt, in history at school, that people once had wirelesses and once you'd got a station you never dared moved that dial or you'd never get it back again. These days, with digital tuning, switching channels isn't a problem. There are now many more channels to switch to not just the Light, the Home and the Third as it used to be. Also radio drama is in competition with all other forms of drama including theatre and film but especially television. So when you write your plays the imperative is to keep the listener listening, capture the mood in the first minute. That doesn't mean there isn't the time for the slow-build but it should still have something that people can get a hook on from the start. As with all drama the story has to start early.

Radio does some things much better than any other medium and they're always interested in plays that can be done in no other medium. Consider plays that not only can't be done in any other medium but are impossible to do the ironing to.

When were the forms of media created? When did advertising first show up? Who owns the media?

Creation of the various forms of media

* Newspapers & Magazines – 1880
* Movies – 1910
* Television – 1945
* Cable Television – 1980's
* Satellite Television, Internet, Digital Communication – End of the 20th century

  In 1920, radio was first developed, primarily for use by the military, strictly for sending History of the Media-Old Radios messages from one location to another. David Sternoff, the then-president of RCA, first had the idea to sell radio sets to consumers, or what were then called radio receivers. However, consumers needed a reason to buy radios, so RCA was the first to set up radio stations all over the country. Between 1920 and 1922, 400 radio stations were set up, starting with KBKA in Pittsburgh. Stations were also set up by universities, newspapers, police departments, hotels, and labour unions.

* By 1923, there were 600 radio stations across the United States, and $83 million worth of sets had been sold.

  The biggest difference in radio before and after 1923 was that the first advertising was not heard on the radio until 1923. RCA at the time was made up of four companies:

* AT&T
* General Electric
* United Fruit
* Westinghouse

United Fruit was one of the first global corporations, and one of the first to advertise on the radio. The AT&T division of RCA first thought about selling time on the air to companies, which marked the start of "toll broadcasting." WEAF was the first station to operate this way, causing widespread outrage, and accusation of "polluting the airwaves."

Because of this controversy, the practice of selling advertising time was called "trade name publicity." Sponsors linked their name with a program on the air, rather than advertising a specific product in a 30 second "commercial" as we know it today.

Why did AT&T decide to experiment with charging companies for air time?

AT&T was not making any money from broadcasting at the time since they only made transmitters, not receivers. They only made money when new radio stations bought the equipment required to broadcast. They did not make money from consumers buying radios.

AT&T also started the practice of paying performers for their time on the air, rather than only volunteers, which was standard practice for radio content up until that point.

9

THE FIRST RADIO NETWORK

INTRODUCTION

In 1926, RCA set up the first radio network, NBC. They decided it was more effective and efficient to produce shows in New York City, and then link the main radio station with stations all across the country, connected by AT&T (another RCA company) phone lines. (Now television networks are linked by satellite to their affiliates).

This was the beginning of the network affiliates system. The ideal network makes sure everyone in the country is capable of listening to their signal. NBC at the time had two philosophies:

* Radio content was a "public service," whose function was to sell radios.
* Radio content was designed to generate income from advertising.

History of the Media In 1927, the second network was formed. It was CBS, started by William Paley. Paley was the first to think that networks could make money strictly from advertising, not even getting involved in the sales of radios. Like AT&T, CBS did not make radios. From the start, they made their money from selling advertising.

The rising of radio networks caused the Radio Act of 1927 to be passed, which established the FRC, or what is now known as the FCC, to allocate broadcast licenses. The need for such an organization was brought on by the fact that airwaves are limited resources, and broadcasting itself is a scarce public resource. By the 1930's, the structure of radio have been set by the commercial format, although advertising never dominated radio like it would television later on.

In the 1920's and '30's, radio programs were divided into two groups. Sponsored shows, which had advertisers, and unsponsored shows, which did not. The radio station paid for the unsponsored shows. The sponsored shows, on the other hand, were created entirely by the company sponsoring the show; advertisers were totally in charge of the radio station's content. The content became advertising. Radio set the precedent for television, in that the same companies that controlled radio early on went on to control television.

Soon thereafter, television inherited the structure of radio. In the '40's, during the rise of television, RCA also held a monopoly on all television sets sold. By 1945-1955, advertising had taken over all of television. Television was organized around the premise of selling things. The entire television industry was creating a political atmosphere of suspicion and fear. Senator Joseph McCarthy, the founder of McCarthyism, which was based on the fear of Communism, and the HUAC (House Un-American Activities Committee, began to question people involved in television about their beliefs and associations.

What affected television in its early stages?

* Politics (McCarthyism / HUAC).
* Blacklists: From almost the inception of television, many writers, directors, and actors were considered to be pro-Communist and/or un-American.

Certain topics were totally off-limits at the time for television, particularly issues of race relations in the 1960's. Overall, networks were not happy with the political situation for television in the 1960's, both in terms of the blacklists, and of the fact that when every show had one sponsor, that sponsor controlled the entire program. Networks preferred to control the program, by way of moving to multiple sponsors/advertisers, where networks would retain control of the show, and advertisers would buy time in between the programming.

In the 1950's, networks decided to eliminate the practice of sponsors controlling the shows with a move to spot selling, or advertisements between programs, as we know it today. What caused the move to spot selling?

1. Discovery of fraud in the quiz shows on television. Quiz shows were extremely popular at the time, and were liked by the networks, the sponsors, and the viewers alike. It turned out, however, that quiz shows were largely fixed. Charles Van Doren on "21" became a huge star due to his repeated wins, until it came out that the whole thing haa been fixed. In the case of "The $64,000 Question," the owner of Revlon was personally hand-selecting the winners and losers on the show.
2. It was becoming financially difficult for just one advertiser to support an entire show.

Around this same time came the inception of ratings to measure a show's popularity. Ratings, quite simply, measure the number of people watching a show. To understand why ratings are so important, it's crucial to understand how the television industry works, through three questions, and their respective answers:

1. Who owns television? [The networks]
2. What is sold on television? [Viewer's time, not television shows]
3. Who are the customers of television? [Advertisers, not viewers]

This might be a counterintuitive concept for some. The networks, which own television, areHistory of the Media-Old Television the buyers of shows, not the sellers. On the other hand, they sell our eyeballs, so to speak, to advertisers. Networks want the maximum possible profit from buying and selling time, both viewers' time, and advertisers' time.

The primary measure of television ratings, which determine the price of that time being bought and sold, is AC Nielsen, an independent company which provides information as to who watches what on television. Currently, about 4,000 households are used to represent the national viewing of television. In the 1980's, only 1,200 households were used. Some households have an electronic device installed on their television which tracks what they watch, while others keep a diary of viewing habits.

There are two measures for determining a show's audience. One is the rating, and the other is the share.

* *Rating:* Percentage of total homes with televisions tuned into a particular show.
* *Share:* Percentage of those watching television at a particular time who are tuned into a particular show.

The share is always greater than the rating. Ratings are more important for advertisers, and share is more important to the networks.

Example:

* Total households with televisions: 150 million
* Total households watching television at 8pm on Monday nights: 90 million
* Total households watching American Idol at 8pm on Monday nights: 45 million
* Therefore: Rating: 30, Share: 50

It's important to note how many factors can skew the results. Shows cost producers much more than the networks typically pay them for those shows. The way for producers to make money is by getting the networks to renew the show, in order to have a shot at making money from syndication on other channels, also knows as reruns. That is the case when individual stations (say for example, the Miami affiliate of ABC wants to carry Seinfeld), buy the rights to a show from the producers of that show. Shows that last only one season, for the most part, lose millions of dollars. One of the most important factors in whether shows will be renewed or not is their rating.

This brings us to how ratings can be skewed. For example, if a show has a 20 share, and it needs a 25 share to be renewed for another season, what might the producers do? In principle, they need to convince another 5% of the people watching television when their show is on to watch their show; this is no simple task, as that involves convincing millions of people. However, since the ratings are based on those 4,000 Nielsen households, that means that they could convince just 200 Nielsen households to watch their show, which would increase the share from 20 to 25. This is why Nielsen households must be kept totally secret from the networks. When the Nielsen households have leaked to the networks, one way which they got people to watch their show was by offering viewers a small sum of money for filling out a survey about a commercial which they were told would play only during a particular show. Since they had to watch that channel while their show was on, this would boost the share.

Once ratings are determined, advertising prices are set by two factors:

* The size of the audience.
* The demographics (income, age, gender, occupation, etc) of the audience.

In short, the job of television programs is to collect our time as a product, which they then sell to advertisers. Programs have to support the advertising, delivering viewers in the best possible state of mind for buying when the time for the commercials comes, which brings us to the Golden Age of Television.

The 1950's are considered the "Golden Age of Television." During this time, something called the "Anthology Series," where different actors each week took part in a show gained History of the Media-I Love Lucypopularity across the board...that is, with everyone except for advertisers. The anthology series format was not right for advertisers, as it covered topics which involved psychological confrontations which did not leave the viewers in the proper state of mind for buying the products shown to them between program segments. The subject matter of the anthology series was of the type that undermined the ads, almost making them seem fraudulent.

This brought up the question of what to network executives actually want shows to do? The answer is not to watch a program that makes them feel good, makes them laugh, or excites them, but rather to watch the television for a set amount of time. With so many new shows being proposed, standards began to be intentionally, or unintentionally, laid out for what shows could and couldn't do. Risks could only be taken at the beginning and/or end of shows. Laugh tracks were conceived to tell the audience when to laugh. Programs began being tested with audiences prior to being put on television and/or radio. Show writers now had to write shows that would test well.

Naturally, this caused many of the same elements and themes to appear in all shows. This was the beginning of recombinant television culture, where the same elements are endlessly repeated, recombined, and mixed.

This same culture is what perpetuated the idea that people watch television, not specific shows. While people certainly choose to watch certain shows instead of others, people less commonly choose to watch television instead of other things. People watch television. Regardless of what was on, television viewing rates were extremely stable.

CLASSIC STORY STRUCTURE BEGINS WITH PLOT

What do we mean by Plot? Simply, plot is WHAT HAPPENS in a short story, novel, play or film. No more, no less. It isn't description or dialogue, and it certainly isn't theme. In the best stories, plot grows organically out of character, rather than being imposed from above. Specifically, plot is the result of choices made by characters in a story, especially the story's protagonist, or main character.

Even if action is not the most compelling feature of the story to you, the reader must always want to know--actually NEED to know--what happens next. Yes, plots are contrived, but that's what makes for art, not life. A theme--your message or meaning--is revealed through plot. For example, 'Money can't buy happiness' is just an empty threat, unless we observe a rich man who's miserable, as in George Eliot's 'Silas Marner.'

Renowned writer Anne Lamott ('Bird by Bird,' 'Operating Instructions') created a mnemonic device to help writers remember how to write plots that work:

Action

Background

Conflict

Development

End

ACTION means a scene (word-pictures presented in more or less 'real' time). Storytellers begin with Action because it is quite literally dramatic, meaning that, theoretically, it could be performed on-stage. Also, scenes are intriguing as we watch and wonder what's going on here. Beginning with Action also means beginning with an inciting incident or point of attack: an event that sets off the events of the story.

The opening of John Steinbeck's 'The Grapes of Wrath' is Action, as a tortoise tries to cross a road. Even two people sitting in a coffee bar talking is Action. On the other hand, 'The family of Dashwood had been long settled in Sussex...' (the start of 'Sense and Sensibility' by Jane Austen) is not Action. Nothing is actually happening, at least not yet. Begin your story as close to the inciting incident as you can. The inciting incident of Franz Kafka's Metamorphosis occurs very simply when Gregor Samsa awakens having been transformed into a 'monstrous and frightening insect.' That event happens in the story's very first sentence.

BACKGROUND: Many 19th century novels begin with Background. For example, 'A Tale of Two Cities' by Charles Dickens starts 'It was the best of times, it was the worst of times...' This certainly seems like a natural way to open a story since Background happened before Action, at least chronologically. However, Background is boring. It is very literally un-dramatic.

Therefore, provide only enough Background at first so that the Action doesn't confuse your readers. They don't need to know everything, just enough to follow along. Joseph Conrad's 'The Secret Sharer' is instructive in that it withholds Background until the reader needs it. The same is true of Toni Morrison's 'Song of Solomon.'

CONFLICT constitutes what your protagonist wants, but doesn't have. It doesn't matter what your protagonist needs, as long as he or she needs it badly. In James Joyce's 'Araby', the main character wants to go to the bazaar. His desire is apparently trivial, but because he feels it so intensely, we are carried swiftly through the story.

The best Conflicts are dramatic and specific. Don't write about a teenage girl who's looking for love; write about a teenage girl seeking her first kiss. For one thing, focusing on the kiss will focus your storytelling and your readers' attention. Even more important, those readers will know without question at the end of the story whether the heroine has attained what she wants or not.

Hamlet seeks to overcome his late-adolescent malaise, but what makes Shakespeare's play dramatic is his need to kill his uncle to avenge the murder of his father. In Charlotte Bronte's novel of the same name, Jane Eyre seeks a life that is secure and yet stimulating; she desires Mr. Rochester, who can provide just such a life, and we will read her story until she gets him--or doesn't.

Conflict IS story, and, conversely, without Conflict, you have no story. D. DEVELOPMENT is the series of attempts made by the protagonist to resolve his or her Conflict. These attempts should increase with regard to drama and/or suspense, and ideally, each step in the Development should tell us a little bit more about the protagonist.

Development is the 'journey' made by the protagonist toward (or perhaps away from) what he or she wants. Sometimes that journey is literal, actual, physical: Think of 'The Odyssey,' John Cheever's 'The Swimmer' or 'On the Road' by Jack Kerouac. Development can also be a trip through time, like childhood or adolescence, for instance. 'Portnoy's Complaint' by Philip Roth and Susan Minot's 'Lust' are essentially journeys made by characters via other characters. Finally, Development can be an emotional, spiritual or intellectual journey. Often, it is a combination of all of the above.

Development usually accounts for 70 to 80 percent of the mass of the story. In 'The Wizard of Oz,' the protagonist is Dorothy Gale. Her Conflict? She wants to get home. The Development of 'The Wizard of Oz' is the Yellow Brick Road, along which Dorothy encounters various characters and situations that she hopes will lead her to the Wizard, and, thus, home. If you ever lose track, remind yourself of the following: Development is the Yellow Brick Road.

END: Here's where the mnemonic device needs further development of its own, since 'End' isn't an especially helpful term. Let's expand it to include 3 more C's: Crisis, Climax, Consequences

CRISIS is often the final stage in a story's Development. In the best stories, it involves a choice--and not simply a choice between good and evil, since given that choice, we'd all pick good. Crisis is a choice between two options of equal, or nearly equal, value.

In 'Sophie's Choice' by William Styron, for example, Sophie must choose one of her children, thereby, condemning the other to almost certain death. In Ernest Hemingway's 'A Farewell to Arms,' the hero must decide between war and desertion. Crisis is, by definition, the most dramatic point in your entire story.

CLIMAX is not necessarily the most dramatic point, despite the word's colloquial meaning. Instead, Climax is the resolution of Conflict. Does the protagonist get what he wants, or not? Or maybe he gets what he wants, but realizes that his struggle to get it wasn't worth it. That's called irony.

Climax is the point of no return. At the Climax of a story there is simply no turning back; the protagonist is powerless to change his fate. Think of Romeo's suicide, the Climax of Shakespeare's play not because it's dramatic, but because it prevents him and Juliet from living together in love. Or the famous line in Hemingway's 'Hills Like White Elephants': 'Would you please please please please please please please stop talking?'--which signals precisely the same state of affairs.

But you must offer your readers a definite resolution to the story's Conflict. Refusing to do so isn't clever, or modern. It's annoying, exasperating, infuriating. And it violates the unspoken understanding between writer and reader: that the writer will finish telling the story.

Consequences: When the Conflict of a story has been resolved, what's left? The Consequences of that story. How have your protagonist and his world changed--or stubbornly refused to change--as a result of the story? The French call this part of the story the 'denouement' or 'unravelling.' At the end of Dickens's 'A Christmas Carol,' Scrooge shows us that he's changed. How? By climbing out of bed, throwing open his window and asking an urchin on the street below what day it is. When he learns that it's Christmas, Scrooge instructs the boy to buy the biggest turkey in the butcher's window for Tiny Tim's family. When the boy returns, Scrooge pays him, laughing while he hands the money over. That's right--Scrooge laughs while paying for something! He has changed! It's a textbook denouement.

Ditto the uncut grass next door at the conclusion of 'The Great Gatsby' by F. Scott Fitzgerald, which indicates quite literally that the landscape of the book has been altered forever by its Action. Of course, you aren't required to use this structure in telling stories. But if you do, however, your stories, novellas and novels will work. That is, when people are done reading one of your pieces of fiction, they will feel as if they've been told a story. Not a 'character sketch,' but a real story.

But if it doesn't have Conflict, Development, and Climax, it isn't a story. If you don't believe that, just try to tell a satisfying anecdote that lacks these components. Or tell a joke that lacks classic story structure, and see if anyone laughs.

VICTORIANS' SECRETS

It may seem peculiar in the 21st century to discuss screenwriting in the same breath as anything that had to do with the 19th century. What does one have to do with the other? After all, the only visual representation that remotely resembled a motion picture was Muybridge's zoopraxiscope: a revolving device consisting of a series of still shots photographed in sequence that appeared to move when viewed through a narrow viewing port. It had no story, only the novelty of movement. The imagination of the viewer filled in the rest.

Once motion pictures began telling stories, filmmakers looked to familiar models on which to build screenplays. The modern novel born in the 19th century gave them the model they needed.

In order to understand how Victorian fiction created the basic structure of motion pictures, we have to examine the times in which those novels were written. The years between the mid-19th century and the early teens of the 20th century resonate with us into the 21st century. Parallels exist between our time and an age that we have romanticized out of all proportion to the truth.

The so-called Victorian Era was rife with upheaval. The Industrial Revolution roared into Western civilization much the same way as the Technological Revolution roared into our own lives. It brought with it a disruption of social values. Middle class entrepreneurs found themselves swimming in money. Think dot-commers. Greed and wealth went hand-in-hand. Think Enron.

Aside from money, society also saw changing values in many other ways. While we look on Victorians as sexually corseted, diaries and newspapers of the time reported increases in violent sex crimes. A plague of sexually transmitted diseases--notably syphilis--affected every strata of society. Consider that HIV-AIDS and other sexually transmitted diseases are with us today.

Victorian-era writers reacted to their world in a number of ways. Jane Austen surveyed the scene with a deep sense of irony--an irony that finds itself at its height with 'Emma.' The theme of the novel is so modern that it became the source for a contemporary motion picture, 'Clueless,' written and directed by Amy Heckerling, as well as a film written and directed by Douglas McGrath that takes place within its own time.

Edith Wharton's 'Age of Innocence' examines New York society in 1870 with a satiric eye, but it could be New York or Los Angeles, 2002. Success necessitates that an attorney marry a trophy wife. But he has a wandering eye and searches for the seductiveness of an illicit love affair with an exotic woman who has a checkered past.

The great Victorian writer, Charles Dickens, examined every aspect of life during those times: From the grimiest London cesspool to the heights of courage and daring. Although 'A Tale of Two Cities' takes place during the French Revolution of

1775, it reflects the mores and values of his time. Dickens constantly searched for soul in an age gone mad. So, too have we searched for soul within the confines of Vietnam or the Gulf War or Bosnia-Herzogovina or in the Middle East. In the same way that Dickens reverted to an earlier time where heroism could be accepted, in our time, we turn back to 'Saving Private Ryan' or 'Band of Brothers' where we can espouse simpler truths even if the veil of time obscures the terrible details of war's horrors.

With his novels of the first decade of the twentieth-century, E. M. Forster predicted enormous changes in society. Pretense, Forster believed, was the mask behind which polite society hid its prejudices against the poor, against ethnic minorities, against all those 'others' who didn't fit within the framework of the 'haves.' His stories peeled away pretence and echo our own times in which prejudice still raises its ugly head. We continue, as they did in 1910, to claim that the 'other' will destroy our society. Today, France votes for a Fascist in reaction to its minority population. Italy votes for a radical right wing government with its attendant bigotry.

Most novels of the era have an episodic structure. Almost every chapter ends with a hook to get the reader back into the story much the same way that screenwriters use hooks, large and small, to lead viewers from one scene to another.

Scenes carefully lay out with precision descriptions of the environment and carefully delineate characters who drive the story forward rather than go along for the ride. It's as if the writers understood that visual elements of stories are as important as their literary qualities.

And why not? Museum art and calendar art or daguerreotypes and tintype photos were the only visuals available. Perhaps some people had a stereopticon. But storytelling was the main source of entertainment.

Even if a person couldn't read, someone could read to them. Therefore, it became necessary to conjure up wonderful images of places and people who occupied those spaces. And since one did not read a novel all at once, it had to have cliffhangers so that the listener yearned to come back for more.

Writers such as Charles Dickens first published their novels a chapter at a time in weekly newspapers. The object was to make sure readers always bought the next instalment. Something interesting had to happen at the end of each chapter. Since most writers were paid by the word, Dickens made sure he wrote enough to cover his bills.

How cinematic was Dickens? He understood one of the main conventions of a motion picture. He understood the 'inciting incident' necessary to start the action. The inciting incident produces the central core of the story--the reason for the story's existence. As a result of this incident, the main character or characters must fight or claw toward the resolution that appears in the third act.

Most of us, who were forced to read 'A Tale of Two Cities' when we were in high school or college, only remember the opening of the novel: 'It was the best of times, it was the worst of times, it was the age of wisdom, it was the age of foolishness, it was the epoch of belief, it was the epoch of incredulity, it was the season of Light, it was the season of Despair, it was the season of hope, it was the winter of despair, we had everything before us, we had nothing before us, we were all going straight to Heaven, we were all going direct the other way...'

And the end with Sidney Carton's heroic, melodramatic speech as he approached the guillotine in place of the romantic lead: 'It is a far, far better thing that I do, then I have ever done; it is a far, far better rest I go to than I have ever known.'

But what starts it all? Above all things, the theme of 'Tale' is that of rape. Real and metaphoric rape creates the dynamics of the story. An evil aristocracy entombs Dr. Manette in the Bastille when he discovers they have raped and murdered a young peasant woman. Everyone becomes victim of the rape: Manette's daughter, Lucy, married to Charles Darnay, a son of the aristocrats who is condemned to death by the French Tribunal, and, lastly, Sidney Carton who takes Darnay's place. Metaphorically, the book describes in vivid detail the rape of a nation gone made with bloodlust.

Dickens writes the book in classic three-act structure. Book One titled 'Recalled to Life' sets up the conflict to come. Book

Two, 'The Golden Thread,' the longest section, presents the conflict and tension. Book Three, "The Track of the Storm' brings the romantic, heroic, melodramatic resolution to a close.

W. P. Lipscomb and S. N. Behrman, the screenwriters of the 1935 version of 'A Tale of Two Cities,' follow the book almost word for word, image for image. It's as if the novel was a detailed treatment, including the dialogue. Dickens used dramatic hooks or dramatic dialogue to draw us from one chapter to another--or from one scene to another.

At the end of Chapter Three, Book One, Dr. Manette, now rescued and riding in the Dover Mail stage, raves about his burial in the Bastille. A disturbed passenger blurts out: 'Eighteen years...Gracious Creator of the day! To be buried alive for eighteen years!'

The last paragraph of Book Two that leads us into the third act has Charles Darnay shipping out from Dover to France in order to save the life of a servant accused of being a monarchist because he served Darney's family. Darnay, convicted in absentia by the Revolutionary Tribunal, places his life in jeopardy for a noble cause.

Edith Wharton's novel 'Age of Innocence,' written during the Edwardian period, maintains many of the Victorian forms. To capture how Wharton and other writers of the period wrote cinematically, all we have to do is read a scene from the book and then take a look at how Jay Cocks and Martin Scorsese translated it to the screen. Very little changes. The screenwriters make a few juxtapositions and deletions because they deal with a different medium, and it requires its own language--the language of cinema.

Wharton carefully peels back layer upon layer of each character until they become revealed or exposed. Surprises arise, but always based on a careful foreshadowing of events. The author explores character as if she held an advanced degree in psychology. She isn't alone. Austen, Dickens, Forster and others in the pantheon of writers of 100 or 120 years ago exhibited the same insight.

In 'Howards End,' E.M. Forster introduces a modern woman--Margaret--who makes the first advance against the wealthy tradesman, Wilcox. The author sets the scene with the Schlegel sisters, Margaret and Helen. Margaret will eventually marry the newly rich and widowed tradesman Henry Wilcox, setting off a chain of events that will change views on class and attitudes toward society.

Cinematically, Forster often opens each chapter with a piece of action or dialogue that grabs the reader immediately. He doesn't tiptoe around and wait for something to happen. He engages the reader immediately. A lesson that screenwriters use over and over again to keep the action moving.

In one chapter, he begins with a shocking statement: 'We are not concerned with the very poor. They are unthinkable, and only to be approached by the statistician or the poet.' The screenwriter, Ruth Prawer Jhabvala, restates the prose as dialogue: 'A word of advice. Don't take up a sentimental attitude over the poor. The poor are poor. One is sorry for them, and there it is.'

The line expresses everything there is to know about Henry Wilcox, one of the newly wealthy merchants of England who, having amassed wealth, now takes his place in the House of Parliament. 'Howards End' explores the breaking down of a rigid class system.

Another chapter begins with 'Leonard accepted the invitation to tea next Saturday. But he was right; the visit proved a conspicuous failure.' The reader is set up for the coming storm in which Leonard feels used by Margaret and Helen Schlegel. The storm that bursts forth eventually changes Henry Wilcox who comes to accept, through Margaret, that the poor are poor, but are not necessarily doomed to perpetual poverty. He also comes to accept that women have capabilities beyond that of mothers and wives.

Those wishing to write screenplays would do well to study these writers and others from the period to understand structure, character and story development. How-to books have their uses--certainly as references--but nothing can take the place of reading novels by writers who understand and explore the human condition. To understand both text and subtext in a story, you have to read these authors along with Emily Brontë, whose 'Wuthering Heights' and 'Jane Eyre' have been reborn again and again in film and television. You should study Joseph Conrad whose 'Heart of Darkness' was reincarnated by John Milius and Frances Ford Coppola as 'Apocalypse Now.' Digest Mary Shelley, who wrote one of the definitive horror novels/ social commentaries with "Frankenstein.' Discover the melodramatic, gothic George du Maurier, not as well known, but who gave us a character film and TV writers use over and over again: 'Svengali' from his book, 'Trilby.'

Without them, cinema might not exist in its present form. Filmmakers in the nascent years of the industry had only those references for making motion pictures. That alone might be the reason so many early films were loaded with melodramatic devices. Unfortunately, the lessons learned from reading the books--or just hearing about them--only touched the surface of the material rather than delving deep into the subject matter.

Part of the reason came from a distrust of the audience. Filmmakers, no matter if they made dramas or pie-in-the-face comedies, felt that their audiences wouldn't sit still for thought-provoking cinema.

They presented 'amusements' rather than subtext. It took Griffiths in the United States, Lang in Germany, Abel in France and other great storytellers to understand that the great novels they read contained lessons they could use in the creation of a new language of cinema. Those lessons became the mainstay of motion pictures into the sound era where screenwriters extracted methodologies with which we have become familiar from storytelling of the previous 30 to 50 years.

We might have discovered all this without the modern novel that began in the 19th century. Or it may have taken a different direction.. Certainly, the three-act structure has been with us since humans started telling stories around the smoking embers of campfires. However, the way in which we develop characters, the way in which we create dramatic devices to draw viewers deeper into the story, was the result of novels written for a public anxious to read about class struggle and struggles within class or who wanted to smile with the author's satiric or ironic view of the world.

The Power and Importance of Human Connection to a Great Screenplay

For years I gently browbeat my students. "Dig deeper," I said. "The best stories are about the human heart."

I wasn't quite sure what I meant. I knew I didn't mean that old Hollywood saw-throw in some love interest! I meant something closer to Samson Raphaelson's remark about Shakespeare in The Human Nature of Playwriting, "[He] is not a realistic writer but he is overwhelmingly real because he reports the hearts of human beings." I was teaching dramatic technique: first, playwriting in the English Department at Florida State, then screenwriting when the Film School began. I was rounding up the usual suspects-conflict, crisis, and climax-but I had this nagging sensation that these overlooked something important in stories. I couldn't figure out what it was, so I hoped, if sufficiently coaxed, my students could.

What We Talk about when We Talk about Drama

Derived from the Greek dran-"to do"-drama means someone strives. Will meets obstacle, and this creates conflict. For two hundred years, perhaps more, we have talked about dramatic stories this way. George Bernard Shaw defined drama as "the conflict between man's will and his environment." Across the channel, Ferdinand Brunetiere said it was "the will of man in conflict." And so it has gone, like a roll call, each person casting a vote for drama's conventional wisdom.

"Since the early nineteenth century the 'conflict theory' of drama has dominated dramatic criticism and, to a considerable degree, the practice of playwrights," Eric Bentley says in Concepts in Dramatic Theory. "It is a central assumption of most Twentieth-century dramatic theory." In film, where the budgets (and insecurities) run wilder and the flops are more catastrophic, the rule of the game is more rigid.

> *"The basis of all drama is conflict," Syd Field says in almost every one of his books. "Without conflict there is no action; without action there is no character; without character there is no story. And without story there is no screenplay."*

Most screenwriting books-about long or short screenplays-say essentially the same thing, though in Screenwriting Tricks of the Trade, William Froug is the most emphatic:

> *"Without conflict, you might as well pack it in-you are in the wrong field of endeavour. Without conflict, your reader will fall asleep and you will never have to think about having an audience. The ballgame is over."*

Conflict has shaped the way that we think about drama and the way that we think to shape it. In Writing Great Screenplays for Film and TV, Dona Cooper offers a new improved metaphor for the screenplay: a roller coaster.

It's a rollicking image, more energetic and imaginative than most I have found in screenwriting books, but the author's graphic depiction-action that rises and rises and rises then falls-is merely a remake of a nineteenth century model, Freitag's Pyramid (conflict, crisis, and resolution), which keeps cropping up in all kinds of books about writing, including former editions of Janet Burroway's Writing Fiction.

But Janet-a friend and colleague-was increasingly uncomfortable, too, with this conflict-bound way of seeing the story. Other writers, most of them women, were also uneasy.

But Ursula LeGuin came closest to articulating what I was feeling: "People are cross-grained, aggressive, and full of trouble, the storytellers tell us; people fight themselves and one another, and their stories are full of their struggles.

But to say that, that is the story is to use one aspect of existence, conflict, to subsume all other aspects, many of which it does not include and does not comprehend. Romeo and Juliet is the story of the conflict between two families, and its plot involves the conflict of two individuals within those families. Is that all it involves? Isn't Romeo and Juliet about something else, and isn't it the something else that makes the otherwise trivial tale of a feud into a tragedy?"

Conflict was not incorrect; it was incomplete. It didn't get to the heart of the matter, to that level of story that engages most deeply. It was half the story, but I couldn't figure out what the other half was.

HERO VS. VILLAIN

We've seen how both Hero and Villain are actually composed of several different qualities. And, we've seen that for every quality the Hero possesses, the Villain has a counterpart. When these qualities are combined in this classic manner, Hero and Villain become stereotypes. When these traits are expressed to the extreme, they become melodramatic.

We have also indicated that the elements of Hero and Villain might be distributed among other characters to break out of the stereotypical mold. One of the most powerful examples of this is to simply swap traits between the Hero and Villain themselves.

In this article, we're going to have the Hero and Villain "Mix it up," to show how relatively minor alterations in the stereotypical arrangement can open up a huge new realm of creative opportunities.

To begin, let's list the qualities of the Hero and Villain for comparison:

Hero: Protagonist, Main Character, Central Character, Good Guy

Villian: Antagonist, Influence Character, Second-Most Central, Bad Guy.

To recap, by the definitions we have been using: Protagonist is the Prime Mover or Driver of the effort to achieve the story's goal. Antagonist is the chief force opposed to the Protagonist achieving the goal.

Main Character represents the audience position in the story and carries the moral attitude being explored in the story. In contrast, the Influence Character represents the opposing moral viewpoint.

The Central Character is the one most prominent in the story, either by pages, screen time, or the intensity with which it is drawn. The 2nd Most Central character is right behind it in prominence.

Finally, the Good Guy character seeks to help others even at its own expense, while the Bad Guy character seeks to help itself, even at the expense of others. As we can see, these two classic character types are well balanced against each other in their stereotypical arrangement.

Protagonist / Antagonist Swap

But what happens if we maintain that balance yet swap some qualities between the two? Lets begin by swapping the first qualities-Protagonist and Antagonist-to create an arrangement like this:

Hero: Antagonist, Main Character, Central Character, Good Guy

Villian: Protagonist, Influence Character, Second-Most Central, Bad Guy

In the case shown above, we have created a modified Hero character who represents the audience or reader in the story, is the most important character, and is a Good Guy, but is trying to stop or prevent something rather than make something happen.

We also now have a modified Villain character who tries to change the Main Character's point of view, is second most important, and is a Bad Guy, but is trying to achieve something, rather than prevent something.

In fact, this is the arrangement of character traits in almost all of the James Bond films! It is the "Villain" who has a dastardly plan and puts it into action, making him the de facto Protagonist. The Villain is the one with initiative in 007 movies, and it is Bond who is the reactionary, trying to stop the Villain before he can successfully complete his evil scheme.

This is the primary character reason that the Bond films feel so uniquely Bond. Our Hero is actually the Antagonist! Now, some might argue that once the Villain begins his efforts, then Bond is the one with the goal-to stop him. But it really boils down to what is called "Point of Attack." That phrase describes the moment at which the story begins.

If the story began after the Villain's scheme was already a known problem, then perhaps we could say that was the status quo, and Bond is taking the initiative to change it, thereby making him the Protagonist. But most Bond films set the status quo as a peaceful world scene into which the Villain interjects an element of threat. Only then does Bond spring into action, to stop what the Villain is trying to do.

So, Bond remains a Good Guy, is still the Central Character, continues to carry the story's moral position, but is an Antagonist, rather than a Protagonist.

In a story, the Protagonist represents our own initiative-the motivation to shake things up, change the order, alter the course.

In contrast, the Antagonist represents our reluctance to change-the motivation is to maintain the status quo or to return things to the state in which they had been. The battle between them illustrates the inner conflict we all experience when trying to decide if it is better to try something new or to let sleeping dogs lie.

So, simply swapping the qualities of being Protagonist and Antagonist will have a tremendous effect on a Hero and Villain, even though all the other qualities remain the same. If you have only been creating the standard Hero and Villain, this one technique alone will open many new creative avenues.

Main / Influence Swap

Now how much would you pay? But wait! There's more.... Suppose we put the Protagonist and Antagonist qualities back in their usual places and try another kind of swap:

Hero: Protagonist, Influence Character, Central Character, Good Guy

Villian: Antagonist, Main Character, Second-Most Central, Bad Guy

Here we have set the Villain up as the Main Character, which basically means that the reader or audience experiences the story through the Villain's eyes, and, that the Villain is the one grappling with the moral dilemma and the Hero is the one trying to change his world view.

Now that's interesting, isn't it? A good example of this arrangement is A Christmas Carol, in which Scrooge is the Bad

Guy, suffering the Moral Dilemma, we see things from his position, and he is the Antagonist, trying to put a stop to the meddling of the ghosts and get the status quo back to normal.

The Ghosts, collectively, form the Hero of the story, taking the initiative to change Scrooge's life-course, tying to change his attitude, and trying to do the right thing for someone else, even though they can't help themselves (classic Good-Guy mentality).

There's one other change in that story that doesn't match the line-up listed above, however. Scrooge is also the Central Character and the Ghosts are the Second Most Central. So, the proper arrangement of qualities in A Christmas Carol would look like this:

Hero: Protagonist, Influence Character, Second-Most Central, Good Guy

Villian: Antagonist, Main Character, Central Character, Bad Guy

This example has served to illustrate that you don't have to limit yourself to swapping just one quality, but in fact, can mix and match them in any combination you want! Imagine the possibilities!

Good Guy / Bad Guy Swap

Still, there's one more kind of alteration in the classic Hero and Villain we have not yet addressed at all: Good Guy and Bad Guy. Based on what we have done so far, you might assume we would simply want to swap those two traits and, to be sure, we could do that:

Hero: Protagonist, Influence Character, Central Character, Bad Guy

Villian: Antagonist, Main Character, Second-Most Central, Good Guy

Now you have a Hero that is, perhaps, more of the classic Anti-Hero, something like the Main Character in Taxi Driver. Here's a disturbed individual who is under such personal pressure that he snaps into a fantasy world and acts to the harm of others. But, he is definitely the Central Character, and he is the Main Character because we see the story through his eyes and he grapples with the moral dilemma, He is also the Protagonist, because he is the one who take the initiative.

Now, while we could do that simply Good Guy/Bad Guy swap, there's something a little different that really opens up the game...

What if we make both characters Good Guys? You know, just because two people disagree doesn't mean one of them has to be operating from ill intent. They might both have the best interests of others paramount in their minds, yet differ in their views of how to accomplish that.

So, if one wants to build a dam on the river that runs through the small town in which he grew up in order to end the poverty under which his people are suffering, another of the town's citizens might be dead-set against it because he believes it would ruin the small-town atmosphere, and even if the people have more money, it wouldn't be worth living there anymore.

Clearly both are Good Guys, yet in the effort to achieve the goal, they are diametrically opposed. The man trying to build the dam is the Protagonist. The man trying to stop it is the Antagonist.

Putting it All Together

Okay, let's take the example above and use the freedom of all that we have learned to fashion two completely non-stereotypical characters.

First, we already have the Protagonist trying to build the dam and the Antagonist trying to stop it. Next, you pick one as Central Character and make him the more important and memorable of the two. You make this choice by picking the one you find most interesting to be Central, because your own interest in the character will almost automatically cause you to give him more media real estate and to draw him with the greatest passion.

Choosing which one you want as your Main Character may be trickier, since it doesn't necessarily have to be the Central Character nor the Protagonist. Often, a charismatic Antagonist makes a good Main Character, but so does a dull bystander who simply provides a good perspective on the story for the reader or audience to adopt.

Finally, you determine if both are Good Guys, Bad Guys, or if one is Good and the other Bad. This choice will depend on whether you want your audience or reader to stand in the shoes of a Good perspective, as with Dr. Richard Kimble in The Fugitive, or in the shoes of the Bad perspective as with Scrooge in A Christmas Carol.

In the Good scenario, you make your reader or audience feel self-righteous, and teach by example. In the Bad scenario, you accuse your reader or audience and teach by encouraging them to deny it in their own lives and prove you wrong. Then, you use your plot to explore both characters' points of view, ultimately passing your judgment upon them as your story's message.

Well, you get the idea. All this might seem pretty obvious by now, but recall back to the beginning in Part One, one of this trilogy of articles when we were only talking about the classic Hero and Villain. At the time, they might have seemed the best way to go for any story, but now... Well, Hero is a four-letter word, and by breaking him and his Villainous counterpart into their various components, you can now create far more interesting, unpredictable and believable characters than you could before.

HOW TO CREATE PASSION, SUSPENSE, AND OTHER ENTERTAINMENT DIMENSIONS

The entertainment dimensions are the pleasant sensations the audience feels when they experience your story. The most important of these feelings are those associated with the actions of the genre structures. When you isolate the plots and subplots of your story, you isolate actions that are directly linked to specific feelings that are associated with romance, mystery, adventure or some other particular activity. Among the more desirable feelings associated with these genres are laughter and tears, love and hate, passion, excitement, suspense, fear and joy.

Laughter and tears need no explanation. Love and hate means getting your audience deeply involved with your characters. Passion, in this sense, doesn't just mean romance, it means giving the audience an intense emotional experience. Suspense means moving them to the edge of their seat, excitement gives them a physical thrill, magic fills them with a sense of wonder and awe, surprise startles and delights them, and fear scares their pants off. The promise of these feelings helps to lure the audience into the experience and the fulfillment of that promise gives them pleasure and a sense of having been entertained.

The emotional values that make up these dimensions are enhanced by a number of factors, among them make-believe. Make-believe separates the intriguing aspects of a given situation from the fear of the consequences we might experience in real life. In real life, nothing could be less entertaining than a real serial killer stalking your neighbourhood. Your only concern would be to get rid of him as soon as possible. When you're experiencing a story, the fear of consequences is eliminated, and you are left with the pleasant sensations associated with the hunt, and you can study the mechanics of that experience objectively. Using this separation, a story can artistically treat and translate even the most horrible real crimes into an intriguing entertainment that conceals an important truth in a powerful metaphor.

Another factor is structure. Separated from the fear of consequences, the archetypal struggle between good and evil, which can be so deadly in real life, becomes a game in story. The same structures, in fact, that make a game fun help to make a story fun--i.e. the fact that it involves opposing sides, important things at stake, a marvellous element, possible victories or defeats, and a ticking clock.

Two other factors are the technical and aesthetic dimensions. The aesthetic dimensions--clarity, beauty, elegance, harmony, rhythm and grace are the pleasing effects created by the skilful use of the technical dimensions--variety, contrast, proportion, timing, symmetry and tempo. Contrast, for example, is a major factor in creating clarity. When you contrast such things as good and evil, spiritual and physical, rich and poor, light and dark, silence and sounds, you heighten the effect of both and greatly increase the clarity.

Each of the hundred or so powerful dimensions of a story has an impact on the entertainment values of the story, so the more dimensions you can add and perfect, the greater the emotional impact on the audience. The more substance you can put behind it, the more powerful your story is going to be--the better the audience will enjoy the ride and the more often they will come back to experience it.

If you are creating a drama, the characters will behave as they do in real life. This puts the audience in touch with reality, and they experience the sensations of real life. If you are creating a tragedy or a romance, you are exaggerating the nobility of the characters. You are making them bigger than life. They become role models the audience can identify with and strive to emulate. King Arthur is such a character, and so is Mel Gibson in 'Braveheart.' They put the audience in touch with their own true potential. It gives them a taste of who they really are and the desire to become what they could really be.

If you're creating a comedy, the basic situation will be real, but you are isolating and exaggerating a character's foibles and flaws, the frequency with which errors occur, and the irony experienced by your characters. Woody Allen makes people laugh by exaggerating his own hypochondria and neurosis. Laurel and Hardy exaggerated the frequency with which mishaps and catastrophes can occur. Charles Dickens exaggerated the ignorance and belligerent slowness of his bureaucrats and the difficulties his heroes had in trying to deal with them, and this makes it funny--and that helps us to laugh at ourselves. Even serious plays like Hamlet have, or should have, a great deal of humour. A story without humour is not about human beings.

If you separate or reunite two characters the audience cares deeply about, that will put them in touch with the tragedy of separation and the joys of reunion hidden deep within their own souls, and that will make them cry. Do you remember how you felt at the end of 'E.T.' when the little boy and his extraterrestrial friend are separated? The tears of sorrow that you shed? Or the tears of joy you experienced at the end of 'I

Am Sam,' when Sean Penn and his daughter are reunited with the help of Laura Dern?

Passion, in the present sense, is not just romance, it is emotional intensity. It is our feeling potential. It increases the emotional involvement. So, if you want to increase the passion your audience is feeling, fill your characters with deep emotional feelings of love or passion for some activity like patriotism, and you will arouse those feelings in your audience. You can easily see this demonstrated in 'Braveheart,' or 'Shakespeare In Love.' Increasing the passion of your characters puts the audience in touch with similar feelings hidden within themselves.

Audiences love it when characters show their feelings--especially changes of heart, forgiveness, acts of love and kindness, and self sacrifice. If you want to increase the love the audience feels toward your heroes, let the hero do kind, humane and loving things. And let him or her show courage and be willing to sacrifice themselves for the sake of others. If you saw 'Armageddon,' do you remember how you felt when Bruce Willis suddenly sacrifices his life for the sake of his future son-in-law and the world? For an instant, at least, we all wanted to be heroes, too. That's passion in the characters transferred to us in the audience. If your characters could care less about each other, the audience will feel the same about them.

If you want the audience to hate your villains, make the villains more villainous. Isolate their negative qualities and conjure them until you have thoroughly vilified them. That will intensify the loathing the audience will feel toward them, and it will also intensify the rejection the audience will feel toward similar impulses arising in themselves. To be truly effective, of course, the villain's villainy has to be in the context of a full human being.

If you want to increase the excitement of your story, isolate and artistically treat the physical action and intensify it. Raise the stakes, increase the urgency and the danger and quicken the pace. And save the greatest burst of energy for the climax of the dominant plot. The chase is an obvious example.

If you want to increase the suspense, make us anxious over how things will turn out and delay the result. Excite interest or curiosity; then hold back the resolution. Anything that causes tension and anxiety causes suspense if it's unrelieved. And what causes tension or anxiety? Anything intriguing or threatening that's unresolved. The more there is at stake, the greater the tension and suspense. And if everything is at stake and there's no time to lose, and the odds are overwhelming, and success is highly unlikely, you will maximize the tension and suspense. And all of this is a reflection of reality. In real life, everything is always at stake. There really is no time to lose, and the outcome is always extremely uncertain. When nothing is at stake, it's not about life, and there is very little tension and suspense.

As for the aesthetic and technical dimensions, you only have to realize they are important, and they will begin to work for you. The moment you realize that timing and variety are important you will begin to develop a sense of how they are created. And the more you work with them, the more effective they will become.

So learn as much as you can about what an audience feels and why and how those feelings are created. Be aware of what works for you, then figure out why it works. What just happened? What caused those feelings or that laughter? And you will quickly develop an instinct for it. Remember the promise of these feelings lures the audience into the experience. And you're not manipulating them, you're putting them in touch with themselves, with their own feelings. And that's a very good thing.

10

Radio Broadcasting

Radio broadcasting is an audio (sound) broadcasting service, traditionally broadcast through the air as radio waves (a form of electromagnetic radiation) from a transmitter to an antenna and a thus to a receiving device. Stations can be linked in radio networks to broadcast common programming, either in syndication or simulcast or both. Audio broadcasting also can be done via cable FM, local wire networks, satellite and the Internet.

HISTORY

The earliest radio stations were simply radio and audio telegraph systems and did not carry audio. The first claimed audio transmission that could be termed a broadcast occurred on Christmas Eve in 1906, and was made by Reginald Fessenden. While many early experimenters attempted to create systems similar to radiotelephone devices where only two parties were meant to communicate, there were others who intended to transmit to larger audiences. Charles Herrold started broadcasting in California in 1909 and was carrying audio by the next year.

For the next decade, radio tinkerers had to build their own radio receivers. KDKA AM of Pittsburgh, Pennsylvania (owned by Westinghouse) started broadcasting as the first licensed "commercial" radio station on November 2, 1920. The commercial designation came from the type of license-they didn't start airing advertisements until a few years later.

The first broadcast was the results of the U.S. presidential election, 1920. The Montreal station that became CFCF-AM began program broadcasts on May 20, 1920, and the Detroit station that became WWJ began program broadcasts beginning on August 20, 1920, although neither held a license at the time.

Radio Argentina began regularly scheduled transmissions from the Teatro Coliseo in Buenos Aires on August 27, 1920, making its own priority claim. The station got its license on November 19, 1923. The delay was due to the lack of official Argentine licensing procedures before that date. This station continued regular broadcasting of entertainment and cultural fare for several decades.

When internet based radio became feasible in the mid '90s, the new medium required no licensing and the stations could broadcast from anywhere in the world without the need for "over the air" transmitters. This greatly reduced the overhead for establishing a station, and in 1996, 'A' Net Station (A.N.E.T.) began broadcasting commercial free from Antarctica.

M.I.T. developed the "Radio Locator" List of Radio Stations. After stations started streaming audio on the internet, Radio-Locator added this to their search engine so anyone could locate a station's website and listen to a station offering a worldwide stream. This list also tracks "terrestrial" radio stations who may not have live audio on the net, or even a website, but are able to find station information by various other search queries.

TYPES

Radio stations are of several types. The best known are the AM and FM stations; these include both commercial, public and nonprofit varieties as well as student-run campus radio stations and hospital radio stations can be found throughout the developed world.

Although now being eclipsed by internet-distributed radio, there are many stations that broadcast on shortwave bands using AM technology that can be received over thousands of miles (especially at night). For example, the BBC has a full schedule transmitted via shortwave. These broadcasts are very sensitive to atmospheric conditions and sunspots.

AM STATIONS

AM stations were the earliest broadcasting stations to be developed. AM refers to amplitude modulation, a mode of broadcasting radio waves by varying the amplitude of the carrier signal in response to the amplitude of the signal to be transmitted. One of the advantages of AM is that its unsophisticated signal can be detected (turned into sound) with simple equipment. If a signal is strong enough, not even a power source is needed; building an unpowered crystal radio receiver was a common childhood project in the early years of radio.

AM broadcasts occur on North American airwaves in the mediumwave frequency range of 530 to 1700 kHz (known as the "standard broadcast band"). The band was expanded in the 1990s by adding nine channels from 1620 to 1700 kHz. Channels are spaced every 10 kHz in the Americas, and generally every 9 kHz everywhere else.

Many countries outside of the U.S. use a similar frequency band for AM transmissions. Europe also uses the longwave band. In response to the growing popularity of FM radio stations in the late 1980s and early 1990s, some North American stations began broadcasting in AM stereo, though this never really gained acceptance.

AM radio has some serious shortcomings.

- The signal is subject to interference from electrical storms (lightning) and other EMI.
- Fading of the signal can be severe at night.

AM signals exhibit diurnal variation, travelling much longer distances at night. In a crowded channel environment this means that the power of regional channels which share a frequency must be reduced at night or directionally beamed in order to avoid interference, which reduces the potential nighttime audience. Some stations have frequencies unshared with other stations in the U.S.; these are called clear channel stations. Many of them can be heard across much of the country at night. (This is not to be confused with Clear Channel Communications, which currently owns many U.S. radio stations.)

- AM radio transmitters can transmit audio frequencies up to 20 kHz (now limited to 10 kHz in the US due to FCC rules designed to reduce interference), but most receivers are only capable of reproducing frequencies up to 5 kHz or less. At the time that AM broadcasting began in the 1920s, this provided adequate fidelity for existing microphones, 78 rpm recordings, and loudspeakers. The fidelity of sound equipment subsequently improved considerably but the receivers did not. Reducing the bandwidth of the receivers reduces the cost of manufacturing and makes them less prone to interference. In the United States, AM stations are never assigned adjacent channels in the same service area. This prevents the sideband energy generated by two stations from interfering with each other. Bob Carver created an AM stereo tuner employing notch filtering that demonstrated an AM broadcast can meet or exceed the 15 kHz bandwidth of FM stations without objectionable interference. After a few years the tuner was discontinued; Bob Carver had left the company and Carver Corporation later cut the number of models produced before discontinuing production completely. AM stereo broadcasts declined with the advent of HD Radio.

FM STATIONS

FM refers to frequency modulation, and occurs on VHF airwaves in the frequency range of 88 to 108 MHz everywhere (except Japan and Russia). Japan uses the 76 to 90 MHz band. FM stations are much more popular in economically developed regions, such as Europe and the United States, especially since higher sound fidelity and stereo broadcasting became common in this format.

FM radio was invented by Edwin H. Armstrong in the 1930s for the specific purpose of overcoming the interference (static) problem of AM radio, to which it is immune. At the same time, greater fidelity was made possible by spacing stations further apart. Instead of 10 kHz apart, they are 200 kHz apart-the difference between the lowest current FM frequency in the

U.S., 88.1 MHz and the next lowest, 88.3 MHz. This was far in advance of the audio equipment of the 1940s, but wide interchannel spacing was chosen to reduce interference problems that existed with AM.

In fact 200 kHz is not needed to accommodate an audio signal-20 kHz to 30 kHz is all that is necessary for a narrowband FM signal. The 200 kHz bandwidth allowed room for ±75 kHz signal deviation from the assigned frequency plus a 50 kHz guardband to eliminate adjacent channel interference. The larger bandwidth allows for broadcasting a 15 kHz bandwidth audio signal plus a 38 kHz stereo "subcarrier"-a piggyback signal that rides on the main signal. Additional unused capacity is used by some broadcasters to transmit utility functions such as background music for public areas, GPS auxiliary signals, or financial market data.

The AM radio problem of interference at night was addressed in a different way. At the time FM was set up, the only available frequencies were far higher in the spectrum than those used for AM radio. Using these frequencies meant that even at far higher power, the range of a given FM signal was much lower, thus its market was more local than for AM radio. Reception range at night was the same as daytime, and while the problem of interference between stations has not disappeared, it is far less.

The original FM radio service in the U.S. was the Yankee Network, located in New England. Broadcasting began in the early 1940s but did not pose a significant threat to the AM broadcasting industry. It required purchase of a special receiver. The frequencies used were not those used today: 42 to 50 megahertz. The change to the current frequencies, 88 to 108 megahertz, began at the end of World War II and was to some extent imposed by AM radio owners so as to cripple what was by now realized to be a potentially serious threat.

FM radio on the new band had to begin from step one. As a commercial venture it remained a little used audio enthusiast's medium until the 1960s. The more prosperous AM stations, or their owners, acquired FM licenses and often broadcast the same programming on the FM station as on the AM station (simulcasting). The FCC limited this practice in the 1970s. By the 1980s, since almost all new radios included both AM and FM tuners (without any government mandate), FM became the dominant medium, especially in cities. Because of its greater range, AM remained more common in rural environments.

DIGITAL RADIO BROADCASTING

Digital radio broadcasting has emerged, first in Europe (the UK in 1995 and Germany in 1999), and later in the United States. The European system is named DAB, for Digital Audio Broadcasting, and uses the public domain EUREKA 147 system. In the United States, the IBOC system is named HD Radio and owned by a consortium of private companies called iBiquity. An international non-profit consortium Digital Radio Mondiale (DRM), has introduced the public domain DRM system.

It is expected that for the next 10 to 20 years, all these systems will co-exist, while by 2015 to 2020 digital radio may predominate, at least in the developed countries.

Satellite

Satellite radiobroadcasters are slowly emerging, but the enormous entry costs of space-based satellite transmitters, and restrictions on available radio spectrum licenses has restricted growth of this market. In the USA and Canada, just two services, XM Satellite Radio and Sirius Satellite Radio exist.

Other

Many other non-broadcast types of radio stations exist. These include:

- base stations for police, fire and ambulance networks
- military base stations
- dispatch base stations for taxis, trucks, and couriers
- emergency broadcast systems
- amateur radio stations

PROGRAM FORMATS

Radio program formats differ by country, regulation and markets. For instance, the U.S. Federal Communications

Commission designates the 88-92 megahertz band in the U.S. for non-profit or educational programming, with advertising prohibited.

In addition, formats change in popularity as time passes and technology improves. Early radio equipment only allowed program material to be broadcast in real time, known as live broadcasting. As technology for sound recording improved, an increasing proportion of broadcast programming used pre-recorded material. A current trend is the automation of radio stations. Some stations now operate without direct human intervention by using entirely pre-recorded material sequenced by computer control.

INTERNATIONAL BROADCASTING

International broadcasting is broadcasting deliberately aimed at a foreign, rather than a domestic, audience. It usually is broadcast by means of longwave, mediumwave, or shortwave radio, but in recent years has also used direct satellite broadcasting and the Internet as means of reaching audiences.

Although radio and television programs do travel outside national borders, in many cases reception by foreigners is accidental. However, for purposes of propaganda, transmitting religious beliefs, keeping in touch with colonies or expatriates, education, improving trade, or increasing national prestige, broadcasting services have operated external services since the 1920s.

The early Years 1914-1939

The Dutch started regular international broadcasting on short-wave in 1927, following experiments in Eindhoven in 1925. This was followed by the BBC with the BBC Empire Service in 1932.

Other notable early international broadcasters included Vatican Radio (February 12, 1931), Radio Moscow, the official service of the Soviet Union which began broadcasting on long-wave in 1923 (this has since been renamed the Voice of Russia, following the collapse of the Soviet Union). Broadcasting in South Asia was launched in 1925 in Ceylon-Radio Ceylon, now the Sri Lanka Broadcasting Corporation is the oldest in the region.

In the 1930s, international broadcasting was a key means of promoting Nazi Germany foreign policy. German propaganda was organized under Joseph Goebbels, and played a key role in the German occupation of Austria and the Munich Crisis of 1938. During the Spanish Civil War, the Nationalist forces received a powerful Telefunken transmitter as a gift of Nazi Germany to aid their propaganda efforts, and until 1943 Radio Nacional de España collaborated with the Axis powers to retransmit in Spanish news from the official radio stations of Germany and Italy.

During the Second World War, Russian, German, British, and Italian international broadcasting services expanded and in 1942 the United States initiated its international broadcasting service, the Voice of America. In the Pacific theater, General Douglas MacArthur used shortwave radio to keep in touch with the citizens of the Japanese-occupied Philippine Islands.

World War II–modern International Broadcasting Begins

Shortwave programming was a low priority in the Weimar Republic. Once Hitler assumed power in 1933, shortwave, under the Rundfunk Ausland (Foreign Radio Section), was regarded as a vital element of Nazi propaganda. German shortwave hours were increased from two hours a day to 18 per day, and eventually twelve languages were broadcast on a 24 hour basis, including English. A 100 kilowatt transmitter and antenna complex was built at Zeesen, near Berlin. Speciality target programming to the United States began in 1933, to South Africa, South America, and East Asia in 1934, and South Asia and Central America in 1938.

Mediumwave transmitters on the periphery of the Third Reich provided speciality programs to listeners in neighbouring countries. Nevertheless, the Germans always had a problem staffing their foreign services with announcers who were both technically competent and loyal to Nazi ideas.

Several announcers who became well-known in their countries included British Union of Fascists member William

Joyce, who was one of the two "Lord Haw-Haw"s; Frenchmen Paul Ferdonnet and Andre Olbrecht, called "the traitors of [Radio] Stuttgart"; and Americans Frederick William Kaltenbach, "Lord Hee-Haw", and Mildred Gillars, one of the two announcers called "Axis Sally". Listeners to German programs often tuned in for curiosity's sake--at one time, German radio had half a million listeners in the U.S.--but most of them soon lost interest.

The British launched Radio SEAC from Colombo, Ceylon (Sri Lanka) during World War II. The station broadcast radio programs to the allied armed forces across the region from their headquarters in Ceylon.

Following the war and German partition, each Germany developed its own international broadcasting station: Deutsche Welle, using studios in Cologne, West Germany, and Radio Berlin International (RBI) in East Germany. RBI's broadcasts ceased shortly before the reunification of Germany on October 3, 1990, and Deutsche Welle took over its transmitters and frequencies.

The Cold War Era (1945-1991): Modern Practices, Modern Technology

The Cold War led to increased international broadcasting, as Communist and non-Communist states attempted to influence each other's domestic population. Some of the most prominent Western broadcasters were the Voice of America, the BBC World Service, and the (covertly) CIA-backed Radio Free Europe/ Radio Liberty. The Soviet Union's most prominent service was Radio Moscow (now the Voice of Russia) and China used Radio Peking (then Radio Beijing, now China Radio International). In addition to the U.S.-Soviet cold war, the Chinese-Russian border dispute led to an increase of the numbers of transmitters aimed at the two nations, and the development of new techniques such as playing tapes backwards for reel-to-reel recorders.

In addition to the superpower states, international broadcast services grew in Europe and the Middle East. Under the presidency of Gamal Nasser, Egyptian transmitters covered the Arab world; Israel's service, Kol Israel, served both to present the Israeli point of view to the world and to serve the

Jewish diaspora, particularly behind the Iron Curtain. Ironically, the isolationist Albania under Enver Hoxha, virtually a hermit kingdom, became one of the most prolific international broadcasters during the latter decades of the Cold War, with Radio Tirana one of the top five broadcasters in terms of hours of programming produced (Although Radio Tirana's programming was almost universally regarded as insufferably dull).

At the end of the Cold War, many international broadcasters cut back on hours and foreign languages broadcast, or reemphasized other language services. For example, in 1984, Radio Canada International broadcast in English, French, German, Spanish, Czech/Slovak, Hungarian, Polish, Russian, and Ukrainian. In 2005, Canada broadcast in English, Chinese, Arabic, Russian, and Spanish There is a trend towards more TV (e.g. BBC World, NHK World, CCTV-9), and news websites. Some services, such as Swiss Radio International, left shortwave altogether and exist in Internet form. In addition, new standards, such as Digital Radio Mondiale, are being introduced, as well as sending programs over the Web to be played back later, as "podcasts."

Daily developments are followed in Radio Netherlands' Media Network blog.

Transmitter power increased during this period to guarantee better reception (and in some cases in an attempt to counteract jamming).

- 1950s: 100 kW
- 1960s: 200 kW, early 1960s (2 x 100 kW 'twinned')
- 1970s: 300 kW, but many 250 kW transmitters sold
- 1980s: 500 kW sometimes transmitters were "doubled up" to produce 1000 Kw output
- 1980s-Present: 600 kW single, 1200 kW from twinned transmitters.

The move from Shortwave to other Technologies

In previous decades Shortwave (and sometimes high powered mediumwave) transmission was regarded as the main (and often the only) way in which broadcasters could reach an international audience. In recent years the proliferation of technologies such as satellite broadcasting, the internet and rebroadcasts of programming on AM and FM within target countries (Used mainly by Radio Free Europe following the end of the cold war) has meant that this is no longer necessairly the case.

Shortwave does possess a number of advantages over these newer technologies, including the following:

- The difficulty in censoring programming by authorities in target countries
- Low cost Shortwave radios are widely available in all but the most repressive countries in the world
- In many countries (particularly in most third world nations and in the Eastern bloc during the cold-war era) Ownership of Shortwave receivers is widespread (in many of these countries some domestic stations also used SW)
- Many newer SW receivers are portable and can be battery operated making them useful in difficult circumstances such as war-torn regions, disaster struck areas, refugee camps etc.
- Shortwave radios can be used in situations where internet or satellite technology is unavailable (or unaffordable)

But nowadays these benefits are widely regarded as being outweighed by the drawbacks such as these:

- Shortwave broadcasts often suffer from serious interference problems because of overcrowding on the wavebands, Atmospheric disturbances and Electrical interference problems (particularly in cities) from TV sets, computers, poorly designed domestic appliances and substandard electrical installations.
- Even under ideal reception conditions the audio quality of a shortwave broadcast is usually inferior to that of domestic stations (particularly FM stations)

- As more people around the world have access to television and the internet old technologies such as shortwave radio find it difficult to compete for peoples attention.
- In most Western countries ownership of shortwave radios is limited to interested enthusiasts. Therefore audiences are limited
- The dependence of shortwave radio on atmospheric conditions (The best frequency for hearing certain parts of the world varies by time of day and season) means that it can be difficult to use by non technically minded listeners.

Because of this many broadcasters are discovering they can reach a wider audience through other methods (particularly the internet and satellite television) and are cutting back on (or even entirely dropping) shortwave.

Means

Mediumwave and Longwave

Most radio receivers in the world receive the mediumwave band (535 kHz to 1700 kHz), which at night is capable of reliable reception from 150 to 2,500 km distance from a transmitter. Mediumwave is used heavily the world over for international broadcasting on a formal and informal basis.

In addition, many receivers used in Europe and Russia can receive the longwave broadcast band (150 to 280 kHz), which provides reliable long-distance communications over continental distances.

Shortwave

Yet other receivers are capable of receiving shortwave transmissions (2,000 to 30,000 kHz or 2 to 30 MHz). Depending on time of day, season of year, solar weather and Earth's geomagnetic field, a signal might reach around the world.

An international broadcaster has several options for reaching a foreign audience:

- If the foreign audience is near the broadcaster, high-power longwave and mediumwave stations can provide reliable coverage.

- If the foreign audience is more than 1,000 kilometers away from the broadcaster, shortwave radio is reliable, but subject to interruption by adverse solar/geomagnetic conditions.
- An international broadcaster may use a local mediumwave or FM radio or television relay station in the target country or countries.
- An international broadcaster may use a local shortwave broadcaster as a relay station.
- Neighbouring states, such as Israel and Jordan, may broadcast television programs to each other's viewing public.

An international broadcaster such as the BBC, Radio France International or Germany's Deutsche Welle, may use all the above methods. Several international broadcasters, such as Swiss Radio International, have abandoned shortwave broadcasting altogether, relying on Internet transmissions only. Others, such as the BBC World Service, have abandoned shortwave transmissions to North America, relying on local relays, the Internet, and satellite transmissions.

LISTENERS

An international broadcaster may have the technical means of reaching a foreign audience, but unless the foreign audience has a reason to listen, the effectiveness of the broadcaster is in question.

One of the most common foreign audiences consists of expatriates, who cannot listen to radio or watch television programs from home. Another common audience is radio hobbyists, who attempt to listen as many countries as possible and obtain verification cards or letters (QSLs). A third audience consists of journalists, government officials, and key business persons, who exert a disproportionate influence on a state's foreign or economic policy.

A fourth, but less publicized audience, consists of intelligence officers and agents who monitor broadcasts for both open-source intelligence clues to the broadcasting state's policies and for hidden messages to foreign agents operating in the receiving country. The BBC started its monitoring service in Caversham, Reading in 1936 (now BBC Monitoring). In the United States, the DNI Open Source Center (formerly the Central Intelligence Agency's Foreign Broadcast Information Service) provides the same service. Copies of OSC/FBIS reports can be found in many U.S. libraries that serve as government depositories. In addition, a number of hobbyists listen and report "spook" transmissions.

Without these four audiences, international broadcasters face difficulty in getting funding. In 2001, for example, the BBC World Service stopped transmitting shortwave broadcasts to North America, and other international broadcasters, such as YLE Radio Finland, stopped certain foreign-language programs.

However, international broadcasting has been successful when a country does not provide programming wanted by a wide segment of the population. In the 1960s, when there was no BBC service playing rock and roll, Radio Television Luxembourg (RTL) broadcast rock and roll, including bands such as the Beatles, into the United Kingdom. Similar programming came from an unlicensed, or "pirate" station, Radio Caroline, which broadcast from a ship in the international waters of the North Sea.

RESTRICTING RECEPTION

In many cases, governments do not want their citizens listening to international broadcasters. In Nazi Germany, a major propaganda campaign, backed by law and prison sentences, attempted to discourage Germans from listening to such stations. In addition, the German government sold a cheap "People's Receiver" that could not pick up distant signals well. In North Korea, all receivers are sold with fixed frequencies, tuned to local stations.

The most common method of preventing reception is jamming, or broadcasting a signal on the same frequencies as the international broadcaster. Germany jammed the BBC European service during the Second World War. Russian and Eastern European jammers were aimed against Radio Free

Europe, other Western broadcasters, and against Chinese broadcasters during the nadir of Sino-Soviet relations. In 2002, the Cuban government jammed the Voice of America's Radio Marti program and the Chinese government jammed broadcasts made by adherents of Falun Gong.

Yet another method of preventing reception involves moving a domestic station to the frequency used by the international broadcaster. During the Batista government of Cuba, and during the Castro years, Cuban medium-wave stations broadcast on the frequencies of popular South Florida stations. In October 2002 Iraq changed frequencies of two stations to block the Voice of America's Radio Sawa program.

Jamming can be defeated by using very powerful transmitting antennas, carefully choosing the transmitted frequency, changing transmitted frequency often, using Single Sideband, and properly aiming the receiving antenna.

11

Cosmic Rules of Writing for Television

As a veteran writer and a licensed psychotherapist specializing in writers' issues, I know enough to know there aren't any rules when it comes to writing.

Except for the following, which I modestly call the Three Cosmic Rules of Writing. I'm serious. Learn these simple rules, then burn them into your hearts and minds. It couldn't hurt.

YOU ARE ENOUGH

It's a growth industry: there are dozens of seminars, how-to books and audio tapes promising to teach you to write better, faster, more commercially. And there's nothing wrong with most of these. I know; I teach some myself.

Because, frankly, there ARE things a writer needs to learn about craft, the traditions of storytelling and the reality of the marketplace. But for the writer just starting out, there's a hidden danger: namely, the belief that if you just take the right seminars, read the right books or pick the right guru, then you'll be successful. That the person you are right now just isn't enough.

It's a classic belief system...writers who feel they have to be something more to succeed--smarter, better educated, funnier--with more interesting lives, more unique experiences.

As a therapist who works with writers, I see this everyday. Writers who feel they're somehow not enough. Who believe all the other writers are more talented, more confident, less burdened by doubt. It puts me in mind of that famous opening sequence of Woody Allen's 'Stardust Memories.' A glum Woody sits in a dark, dingy train car, with other lost souls. Looking out the window, he sees another train car--shining, brightly lit. Inside, beautiful men and women laugh and drink champagne, a festive vision of wit and privilege out of a Noel Coward play. Woody despairs. Why isn't he in the sparkling car, with the sparkling people?

Once, when a writer client of mine made reference to this scene to explain his feelings, what emerged was not only his sense of himself as inadequate, but something else, more insidious and undermining. Namely, the idea that he'd been dealt a bad hand--'I'm in the wrong car'--because of intrinsic defects in himself. If he were a better writer--smarter, more talented, whatever--he'd be in the right car. Those happy, glittering people were in the shining train car because they DESERVED to be there while he did not.

Thereafter, in our work together, his self-sabotaging behaviours could be understood as a natural result of his belief in himself as basically defective. When this painful self-concept was successfully illuminated and challenged, things began to shift in his view of himself.

What this anecdote illustrates is the real danger to your writing in seeing yourself as less than, not enough. Admittedly, a very common, self-limiting belief. To which I offer this thought, which will save you thousands of dollars in therapy bills and trim years off your spiritual journey: everybody thinks the party's happening somewhere else.

But it isn't. It's happening right here, right now. With you.

You--with all your doubts and fears, joys and sorrows--are enough. You--the one reading these words at this very moment-have everything you need to become the writer you want to be.

'Me?' you may be asking. 'Just as I am?'

Yes, you, who may, at this moment, be feeling scared, frustrated, blocked, discouraged. If so, join the club. Because so does every other writer in the world, even the most successful ones, who, after all, were once struggling writers themselves.

And now that they're successful, guess what? They still struggle. They have the same doubts, fears, longings, worries. They just don't give these feelings the same negative meanings you do. Smart writers recognize their feelings as important information about their inner lives, as the raw material of their writing craft. Just grist for the mill.

Which brings me to the Second Cosmic Rule of Writing: 'Work With What You're Given'

WORK WITH WHAT YOU'RE GIVEN

One of my favourite New Yorker cartoons by George Booth depicts a tormented, obviously 'blocked' writer sitting at his typewriter, crumpled paper strewn about, surrounded by literally dozens of dogs--napping, barking, hanging from the window sills, etc. The writer's wife stands in the doorway, glaring at him in weary disdain. 'Write about dogs,' she says.

Aside from its dark humour, the cartoon's truth is that the frustrated writer often doesn't see that a subject for his writing is right in front of him--the dogs; i.e., the obvious elements that actually inhabit his life.

In other words, work with what you're given. Writers have to practice SEEING, really seeing the world around them. As a writer, your job is to do this consciously and artfully, using craft and imagination as well as memory and reflection. You have to pay attention.

Tolstoy said, 'Love those whom God has put before You'; the Tao says, 'Love the Ten Thousand Things.' In short, love, that is--see--everything.

What do I mean by this? To 'love' the totality of what we experience is to accept all our responses to it, to be enlivened by the variety of ways we experience events, good or bad, painful or joyful. The artist's task is to see every moment--and our reaction to it--as potentially interesting, challenging and worthy of our creative participation.

Viewed from this perspective, a writer is never bored, never longs for things in his or her life to be more exciting, more interesting, more something else than they actually are. Except, of course, when you DO feel that way, in which case you should write about that boredom or that longing. That's your grist for that particular day. It's working with what you're given.

Which brings me to the Third (and, thankfully, last) Cosmic Rule of Writing...namely, 'Writing Begets Writing.'

If you're stuck on a difficult scene, write it anyway.

Write it badly. Write it in verse. Write it as a journal entry, a Dennis Miller rant. If you're frustrated at being stuck, write about that. I don't care. But write.

If you have angry, self-critical feelings, give them to a character in your story. If there isn't a likely candidate, invent one. There IS one, anyway: you. Your anguish, doubt, fears and frustrations are as vital and elemental to what you're writing as any character or plot point. Might as well make use of this fact.

WRITING BEGETS WRITING

Writing begets writing. Just as worrying begets worrying. Obsessing begets more obsessing. Pacing back and forth begets--well, you get the idea.

When you risk writing from where you're at, you set in motion a whole set of internal processes. The first rotten sentence you write has a life you can inhabit, evaluate, cross out. This first attempt can be replaced by a second, hopefully less rotten sentence--maybe a good piece of description or a sharp line of dialogue.

Then again, maybe not. But it doesn't matter. Just keep going. As William Goldman reminds us, some scenes you write are just going to be sludge, but they're important connective tissue. They keep things moving; they're links in a chain. Weak links, perhaps, but you can always go back and strengthen them later.

With what? The knowledge that you've written, for one thing, because writing doesn't just beget writing, it also begets--and reinforces--the reality that you can write; that pages will accumulate.

Look at it this way: Every hour you spend writing is an hour NOT spent fretting about your writing. Every day you produce pages is a day you DIDN'T spend sitting at a coffee shop, bitching about not producing any pages.

Writing begets writing. Not writing begets...well...not writing. You do the math.

There you have it: the Three Cosmic Rules of Writing.

(1) 'You Are Enough.'

(2) 'Work With What You're Given.'

(3) 'Writing Begets Writing.'

THE INS AND OUTS OF TV SERIES WRITER DEALS

The television business has undergone a dramatic change in recent years. In the past, studios would lavishly spend millions of dollars on long-term development deals with TV writers referred to as 'overall deals' in the hope that during the two to four year term of such arrangements (during which the studio is paying the writer's overhead plus a salary), the writer will create a hit show for the studio. Those days are now gone--unless of course you're Dick Wolf or David Kelley!

Nowadays, a writer is typically engaged to perform the initial step of writing a pilot script, and the studio is granted a number of options to engage the writer to render additional services on the pilot episode and/or series (both writing and producing). The benefit of this arrangement to the studio is clear: if the studio is not happy with the script, it can cut its losses relatively early, having committed only to payment of the initial script fee. Such deals, referred to as 'one-off's,' used to represent only a fraction of the deals that studios would enter into when developing television pilots and series, but are now the dominant form of television series writing deals. To give you an idea of what we're talking about and a heads-up for important things to consider when you're negotiating a deal, below is the basic outline of a television 'one-off' pilot/series writing agreement.

Pilot Writing Fee: The first item you would negotiate in connection with these types of agreements is invariably the pilot script-writing fee. Under the WGA Agreement (which governs most television projects, as all of the major networks are guild signatories), union minimum (or 'scale') for such services is approximately $30,000 for a half hour script and $43,000 for a sixty-minute script. For scale, the studio will be entitled to a story, first draft and final draft of the script (also called a teleplay).

In most instances, the studio will bargain for a story, first draft, two sets of a revision and a polish. Usually, the writer/creator will receive more than scale and pilot writing fees can range from $50,000 (for a relatively inexperienced writer) to $250,000 or higher for an A-level television writer (i.e., one who has already created at least one successful series, such as David Milch). As we mentioned above, this is the only money that the writer is guaranteed to receive under the 'one-off' deal.

Pilot Producing Services: The next issue of negotiation you would need to concern yourself with is the nature of the writer's services (if any) in the event that your script is well received and the pilot episode is ordered to production. In many cases, the studio will guarantee the writer employment as an 'executive producer' of the pilot episode at a negotiated fee. Other times (for example, if the pilot writer is not an established television writer or 'show-runner'), the studio might agree to attach the writer to the project at a lower level, such as a consulting or supervising producer. The writer's role in connection with the pilot is ultimately a result of negotiation, taking into account the writer's clout and prior experience. The WGA does not govern producing fees, as such services are not deemed to constitute writing. The fees for such producing services can range anywhere from $15,000 to $100,000.

Series Services/Compensation: If the pilot is 'picked up' by the network (i.e., series episodes are ordered to production), the studio can choose to exercise its option (negotiated up front, as part of the 'one-off' deal) to engage the writer as some type of producer on the series. A writer's series episodic producer fee will generally be lower than the pilot-producing fee, as there is less work to do once the first episode (i.e., the pilot) is completed.

Another point that is negotiated as part of the pilot/series deal is the length of time that the pilot writer (or 'series creator') will be 'locked' or attached to the series, thereby continuing to receive screen credit and a fee. A studio will usually agree to lock the writer/creator to the series for at least one year, and in many cases two years. Again, this depends largely on the writer's status in the television industry. Top writer/producers, such as Steven Bochco, might be guaranteed an executive producer fee and credit for the 'life' (i.e., duration) of the series. A writer/creator might also be guaranteed the opportunity to write (and be paid for) a specified number of episodic scripts during each year of the series.

In addition to series producing fees, you may negotiate for a 'series sales bonus' (i.e., a sum of money payable as a bonus if and when the network orders series episodes based on the pilot). While the dollar amount of a series sales bonus will vary and is subject to negotiation, it is fairly standard today for a series sales bonus of $25,000 to be granted in the event the writer receives sole 'written by' credit on the pilot and sole 'created by' credit on the series. This bonus may be reduced if the writer receives shared credit and/or if fewer than a set number of episodes (usually 12) are actually produced.

Finally, the WGA Agreement requires that the writer or writers accorded 'created by' credit on a series receive a royalty (or payment) for each episode of the series that is produced beyond the pilot. The current WGA required royalty for network prime-time programming is approximately $1,000 per episode. Subject to this minimum, the actual amount of the royalty payable to the series creator is negotiable and may be as high as $6,000 per episode for top guns.

Profit Participation: A writer's profit participation in a television project is typically more significant than with respect to a feature film, and is more likely to generate payment to the writer for two reasons. First, as television writer, you can normally negotiate for a percentage of the profits in excess of five percent (which is the standard participation for motion picture writers with limited exceptions). In addition, television writers are generally more successful than their feature film counterparts in extracting favourable terms from the studios relating to the calculation of such profits. Second, an enormously successful series may generate so much cash relative to its costs, that regardless of the precise definition of the project's 'net proceeds,' it is likely to generate some payment in many cases.

We think it is therefore imperative for a writer's representative to take great care in negotiating the definition of 'project proceeds' in the writer's contract. A top-level showrunner/creator will often be able to negotiate for 15 percent or more of the 'adjusted gross receipts' (gross revenues less certain defined deductions and a reduced distribution fee), or for up to 50 percent of the 'net proceeds,' reducible by net participations granted to third parties. If a project survives the uphill battle toward syndication, these profits may indeed materialize.

Credit: Assuming that the production falls within the WGA's jurisdiction, the Writer's Guild Agreement will determine the form of most writing credits. Typically, the writer or writers receiving 'written by' or 'story by' credit on the pilot will be accorded a 'created by' credit on the series. The WGA does not, however, govern producing credits. The terms and conditions relating to the writer's 'executive producer' or 'supervising producer' or even 'consultant' credit need to be specifically addressed by contract. In recent years, a number of established writers have requested 'logo' credits (which will typically appear in the end titles) in addition to their producer credits. For example, a 'Chase Films' logo appears at the end of every episode of The Sopranos at the request of that series' creator, David Chase.

Perks: As is the case with most talent agreements, writers can usually negotiate for some basic 'perks' (which may or may not be granted, depending upon their status), such as: (i) first-class travel if the studio or network requires the writer to travel; (ii) first class accommodations; (iii) a per-diem; and (iv) ground transportation to and from airports, hotels, and sets. In addition, some writers request that the studio provide an exclusive office and assistant during all periods in which they are expected to render exclusive services. Finally, a reserved parking space is considered a bit of status symbol in Hollywood and is requested by most series creators. This is merely a brief overview of television pilot/series writer agreements. There are several other terms and conditions that vary from deal to deal, which writers should be aware of when entering into such agreements. Before signing any contract, we strongly recommended that writers consult with an experienced entertainment attorney who can review the agreement in detail.

THE ESSENCE OF STORY

What is the essence, or heart and soul, of a great story? There are seven critical elements: the change of fortune, the problem of the story, the complications, crisis, climax and resolution of the classical structure, and the threat, which is by far the most important. In this article, we will examine the threat and its relationship to the other six critical elements that constitute the very essence of story--that without which there would be no story.

The first element is the change of fortune. There is an entity (i.e. an individual, a family, a town, a country, the world, etc.) and that entity goes from a desirable to an undesirable state or condition or the reverse. Or as Aristotle put it: 'The proper magnitude (of a story) is comprised within such limits that the sequence of events, according to the laws of probability and necessity, will admit of a change from bad fortune to good or from good fortune to bad.'

In 'The Exorcist,' a little girl is possessed by the Devil and a state of misfortune exists. Then, the principal action, casting out the Devil, brings about a state of good fortune. In stories that end unhappily, it's the reverse. In 'Othello,' a state of good fortune exists at the beginning. The principal action, perpetrated by Iago, destroys the Moor with jealousy and a state of tragic misfortune is the result.

The second element, the problem, brings about these changes of fortune. This problem is a prerequisite in all stories. You have a problem and that problem is resolved. No matter how big or small the story, it will be focusing on, or related to, a problem. And everyone in that story will somehow be involved in that incident. And everything everyone does in that story will in some way affect the outcome of that incident. And revealing how that problem was created and how it can be resolved is at the very heart of a story.

In 'Kiss The Girls' and 'The Silence Of The Lambs,' a serial killer is on the loose. That is the problem that brings about the change of fortune and that is the problem that has to be resolved. The solution to those problems will be the principal actions that give a unity of action to these stories.

In 'Gladiator,' a tyrant has usurped the Roman Empire, preventing the restoration of the Republic.

In 'The Sixth Sense,' there are two problems: a murdered child psychologist is stuck in limbo, and the spirits of dead people are haunting a little boy's mind.

In 'Independence Day,' aliens have invaded the Earth. In 'Star Wars,' the Evil Empire has taken possession of the galaxy. In 'The Iliad,' the Greek army is being decimated because their best warrior has dropped out of the fight.

In the legend of King Arthur, the kingdom is in a state of anarchy and has to be reunified. In 'Jaws,' it's a shark problem. In 'The Mummy,' it's a mummy problem. In 'The Perfect Storm,' it's a weather problem. In 'Traffic,' it's a drug problem. In 'Armageddon,' it's an asteroid problem.

In 'Indecent Proposal,' it's a temptation problem. In 'Erin Brockovich,' it's an environmental problem. Each of these stories, and hundreds of others I could name, revolve around a problem that has to be resolved.

Can any problem be a story? Technically, any problem can be a story if its solution contains a classical story structure--i.e. complications, a crisis, a climax and a resolution. Generally speaking, however, an audience wouldn't be interested in a story about some minor problem, like finding your lost keys, unless something truly funny or horrendous like the end of the world would happen if you didn't find them.

Story is especially interested in problem-solving actions that involve crises--critical events that threaten life, health, wealth, freedom, love, security, happiness, etc. while testing the limits of human endurance and ingenuity.

Story focuses on problems for the same reason the news only reports the bad things that are happening in the world--and not the good--because problems are where it's at. If everything is in perfect harmony, and there are no problems to worry about--we're in Paradise.

And that's one of the functions of story: to help guide us to higher, more desirable, less problematic states of being. One of the ways that a story does this is by revealing the truth and nature of problems and their solutions.

Next, there's the super important element called the threat. The threat is the agent or perpetrator that creates the problem that brings about the negative state. In 'Kiss the Girls,' the serial killer is the threat, and the act of murder is the inciting action that creates the problem that brings about the change to a state of misfortune.

Equally significant in a great story is the fact that this threat will become the source of resistance that opposes the action when someone tries to solve this problem and restore a state of good fortune. This resistance will create the classical structure that occurs when a problem-solving action encounters resistance.

In 'Harry Potter,' Voldemort is the threat. His efforts in the seven books to take possession of the wizard world create the problem that brings about an undesirable state. And he will be the source of the resistance that creates the classical structure whenever Harry tries to solve these problems and restore a state of good fortune.

In 'The Exorcist,' the Devil is the threat. He takes possession of a young girl and that is the inciting action that creates the problem and brings about the change of fortune. He is also the source of resistance that creates the complications, crisis, climax and resolution when the priest tries to solve that problem.

In 'Ordinary People,' the mother is the cause of the problem that has brought about the negative state, and she will be the source of resistance when the psychiatrist, played by Judd Hirsch, and the boy's father, played by Donald Sutherland, attempt to solve the mystery of the boy's suicidal tendencies.

In 'Jaws,' the shark is the threat that causes the problem. In 'Dracula,' it's the Count. In 'On the Waterfront,' it's Johnny Friendly. In 'Gladiator,' it's Commodus. In 'Braveheart,' it's the British. In 'The Iliad,' it is the Trojan, Paris. In the Egyptian myth of Osiris, it's Osiris' brother Set.

In all of these cases, the threat performs the action that creates the problem that brings about the change of fortune. It also is the source of resistance that creates the classical structure when someone tries to solve the problem and reverse the state of misfortune.

You can see this same pattern at work in real life as well. In World War II, Hitler was the threat, and his 'taking possession of Europe' created the problem and the state of misfortune. He was also the source of the resistance that created the complications, crisis, climaxes and resolutions of the classical structure when the Allies tried to solve this problem.

In our latest war, this is also very evident. Osama Bin Laden, his Al Qaeda terrorist network and the Taliban are the threat. Their attack on the World Trade Center and Pentagon is the inciting action that created the problem that brought a very undesirable state of fear to the United States. And they will be the source of resistance that creates the classical structure as we try to solve this problem.

In all of these examples, the threat is the cause of the problem that brings about a change of fortune and is the source of the resistance that creates the classical structure when the good guys try to solve the problem. The problem, change of fortune and components of the classical structure constitute the very essence of story--that without which there would be no story.

If you think about it, this is easy to see. Without a problem and change of fortune, there is no story. If the story ends in the same place it began, without some significant progress up or down, the audience will wonder what the point of it was. It will be a very unsatisfactory experience.

Without complications and a crisis, there is no story. If Cinderella goes to the ball, falls in love with the prince and marries him without a single hitch, or if Indiana Jones goes after the Holy Grail and finds it without running into any difficulty whatsoever, there is no story. The audience is left muttering: So what? If there are complications and a crisis, but no climax and no resolution, you will have the same problem. You will leave your audience feeling completely unfulfilled. They will have the distinct feeling that the story was left unfinished.

The threat, then, is not only the heart of the high concept great idea, (see our eZine article on the high concept dated July 21, 2001), it creates the problem that brings about the change of fortune and provides the resistance that creates the classical structure, all of which make up the very essence of story. An element that does all of that is an element worth thinking about and understanding.

IS IT A STORY ANALYST OR A READER?

Question: I keep hearing about these mysterious story analysts who will be charged, hopefully, with reading my script. Who are they and what are they like?

Marisa D'Vari responds: Story analysts (or readers, as they are sometimes called) come in two types. The full-time studio or production company reader is required, in most places, to read and analyze at least two scripts a day. They show up for work like everyone else, have their coffee, put their feet up on the desk and read.

Many are exceptionally well-educated, and have advanced degrees, with law degrees particularly prevalent. Despite their education, however, few actually start off as story analysts. They often fast track their way from being lower inside positions by 'reading on the side' for free.

The other type of reader, the independent or freelance reader, is potentially your worst enemy because she gets paid 'by the pound.' Fast readers make very good money and working fast to accommodate more scripts can be the subliminal motivation to shout 'next' when they see the material isn't going anywhere.

Both types of readers, after reading or scanning the script, create what is called a story analyst's report or 'coverage,' consisting, at most studios, of four pages of paper. Page one is the cover sheet containing basic information like title, name, type of material, which executive it was submitted to, the analyst who's writing the coverage, and something called 'logline' and 'comment.' The logline is a TV Guide-type run-down of what the story is about. The comment is a summary of what the material has to offer. About two lines (a single sentence) is devoted to each.

Executives rely heavily on the loglines and comments, and if there is a flicker of interest, the executive will read the rest of the coverage. If the executives like what they read, they will read the script personally. Executives are looking for material for which to go to bat, material that contains universal appeal. The script must contain the emotional elements that drive us all and to which we can relate. It must be very compelling, with an unusual mix of highly intriguing characters. And it must be the right story at the right time, read by the right reader and given to the right studio executive. Synchronicity plays an enormous part in all of this.

12

Writing for the Television

Chad currently works as a Creative Executive at the Littlefield Company/Paramount Studios. He has previously worked in television development and production at 20th Century Fox, CBS Productions, NBC Studios, and Regency Television.

If you think writing for film and television is essentially the same, here's a helpful hint: Think differently.

Although teachers often lump feature and television writing into one category, they're actually separate, rarely overlapping worlds. This article focuses on the industry and craft of television. We'll explore the industry's structure, how shows work and how writers break in.

UNDERSTANDING THE INDUSTRY

The television industry consists of three main entities: networks, studios and production companies. They may look similar on the surface, but each works in a unique way.

Networks program and broadcast material. The non-cable networks are NBC, CBS, ABC, FBC (Fox), the WB, and UPN. Although they suggest shows to studios and production companies, networks don't always produce their own programming.

Studios hire writers to develop material for networks. While most studios are owned by networks, they may sell product anywhere. Twentieth Century Fox is owned by FBC, but ABC airs Twentieth's The Practice.

Production companies, like studios, produce material for networks. Production companies are independent entities that make deals with studios wishing to partner with valuable producers. Imagines' Ron Howard is an acclaimed director/ producer with a Twentieth deal. Warren Littlefield ran NBC for nine years before partnering the Littlefield Co. with Paramount. By joining forces, studios and production companies can access each other's stables of talent (writers, directors, producers).

Studios and production companies make two kinds of deals with writers:

> *A development deal employs a writer to develop a single idea (paying from $30,000 to $500,000, depending on the writer). Because development deals focus on one project, writers can have simultaneous deals at different companies.*

Overall deals pay more than development deals (usually in the low millions) and bind the artist to a particular entity. Overalls are the holy grails of TV development. Jason Katims (Roswell) has an overall at Twentieth. Although Katims develops only for that studio, Twentieth may sell his shows to any network (Roswell aired on WB and UPN).

Thus is the basic structure of Hollywood's TV machine. But how does this machine work? Let's follow a show from conception to airdate. A show begins in...

Development season. From July through November, writers pitch shows to studios and production companies. Executives rarely meet first-time writers. Most developing writers have sold features or worked on staff. Had Kevin Williamson never written Scream, he wouldn't have sold Dawson's Creek to Columbia-TriStar (which sold the series to WB).

Studios also hire writers to write ideas conceived in-house. Warner Brothers Television owned the rights to Superman before hiring Miles Millar and Alfred Gough to write Smallville.

Studios then work with writers to perfect network pitches. Networks rarely buy scripts; they buy concepts. This allows input in shows' development and spares writers from finishing scripts that don't sell.

After hearing approximately 1000 pitches, networks buy 50 to 75 ideas, or script commitments. Writers then develop scripts and networks receive about 75 pilot scripts. Thus we enter...

Pilot season (January-April). From these scripts, networks shoot 15-20 pilots. Scripts that don't get picked up may be sold to other networks. Ed was developed and axed at CBS before being picked up at NBC.

Networks view finished pilots in April and May. Mid-May brings the upfronts, enormous affairs where networks announce season lineups to advertisers. Each network debuts two to six new shows each fall and a handful more at midseason (January-March). When a show goes, we enter...

Staffing Season. Between April and June series hire writers for the upcoming season. Agents submit clients' materials, and creators and executives meet with writers they like. Of the hundreds of submissions received, most shows staff 4-10 writers. Staffs begin writing immediately. Because most new shows premiere in fall, they commence shooting in early August.

HOW THE STAFF WORK

A staff is the hierarchy of writers that writes a TV Show. At the top of this hierarchy is the showrunner, often the program's creator. Running a show isn't simply visualizing a series; it's hiring, inspiring, and organizing an entire writing team and production staff. Most showrunners have spent years writing television and receive an Executive Producer credit on the series. Before running 8 Simple Rules To Dating My Teenage Daughter, Tracy Gamble paid dues on Home Improvement, My Two Dads and others.

While staffs arrange their hierarchy differently, here's the basic ladder (from top to bottom): executive producer, co-executive producer, supervising producer, producer, co-producer, executive story editor, story editor, staff writer.

Most writers begin as staff writers, or "baby writers."

Each level comes with its own perks and payscale. TV writers are salaried (except for those with overalls), and baby writers make between $60,000 and $80,000 a year. Showrunners-depending on their cache and the show's success-make closer to a million. As writers ascend the ladder, they eventually get offered development deals and-hopefully-overalls.

All shows use staffs, although different staffs work differently. On half-hours (sitcoms), writers write as a group. They sit in "The Room" and discuss jokes, stories, characters, etc. While individuals may write first drafts, scripts are always revised by committee. On hours (dramas) the staff structures the season together before assigning individual episodes. Writers then write alone, often under the showrunner's supervision.

How to break in:

Unless you sell a movie that earns a development deal, there are two basic ways to get staffed:

Have a great agent. As any agent will say, "breaking a baby" (getting a job for a first-time writer) is nearly impossible. Many shows don't hire low-level writers. Those that do want specific voices, and-in an ever-diversifying world-shows strive to find ethnically diverse babies. Even with a great agent, it may take three years to break a baby.

Get promoted from being a writers assistant. Writers assistants do everything from taking notes in the Room to making copies and offering story feedback. Naturally, showrunners like hiring people who know office dynamics and the voice of the show.

Writers assistants begin at the bottom. Jobs as production assistants (grunt work) abound. After a year. P.A.'s graduate to "writers P.A.," slaving away for writers themselves. That leads to a writers assistant gig, which-hopefully-becomes the coveted staff job.

Aspiring writers need two weapons: strong original material, and strong specs.

Original material consists of plays, screenplays or sketch material. Showrunners want writers who have unique voices and can fashion characters and stories. But they also need writers who can mimic others' tones and characters, so it's important to have....

Specs, or sample episodes of shows currently airing. Showrunners use specs to evaluate one's grasp of character voices, the ability to tell stories within a particular structure, and knowledge of a series present state of affairs.

To write a spec, watch and outline several episodes of the show. How are the stories structured? Are there B Stories and runners (subplots and continuing gags or themes)? Write down lines for each character.

Does one character always have the sassy comeback? Does another speak in one-syllable words? Scrutinize the show till you know it in your sleep; if you can't think the characters' thoughts, you're not ready to write.

Outline your spec based on original ideas. Continue watching and revising as you write. With each episode, update the script. The more current your spec, the stronger a showrunner's response.

Also pick a series that's frequented by showrunners and executives (The West Wing, Sopranos, etc.) You may love Yes, Dear, but few people watch it. If readers don't know the show, your spec won't get rave reviews.

Get your material to as many people as possible. In an industry based on networking, you can't shy from peddling your work. If everyone's six degrees away from an agent or executive, you must find those paths.

Don't send specs to their own shows. Showrunners feel they know their show better than anyone, and-regardless of what they actually produce, and regardless of what you may have written-your two visions probably won't connect.

Rather, send your specs to similar shows. CSI specs go to Law & Order, Malcolm in the Middle to Bernie Mac.

Of course, most shows won't accept cold submissions. They take scripts only from agents and mangers and, even then, mostly from agents or managers they know well. Your job, then, is to make friends. Once you know a story editor, an agent's assistant, or even a camera operator, ask them to read your stuff. Or pass it to their boss.

I recommend finding a job in the industry. Even P.A. jobs or studio receptionist gigs provide industry knowledge and access to contacts. This not only helps you move forward, it impresses agents who want clients in positions of upward mobility.

Now that you understand the fundamentals of the industry, there's only one thing left to do. Keep writing. Television, first and foremost, is a medium of storytelling. If you have the chops, you'll get there. It just helps to know the ropes.

SEVEN STEPS TO A SUCCESSFUL SPEC SCRIPT

It's easy to learn the format of writing for television from a book or writing class. It's a much harder thing to capture the voice and the tone of a particular series,Use this exercise to learn what makes your favourite TV series work, then craft a spec script that showcases your writing talent.

And to make your script fit flawlessly into the run of the show. Television is the one medium where you don't want your own unique voice to shine through. The characters' voices and thoughts and ideas need to stay true to the ones already established by the series' creators. Here's an exercise to help you capture the established voice of the show you wish to write.

Videotape a new episode of a show you love and that you watch often. Watch the first half, then shut off the television You are going to write the ending yourself.

Start by brainstorming all the possible ways the episode could end. For example, on the show I work on Sex and the City, in the first half of the episode "Ghost Town," Carrie and Miranda learn that Steve and Aidan are opening a bar together. At the halfway point, Carrie has just run out of the bar after hearing Aidan's voice because she is afraid to face him again. Think up as many ideas as you can for ways to resolve this story. Carrie could see Aidan and discover that he's married to someone else.

She could realize she never loved him. Or maybe she realizes that she loves him still. Maybe she never sees him at all-she goes back to the bar only to discover he's left New York for good. There are dozens of possible resolutions-let your imagination run wild.

Pick the ending you think best suits the characters and the show, then write it out, keeping in mind the way the characters act and talk and behave. You know these characters; how do you think they would solve their problems? You have about 12 pages to resolve the main story line, plus tie up any subplots or "B" stories.

When you finish, put your pages down and turn the television back on. Watch the broadcast ending straight through. Compare the ending you wrote to the one your just watched. As you go through your script, ask yourself these questions.

1. Why did the writers pick the ending they did?

   This particular episode of Sex and the City ends with Carrie discovering she has been in love with Aidan all along and decided to try to get him back. Think about why this particular ending works best for the show. If you ended your script with Aidan having left town, there are fewer possibilities for future stories between the two characters. Carrie scheming to get Aidan back, however, gives the writer plenty of material for many more episodes to come. Does the ending you wrote help move the series forward?

2. Is your ending believable? However you chose to resolve the episode, make sure that your story episode, makes sense in the world set up by the series' creators. You should never have a major character die, move to a different city, or do anything which would have permanent repercussions on the character and the show.

A spec script needs to show that you understand the constraints of the series and are able to work within them.

You might write a hilarious scene where Charlotte and Mr. Big get drunk and get married. Funny though it may be, it would never happen in the world of Sex and the City, and writing a story line like that would hinder your script form being taken seriously by anyone familiar with the show.

3. Did you leave any loose threads in your ending? Contemporary sitcoms are often intricately plotted, with four or five story lines all intertwining and building upon one another, leading to a resolution which affects all the characters. A show like Seinfeld will throw half a dozen plot elements into the mix, and all need to be resolved by the show's end. Make sure the ending you wrote satisfies all the questions raised in the beginning of the script.

   If you have trouble resolving each story line thoroughly and appropriately, try doing this exercise on an older series like Mary Tyler Moore or The Odd Couple. These shows tend to have simpler, more linear story lines and fewer subplots. They are great practice for building up to writing a more complicated script for a contemporary show.

4. Does the language you write fit the character? A joke that would be hilarious on Malcolm in the Middle would fall flat on Fraiser. The character in your script should talk the way you expect them to. If you have Malcom's brother Reese using 25-cent words or Fraiser's brother Niles using poor grammar, viewers will instantly recognize the inconsistency in the characters, and you will lose your audience.

5. Have you taken care of business? All shows have recurring elements they always feature. Each episode of Sex and the City shows Carrie typing a question for her column on her laptop computer. Just Shoot Me

begins scenes by showing words from the cover of Blush Magazine. Frasier always included a scene at the radio station, with Fraiser giving humorous advice to the caller.

Including these elements in your script can ground your story in the world of the series, and establish that you thoroughly understand the parameters of the series for which you want to write.

Many shows also often have recurring "bits'-themes or character which appear frequently but are not mandatory parts of each episode. "Itchy and Scratchy" cartoons are certainly an important part of The Simpsons, but they do not occur every episode. The same goes for Jacks' cabaret act on Will & Grace, and Ross' line "We were on a break!" on Friends. Using some of these elements in your writing can add specificity to your episodes and are a good way to show your understanding of the series' history.

Similar to business that always appears is business that never appears in a show. No one would believe a Sex and the City script which referred to Mr. Big by his real name or a Fraiser episode where we actually see Niles' wife Maris. Make sure you don't break any of the rules of the show by revealing something the staff writers intentionally keep secret.

6. Have you covered the basics? Shows vary in terms of length and number of scenes. The second half of a Fraiser episode might take place in three long scene, one each at the radio station, Fraiser's apartment and café.

   A show like Sex and the City, however, will use 10 or 12 shorter scenes, cutting quickly from the girls' apartments to bars to stores and back again. Only a few lines are said at each location before moving on to the next scene.

   The ending you write should have roughly the same number of scenes as the ending that was broadcast. Also be aware of the number of exterior scene in your show. While there are numerous scenes in Sex and the City of the women walking down the street or sitting in the park, we rarely see the Friends characters outdoors. Make sure the number of exterior shots in your ending is comparable to the broadcast ending.

7. What's the tone of your ending? "Sitcom" is short for situation comedy, and comedies need to be funny. Even sad or moving story lines are invariably lightened with a joke. When Miranda's mother died on Sex and the City, the writers contrasted her sorrow with Charlotte's outrage at the giant, glitter-covered flower arrangement the florist mistakenly sent. And Monica and Chandler's wedding on Friends was all the more touching for Joey not being able to remember all the parts of the ceremony he was officiating.

Be aware of the comic potential in every situation the show's writers have presented. Watch the broadcast ending again and count not only how many jokes are in each scene, but also how many jokes each character says.

And keep in mind that comedy can occur in action as well as dialogue. Kramer's pratfall entrances on Seinfeld got some of the biggest laughs on the show.

By doing this exercise, you learn how the staff writers of sitcoms think, how their minds work in terms of character, voice and story.

As you practice writing the endings of their scripts, you will be learning how to structure your own script. Once you understand the world of the series, you have the necessary tools to write your won episode, which will be true to the characters, their lives and their voices.

When you decide to write an entire spec script of your own, ask yourself these same seven questions. If you can answer each question positively, your spec script will work within the context of the series and demonstrate your understanding of the world of the show.

Spec Script Checklist Use these tips to help you craft a great spec script before you drop it in the mail.

- Consider how your ending affects the rest of the series.
- Make your story believable based on what you know that the characters' actions and language.
- Make your script self-contained. Finish what you start within one episode.
- Use elements from recognizable episodes to show you understand the series.
- Make sure the number of scenes and the locations are consistent with the series.
- Remember the tone of the series. If your spec script is for a sitcom, it needs to be funny.

Bibliography

Alan, B.: *Management of Electronic Media*, Belmont, Wadsworth/ Thompson Learning, 2002.

Atkins, B.: *The Mission: Journalism, Ethics, and the World: International Topics in Media*, Ames, Iowa State University Press, 2002.

Bagdikian, Ben: *The Media Monopoly*, Boston, Beacon Press, 1997.

Baker, C. Edwin: *Advertising and a Democratic Press*, Princeton NJ: Princeton University Press, 1994.

Berry, David: *Ethics and Media Culture*, Woburn, Focal Press, 2000.

Black, Jay: *Mixed News: The Public/Civic/Communitarian Journalism Debate*, Mahwah, Lawrence Erlbaum, 1997.

Bliss, Edward: *Now the News: The Story of Broadcast Journalism*, New York, Columbia University Press, 1991.

Briggs, Asa and Peter Burke: *A Social History of the Media from Gutenberg to the Internet*, Malden, Blackwell, 2001.

Bruce D. Itule: *Visual Editing: A Graphic Guide for Journalists*, Belmont, CA: Wadsworth, 1990.

Carey, W.: *Public Opinion and the Communication of Consent*, New York: Guilford Publications, 1995.

Chermak, Steven M.: *Victims in the News: Crime and the American News Media*, Boulder, Westview Press, 1995.

Cloud, Stanley and Lynne Olson: *The Murrow Boys: Pioneers on the Front Lines of Broadcast Journalism*, Boston, Houghton Mifflin Company, 1996.

Conrad, C.: *Strategic Newspaper Management*, Boston, Allyn and Bacon, 1996.

Cook, T.: *Making Laws & Making News*, Washington, DC: Brookings, 1989.

Copeland, David A: *Debating the Issues in Colonial Newspapers,* Westport, Greenwood Press, 2000.

Craig, Richard: *Online Journalism: Reporting, Writing and Editing for New Media,* Belmont, CA: Thomson/Wadsworth, 2005.

Downing, John: *Ethnic Minority Media: An International Perspective,* Thousand Oaks, CA: Sage, 1992.

Earl, R.: *Writing for Mass Communication,* White Plains, NY: Longman, 1996.

Edwin, C.: *Advertising and a Democratic Press,* Princeton NJ: Princeton University Press, 1994.

Emery, Michael: *The Press and America: An Interpretive History of the Mass Media,* Boston, Allyn and Bacon, 1999.

Ericson, Richard: *Crime and the Media,* Brookfield, Dartmouth Publishing, 1995.

Frank, Reuven: *Out of Thin Air: The Brief Wonderful Life of Network News,* New York, Simon & Schuster, 1991.

Gerald, J. : *News of Crime: Courts and Press in Conflict,* Westport, Greenwood Publishing Group, 1984.

Gillmor, Dan: *We the Media: Grassroots Journalism by the People, for the People,* Sebastopol, CA: O'Reilly Media, 2004.

Good, Howard : *Media Ethics Goes to the Movies,* Westport, Praeger, 2002.

Gordon, A. David: *Controversies in Media Ethics,* White Plains, Longman Publishers, 1999.

Hudson, Robert V.: *Mass Media,* New York, Garland Publishing, 1987.

Hutchison, R.: *Writing for Mass Communication,* White Plains, NY: Longman, 1996.

John Nerone: *The Form of News: A History,* New York, Guilford Press, 2001.

Kellner, Douglas: *Television and the Crisis of Democracy,* Boulder, CO. Westview Press, 1990.

Kessler, Lauren: *The Dissident Press,* Newbury Park, CA: Sage, 1984.

Langman, Larry: *The Media in the Movies,* Jefferson, NC: McFarland & Company, 1997.

Linder, Ken: *Broadcasting Realities*, Chicago, Bonus Books, 1999.

Lynne Olson: *The Murrow Boys: Pioneers on the Front Lines of Broadcast Journalism*, Boston, Houghton Mifflin Company, 1996.

Moore, L.: *Mass Communication Law and Ethics*, Hillsdale, Lawrence Erlbaum Associates, 1999.

Murray, Michael D.: *Encyclopedia of Television News*, Phoenix, AZ: The Oryx Press, 1999.

Ness, Richard: *From Headline Hunter to Superman: A Journalism Filmography*, Landham, MD: Scarecrow Press, 1997.

Newton, Eric: *Crusaders, Scoundrels, Journalists: The Newseum's Most Intriguing Newspeople*, New York, Times Books, 1999.

Peter Burke: *A Social History of the Media from Gutenberg to the Internet*, Malden, Blackwell, 2001.

Quaal, Ward: *Radio-Television-Cable Management*, New York, McGraw Hill, 1998.

Ripley, Jr. Casey: *The Media and the Public*, New York, H.W. Wilson, 1994.

Ross, Lillian: *Reporting Back: Notes on Journalism*, Washington, DC: Counterpoint, 2002.

Sachsman, David B.: *The Civil War and the Press*, New Brunswick, NJ: Transaction Publishers, 2000.

Sterling, John Michael: *Stay Tuned: A History of American Broadcasting*, Mahwah, NJ: Lawrence Erlbaum Associates, 2002.

Teeter, Jr.: *Voices of a Nation: A History of Mass Media in the United States*, Needham Heights, Allyn & Bacon, 1997.

Trahant, Mark N.: *Pictures of Our Nobler Selves: A History of Native American Contributions to News Media*, Nashville, TN: The Freedom Forum, 1995.

Ward, Brian: *Radio and the Struggle for Civil Rights in the South*. Gainesville, FL: University Press of Florida, 2004.

William, G.: *Creativity in TV & Cable Managing & Producing*, Lanham, University Press of America, 1999.

INDEX